Named in remembrance of

the onetime *Antioch Review* editor

and longtime Bay Area resident,

the Lawrence Grauman, Jr. Fund

supports books that address

a wide range of human rights,

free speech, and social justice issues.

The publisher and the University of California Press Foundation gratefully acknowledge the generous support of the Lawrence Grauman, Jr. Fund.

Human Shields

Human Shields

A HISTORY OF PEOPLE IN THE LINE OF FIRE

Neve Gordon and Nicola Perugini

UNIVERSITY OF CALIFORNIA PRESS

University of California Press
Oakland, California

Cataloging-in-Publication Data is on file at the Library of Congress.

ISBN 978-0-520-30184-9 (cloth : alk. paper)
ISBN 978-0-520-97228-5 (ebook)

Manufactured in the United States of America

28   27   26   25   24   23   22   21   20
10   9   8   7   6   5   4   3   2   1

"The goumiers [Muslim soldiers in the French colonies]," said Pierre Lyautey, "are incorrigible. They can't accustom themselves to modern civilization. Even booby-traps are part of modem civilization."

"Throughout North Africa," said Jack, "the natives got used to American civilization straight away. It's an undeniable fact that since we landed in Africa the peoples of Morocco, Algeria and Tunisia have made great progress."

"What sort of progress?" asked Pierre Lyautey in amazement.

"Before the American landing," said Jack, "the Arab used to go about on horseback while his wife followed him on foot, walking behind the horse's tail with her child on her back and a large bundle balanced on her head. Since the Americans landed in North Africa things have altered profoundly. The Arab, it is true, still goes on horseback, and his wife continues to accompany him on foot as before, with her child on her back and a bundle on her head. But she no longer walks behind the horse's tail. She now walks in front of the horse—because, of the mines."

CURZIO MALAPARTE, *The Skin,* 1949

CONTENTS

ILLUSTRATIONS

Introduction

AS PART OF HER SENIOR-YEAR PROJECT at Evergreen College, twenty-three-year-old Rachel Corrie traveled to the Middle East, intending to initiate a sister city project between her hometown Olympia, Washington, and the Palestinian town Rafah, in the Gaza Strip. She flew into the area at the very height of the second Palestinian uprising, and after a two-day seminar in the offices of the International Solidarity Movement (ISM) in the West Bank, she continued on to Rafah to join other ISM activists who were trying to prevent Israel's massive demolitions of houses on the Egyptian border. Less than two months after her arrival, on March 16, 2003, Corrie was crushed to death as she tried to prevent an Israeli Caterpillar D9R military bulldozer from destroying the home of local pharmacist Samir Nasrallah.

During the subsequent trial, the military spokeswoman defended the bulldozer driver and accused the ISM of carrying out "illegal and violent" activities by "serving as human shields for wanted people or for the homes of Palestinians."[1] In the military's eyes, the fact that Corrie had used her body as a shield to try to deter bulldozers from demolishing homes was proof that she had engaged in an act of combat, and thus the person who killed her had not violated any law. Rachel Corrie's horrific death and the acquittal of the soldier who killed her pose a number of questions around human shielding. Why was the killing of a voluntary human shield, an unarmed person who deploys nonviolent forms of protection, deemed legal? Why are voluntary human shields considered criminals by some and heroes by others? And what might a history of people in the line of fire teach us about the laws of war and the changing political and social forces that have shaped the global order?

The phrase "human shield" actually emerged only following the Second World War, even though the practice of human shielding had been common for a very long time. In the seventh century, for example, the Chinese used "barbarian" tribes on the Turko-Mongol frontier as human buffers, while the Mongols deployed prisoners as shields during their conquests.[2] In the eleventh century, Crusaders were advised to set "their Muslim captives out naked in chains to take the force of enemy missiles," and throughout the Middle Ages hostages were used as human shields in different battles and conflicts.[3] Unlike Rachel Corrie, these were involuntary human shields, people who were coerced to serve as a buffer, and a careful reading of the historical records revealed that their use was not uncommon.

The practice of human shielding also appears in many notable novels, memoirs, poems, and films, but since it's not explicitly mentioned, it's easy to miss. Human shielding occurs in one of the key scenes in Harper Lee's novel *To Kill a Mockingbird,* for example. Set in a southern United States town in the early 1930s, the story follows the lives of two children and their lawyer father, Atticus Finch, who is charged with defending Tom Robinson, a black man wrongfully accused of raping and beating a white woman. The night before the trial, Robinson is brought back to the local jail, and Atticus, who thinks that some of his white neighbors might want to murder the prisoner, decides to sit in front of the jailhouse to protect his client with his own body. Sure enough, an angry mob of men arrive and demand that Atticus move aside so that they can carry out the lynching, but his two children and another boy suddenly appear, and by standing on the steps of the jailhouse, unwilling to budge, the lawyer and the three children manage to fend off the would-be killers (figure 1).[4]

This scene pre-dates the activities of the International Solidarity Movement in Gaza, but it too depicts an action that today we would call voluntary human shielding, where a person or group of people risks their lives to protect someone or something that is under attack. It is a nonviolent act of resistance not only against the deployment of violence but, as Lee's novel suggests, also against oppressive social norms—in this case the white supremacy that dominated the southern US town. This is but one of many instances of voluntary shields who challenged militarism, imperialism, racism, sexism, capitalist exploitation, and environmental plunder. Such people willingly put their lives in the line of fire to advance a cause they perceive as ethical.

FIGURE 1. In *To Kill a Mockingbird,* Atticus Finch and the children shielding Tom Robinson from an angry mob. Credit: YouTube clip.

The dual connotation whereby human shields create a buffer to protect a target and simultaneously expose structures of power sustaining a particular social reality is captured by the phrase *human screens,* which is the name given to human shields during the First World War. In the literal sense, human shields serve as a screen to protect a target, but they can also serve as a screen that renders something visible, like a television screen. They help uncover institutionalized relations of power and violence. By defending Tom Robinson, Atticus and the children were taking a stand against the deep-seated racism embedded in their society while at the same time helping to lay bare this racism. An analysis of human shielding helps to illuminate the political and legal order informing any society.

WEAPONIZATION

In the history of warfare, involuntary human shields have played a more prominent role than their voluntary counterparts, having long been manipulated by both state militaries and insurgents. Analyzing a series of historical events, including horrific testimonies recounting how civilians in conflict zones have been weaponized, this book outlines who was forced to serve as shields, why they were chosen rather than others, as well as the different types of shielding practices that have been adopted over the years, how they were portrayed by different political actors, and what kind of political and legal work human shields do.

Consider the newspaper articles portraying the fighting in the Syrian city Raqqa. As the US-led coalition began its campaign to recapture Raqqa from the hands of the Islamic State (ISIS), numerous descriptions appeared in the press of how the militants dragged along terrified civilians, "intentionally endangering the lives of innocents" while using them for cover against the ferocious onslaught.[5] In October 2017, a few Syrians who had managed to flee the ravaged city described being herded from one damaged building to another as the extremists retreated into the city's Al-Badu district. "They were holding us as human shields. They were keeping us there to protect themselves," said one survivor, whose oversized trousers hanging from his bony frame suggested that he had not had a hearty meal for a very long time.[6]

Umm Mohammad, a heavyset woman who had also managed to escape from Al-Badu, recounted how civilians were not allowed to leave the buildings except to draw water from nearby water wells, and, even then, ISIS fighters would use the civilians as cover when they moved from one place to another. "At the wells," she explained, "[ISIS] would allow its fighters to fill up water first and made civilians wait for hours to protect them from air strikes." Her eldest son, Mohammad, would leave the building at 4:00 in the morning to draw water from a nearby well, and it would be hours before he came back. Several days before she escaped, he had left as usual but had never returned. "We learned there was an air strike there," she says. "I couldn't even find his sandals."[7]

Such testimonies, alongside those of the international volunteers who went to Iraq in 2003 to try to protect civilians from imminent attack, show how the history of human shields is also a history of the human body, and how the body has been mobilized to advance both domination and resistance. This history is marked not only by numerous incidents of people subjected to cruel and inhumane treatment by those who deployed them as shields, but also by incidents of immense courage, such as when activists have risked their own lives in order to save the lives of others.

Between the First and Second World Wars, for instance, pacifists, humanitarians, and anticolonial activists such as Mahatma Gandhi developed the idea of human shielding as a tool of resistance. This suggests that human shields can serve not just as weapons of war but also as weapons of peace. And as they are used to advance different political and military goals, human shields have come to embody a historical repository that reflects diverse social and ethical relations.

HUMAN VULNERABILITY

During its occupation of France in 1871, the German military tied French dignitaries on trains transferring soldiers and supplies to the front lines in the hope that this would shield the trains from enemy fire, not unlike the way ISIS used civilians to protect its convoys in Syria and Iraq (figure 2). These human shields have functioned as defensive tools, but in a profoundly different way than inanimate shields, such as land mines used to defend a border or antiaircraft missiles protecting an airfield. Generally speaking, inanimate shields are an integral part of any weapon arsenal and are used to protect vulnerable targets. Their particular physical or technological capacities determine their function as instruments of protection within armed conflict. By comparison, human beings seem an unlikely choice for a shield, since as beings made of flesh and blood they can be easily killed. Clearly, for human shields to be able to serve as effective deterrents, some other capacities or warfare strategies come into play.

When ISIS militants forced men, women, and children to walk in front of them, their hope was that the value attributed to these people as defenseless civilians protected by international law would deter and prevent their enemies from bombing. In Palestine, Rachel Corrie and other international activists volunteered to stand in front of bulldozers, hoping that their privilege as white protestors holding Western passports would stop Israel from demolishing Palestinian homes. While the value that has been ascribed to people from different social, economic, and geographical settings who became shields has shifted over the course of history, the vulnerability of those whose lives were considered valuable by the attackers has continued to serve as an effective shield within theaters of violence.

This suggests that the seemingly neutral term *human* in the phrase *human shield* denotes not merely an ostensibly universal biological condition but also a political one. The term both reflects and is constituted through social and political hierarchies. It is the value ascribed to the lives of some people that explains why their vulnerability can become a weapon of deterrence, while the lives of others are perceived to be expendable and therefore they cannot

SDF Press Center @SDF_Press_1 · Aug 19, 2016

بالصور لحظة فرار داعش مع المدنيين من #منبج

#Manbej **Daesh pictures how to use civilians as human shields** to flee

syrian democratic forces
you tube//SDF PRESS CENTER
TWITTER//@SDF PRESS 1

◯ 10   ↻ 206   ♡ 102   ↑

FIGURE 2. ISIS using civilians as human shields to protect its convoys. Credit: Syrian Democratic Forces Twitter account.

be used as shields. Unique forms of reckoning and ethical calculations enter the picture when humans become shields within a conflict zone.

Both involuntary and voluntary forms of shielding are fundamentally part of a politics of human vulnerability: a form of politics in which vulnerability is used as a strategy to achieve a range of political, military, and legal gains.[8] Deterrence is successful only when the attacking party values the shield's humanity and feels morally compelled to stop the attack in order not to harm the person who serves as a shield.[9] Deterrence fails when the value of the shield is considered negligible. The story of human shields is also the story of those who have been included and those who have been excluded from the fold of humanity, revealing that humanity is a political rather than universal category.

The history of human shielding touches several nerves. It describes who deserves to be treated humanely at a given historical moment and who does not. It also illustrates how racial, class, religious, sexual, and gender orders help shape our understanding of the human and thus the ethics of violence and how legal frameworks, particularly the laws of war, reflect, reinforce, and even produce these orders and their ethical valence.

The laws of war are a crucial aspect of the history of human shields. This body of laws regulates the deployment of violence during armed conflict, but it is also an instrument that is used by warring parties to establish the legitimacy of power and the forms of humane violence.[10] The principle of distinction is arguably the bedrock of these laws, distinguishing between combatants, who can be legally killed during armed conflict, and noncombatants, who are characterized as protected persons. The human shield, however, does not fit in either of these axiomatic "legal figures," or groups of people whose specific characteristics are classified and defined by law.

Because the human shield elides the law's two primary classifications of human beings—combatants and noncombatants—it destabilizes the order regulating the use of lethal violence in war. Examining the laws of war from the vantage point of this marginal and controversial legal figure provides insight into how the laws of armed conflict function and how they not only limit, regulate, and justify violence but can also facilitate and enhance it. Incidents of human shielding can serve as a lens to investigate the law's inner workings and thus produce a legal history from the margins, one that is often not apparent when studying the law from within the canon.

The story begins with the first detailed code to regulate fighting in a manner that was considered humane. The code was drafted during the American Civil War by Francis Lieber, a professor at Columbia College in New York, at the request of President Abraham Lincoln, who was troubled by the conflict's ethical implications.[11] As the horrific effects of the war became manifest, both sides tried to claim the moral high ground and present themselves as civilized. These claims were influenced by the international attention the war was drawing—especially from European powers such as France and Great Britain that considered themselves the champions of liberal humanity—and each warring party aspired to gain international legitimacy.[12] Although Lieber wrote the document within the context of a civil war, it ended up influencing the international debates leading to the first two Hague Conventions of 1899 and 1907, and some argue that it served as their blueprint. It is also with the appearance of the Lieber Code that the figure of the human shield began to acquire a certain legal, political, and conceptual depth it did not have in previous centuries.

Lieber acknowledged that civilian populations should be treated humanely, but he also framed them as an "object of warfare," claiming that in certain circumstances enemy civilians could become legitimate targets.[13] Thus the Lieber Code contains a foundational tension surrounding the status of civilians in armed conflict. In cases of human shielding, the issue becomes even more complicated. Civilians who either volunteer or are forced to become human shields produce an ethical uncertainty or ambiguity in the laws of war precisely because they can, at times, be legitimately killed.[14] Fierce debates about human shields commenced in the wake of the 1871 Franco-German War, not long after the Lieber Code was first drafted, and continued well into the twenty-first century, not least after the publication of the 2015 *Law of War Manual* in the United States.

Because human shields fall between the laws of armed conflict's two axiomatic legal figures, they challenge the laws of war's basic structure and logic, which is based on the possibility of distinguishing between combatants and noncombatants. Ethical questions concerning the circumstances allowing human shields to be killed as well as who is responsible for the life and potential death of human shields arise because human shields cannot be easily captured by the law's framework.

Acts of human shielding also expose operations of power and ideology within the law. An interrogation of human shields can, for instance, help us trace the changing status of civilians—those who can become shields—both in war and within the laws of armed conflict. In certain periods nonwhites could not be deployed as human shields because they were not considered civilians, while in other periods almost all the people who were forced to become shields were nonwhites. The changes in the political significance of "the human" who can serve as a shield are as intriguing and disturbing as the ethical implications of these changes.

Voluntary human shielding is particularly tricky, since the laws of war create a clear opposition between combatants, who are considered to be active actors, and civilians, who are understood to be innocent and passive bystanders.[15] The laws of war do not have the vocabulary to address civilians who are active in armed conflict, especially those who act to protect other civilians. Voluntary human shields are therefore often legally conflated with combatants even though they deploy nonviolent forms of resistance. Like Rachel Corrie and the activists who travelled to Iraq during the Gulf Wars, frequently voluntary shields are nonviolent and antimilitaristic and use direct action to defend vulnerable civilians trapped in a war zone.

LEGITIMIZING VIOLENCE

In addition to revealing the shifts in the value ascribed to different people and illuminating the laws of war, human shielding also exposes the relationship between the changing nature and methods of warfare and the ethics of violence. The testimonies from Raqqa not only provide a glimpse of the people who are most frequently being used as human shields in contemporary conflicts, but they also reveal why human shields have been mobilized at a greater rate in the past couple of decades. One of the reasons is the "disappearance of the battle-field"; in the global and perpetual war on terror, fighting is no longer confined within demarcated spatial boundaries or a circumscribed time frame.[16]

This shift to warfare that has no borders and an unlimited time frame has also pushed human shields to the forefront of several theaters of violence. New surveillance technologies and enhanced weapon systems enable high-tech militaries to search, find, and kill militants anywhere around the world, forcing these militants to find new ways to hide.[17] Militants are reacting to cutting-edge technologies of warfare by moving into urban settings where they can conceal themselves by intermingling with civilian populations.[18] Consequently, the major battles against ISIS over the past years have been not in open terrain but in cities like Mosul, Kirkuk, and Raqqa. The move to the city not only undermines the ability to distinguish between combatants and civilians, but also provides a ripe terrain for the deployment of human shields by militants striving to hide from the lethal weapons of states with high-tech militaries.[19] The ways wars are fought thus determine the prevalence of human shielding.

These new wars have produced new ways to legitimize the use of lethal force. Following strikes against ISIS and other rebel groups, high-tech states have increasingly appealed to a variety of legal classifications to help justify the deaths of civilians. "Collateral damage," "military-aged males," "enemies killed in action," and "human shields" are some of the legal figures describing people who were not the intended target but, nonetheless, were killed during attacks.[20] The proliferation of such figures is not incidental, and they have become tools in the political struggle over the ethics of violence.

Human shields have emerged as one of the key legal figures marshalled to legitimize the use of lethal violence against innocent people. When those who die are classified as human shields, then the party who deployed them rather than the one who killed them is most often framed as the one responsible for their death. Human shields, in other words, can be mobilized as a weapon of denial and of allocating blame to other warring parties.[21]

If ISIS militants forced a civilian to serve as a human shield as they changed positions in Raqqa and enemy missiles killed both the militants and the shield, then, according to the laws of armed conflict, the militants are the ones likely to be blamed for the civilian's death and not those attacking them. But if the militants were moving in the city and the missiles killed civilian bystanders, then the party launching the missiles is deemed responsible for the deaths. While determining exactly what transpired during a conflict is often difficult, it is clear that the attacking party has a vested interest in classifying civilians who are killed as human shields, since this assigns the blame to the militants. Conversely, it is in the militants' interest that these same people be classified as civilians. The ethics of violence is, at least in part, determined by the way the violence is framed, and human shielding has become a useful instrument for assigning guilt in contemporary wars.

BLURRING REALMS

Most people associate human shielding with warfare. But historically, human shields have often appeared in the civil sphere—and not only during armed conflict. Atticus Finch's courageous effort to defend Tom Robinson in *To Kill a Mockingbird* is an example, but one of the earliest historical instances of human shielding that we encountered comes from environmental activism in eighteenth-century India, where members of the Bishnoi community hugged trees in an effort to prevent a local king from uprooting them. Two hundred fifty years later, Greenpeace adopted shielding as its major eco-tactic in struggles against nuclear testing and whaling.

Human shielding has also been an important strategy in the history of labor struggles, as workers in numerous countries across the globe have created human barricades to shield factories from scabs and other strikebreakers. By so doing, they strove to protect themselves and future generations of workers from capitalist exploitation.

Human shields have even made their way into our homes, not only through their portrayal in television series such as *Homeland* and *Games of Thrones* but, more significantly, through popular computer games such as *The Last of Us* and *Army of Two*. Computer games very similar to those that are employed to train soldiers preparing for combat are being used by millions of people from the comfort of their homes, and some even invite their users to deploy human shields. More than simply another indication of how the line between war and civil space is being blurred, the appearance of human shields within virtual war games provides insights into our cultural moment.

In December 2016, two thousand US veterans travelled to Standing Rock Sioux Reservation in North Dakota to defend Native Americans. After seeing footage of peaceful indigenous water protectors being brutally attacked by security dogs, blasted with water cannons in subzero temperatures, and fired on with rubber bullets, thousands of veterans decided to shield the indigenous citizens from the violence deployed by their fellow uniformed officers. These powerful images were followed not long afterward by a viral picture of Ieshia Evans, an African American demonstrator, standing in the middle of the street to shield fellow Black Lives Matter protestors from an advancing row of officers dressed in battle gear like Robocops. In these and many other civil protests, human shielding was used to expose not only social relations of power but also the increasing militarization of policing and the ways that forms of violence used by militaries against civilian populations in foreign conquests are migrating home and into the civil sphere, blurring the distinction between armed conflict and civil protests.[22]

HUMANE VIOLENCE

The figure of the human shield has always generated contentious claims and counterclaims about the ethics of using violence, while the history of human shielding is inextricable from a history of how violence has been justified as humane.[23] The figure of the human shield embodies two central and seemingly opposed elements: the *human,* which evokes the notion of humanity in its twofold meaning of being human as well as being humane toward the vulnerable other, and the *shield,* which is an instrument of war and violence. Human shields present a duality and even a conceptual and ethical tension between the moral virtue of being benevolent and just towards fellow human beings, on the one hand, and the employment of violence, on the other.[24]

This duality is often disturbing because it produces a series of ethical quandaries about the use of violence, how it is justified, and how it can be resisted in moral ways. For instance, how should a humane warring party react when confronted by enemy combatants who hide behind civilians? Should it refrain from shooting to protect the civilians who are being exploited by its enemy? But if the warring party withholds its fire, won't the enemy be incentivized to continue using civilians as shields? Or how is it possible that residents who are trapped in an embattled city are, at times, portrayed as human shields while on other occasions they are presented as innocent civilians? How does framing civilians as shields operate to legitimize violence? From a different perspective, does volunteering to become a human shield in an attempt to stop state violence constitute a humane or inhumane act? Questions like these have triggered heated debates because the figure of the human shield unsettles the ethics of violence, particularly for those who identify as humane. Indeed, such questions accentuate the inextricable tie between notions of humanity and being humane and the modern history of violence.

The figure of the human shield thus serves as a prism through which to interrogate the ethics of violence, how this ethics is produced and reproduced over time and to what ends. Recounting incidents of human shielding over a span of 150 years while looking at how the laws of armed conflict have dealt with the phenomenon, this book explains when, why, and how certain manifestations of violence come to be conceived as humane while others are perceived as immoral. Human shields are the book's main protagonists, and the production of humane violence is its plot.

Human shields are thus fascinating not only because they take on multiple meanings and uses but also because they serve as a crucial site for interrogating some of today's most urgent political questions around the ethics of violence. Human shielding reveals the precarity of civilians both in war zones and in the civil sphere and how the law often enhances this precarity by facilitating violence while portraying it as humane. It also reveals how people can and do use this precarity to resist this violence. The human shield's precarious position between combatant and civilian and between a weapon of war and a weapon of peace unsettles our common ethical assumptions about violence and urges us to imagine entirely new forms of humane politics.

. . .

The book begins with the use of prisoners of war as shields during the American Civil War (chapter 1, "Civil War") and then crosses the Atlantic to the Franco-German War, where some of the greatest legal minds of the day argued that tying French dignitaries to trains was legal because the trains were attacked by irregulars (chapter 2, "Irregulars"). Heading next to South Africa, we examine how race pervades the ethics of violence, describing how during the Second Boer War British humanitarians took the Boer settlers' side against their own government, denouncing its use of human shields while ignoring British crimes against the black indigenous population (chapter 3, "Settlers"). We then turn to the German use of human shields during the occupation of Belgium in the First World War, focusing on the first governmental reports that used international law to assess the deployment of violence while showing how they classified the Germans as barbaric (chapter 4, "Reports").

The next chapter describes the attempt of the British pacifist feminist Maude Royden to create an army of voluntary human shields to stop the Japanese occupation of Shanghai in 1932 and to use shielding as a weapon of peace (chapter 5, "Peace Army"). Highlighting the debates surrounding the bombing of hospitals during the Italian colonization of Ethiopia in the mid-1930s, "Emblem" (chapter 6) shows how the fascist Italian regime justified its aerial strikes against Red Cross medical units by presenting the Ethiopian combatants as barbarians who used field hospitals as shields because they did not understand the moral significance of distinguishing between military and civilian sites.

The horrors of the Second World War led to the trials at Nuremberg (chapter 7, "Nuremberg"), where two Nazis were tried for deploying prisoners of war as human shields, but no one was tried for deploying civilians as shields because the laws of armed conflict had not yet registered the act as a crime. We then turn to the massive post–World War II introduction of an array of civilian protections, when for the first time in history the use of civilians as shields was outlawed (chapter 8, "Codification"). In "People's War" (chapter 9), we show how the United States reduced Vietnamese resistance to an act of human shielding to justify its use of lethal violence against thousands of civilians. "Environment" (chapter 10) turns away from war and focuses on shielding actions carried out by Greenpeace that expanded the notion of ethics beyond the human realm to include nonhuman organisms, while "Resistance" (chapter 11) describes how civilians in the two Gulf Wars and in Palestine became active political agents who challenged the whole framework of humane violence by rejecting violence itself.

"Humanitarian Crimes" (chapter 12) illustrates how the International Criminal Tribunal charged with investigating war crimes in the former Yugoslavia selectively handed out human shielding accusations so as to shield NATO from allegations that its aerial strikes were inhumane. "Manuals" (chapter 13) examines the coverage of human shields in military manuals, showing how these handbooks are lawmaking tools that can end up legitimizing the killing of shields. In "Scale" (chapter 14) we look at the Sri Lankan civil war, in which accusations that the Tamil Tigers were using human shields played a crucial role in interpreting the principle of proportionality, leading to assertions that the killing of an estimated forty thousand civilians during the war was not a crime.

"Hospitals" (chapter 15) shows how belligerents have consistently justified attacks on medical units by claiming that they are being used as shields to hide combatants or weapons and how the laws of war lend themselves to such claims. This leads us to the battles to capture the Iraqi city of Mosul and the framing of civilians trapped in conflict zones as shields (chapter 16, "Proximity"), followed by Israel's use of infographics to frame Palestinian homes, schools, hospitals, and mosques as shields in order to legitimize the killing of civilians during its attacks on Gaza (chapter 17, "Info-War").

We then turn to an examination of new surveillance technologies, demonstrating how shielding is cast as a perfidious weapon of the weak—who are also portrayed as barbarians—to deter powerful high-tech states from launching "surgical" strikes (chapter 18, "Posthuman Shielding"). "Women and Children" (chapter 19) explains why ever since the war on terror nonwhite women and children have become the protagonists of shielding accusations, a charge that helps reinscribe the colonial trope of brown men as uncivilized human beings. The notion of barbaric violence also emerges in viral video clips showing ISIS fighters parading dozens of civilian shields locked in metal cages through the rubble-laden streets of a Syrian town and others showing soldiers patrolling towns in Kashmir with an Indian citizen tied to the hood of a military jeep (chapter 20, "Spectacle"). Barbaric violence even appears in interactive computer games, where the usual reasoning is turned on its head: the deployment of involuntary human shields is not only presented as legitimate but, at times, even romanticized as a means for achieving the liberation of those who are considered humane (chapter 21, "Computer Games"). Finally, human shields figure increasingly in civil protests, where they protect targeted civilians from violence exerted by security forces while simultaneously defending the public sphere—the space where people can join together to challenge or resist governmental or corporate violence (chapter 22, "Protest"). Voluntary human shielding as a strategy of resistance aspires not only to expand and deepen the ethical terrain but also, as we will show, to subvert the very notion that violence can be humane.

ONE

────────

Civil War

Humane Warfare in the United States

ON A HOT AND HUMID DAY IN MID-JUNE 1864, just over three years following the outbreak of the American Civil War, the *Charleston Mercury* published an article about the deployment of prisoners of war as human shields in the city of Charleston, South Carolina. Owned by a secessionist South Carolinian family, the *Mercury* had been instrumental in shaping public opinion against the federal government's efforts to alter the Southern way of life, including the right to hold slaves and the necessity to separate from the Union.[1]

Although the city had already been under siege for over three hundred days and it was becoming apparent that the Confederate forces were destined to lose the war, the *Mercury* did not abandon its ideological line. "For some time past," the article notes, "it has been known that a batch of Yankee prisoners, comprising the highest in rank now in our hands, were soon to be brought hither to share the pleasures of the bombardment. They accordingly arrived on Sunday." The newspaper goes on to provide the names of fifty Union officers, concluding: "These prisoners we understand will be furnished with comfortable quarters in that portion of the city most exposed to the enemy's fire. The commanding officer on Morris Island [which was controlled by Union forces] will be duly notified of the fact of their presence in the shelled district, and if his batteries still continue their wanton and barbarous work it will be at the peril of the captive officers."[2]

A day before the article's publication, Confederate Major General Samuel Jones, a graduate of Princeton University who had served as an assistant professor of mathematics at West Point before the war, wrote a short letter to the commanding Union officer stationed in Hilton Head just outside Charleston:

FIGURE 3. The shelling of Charleston by Union forces, 1863. Credit: Alpha Stock / Alamy Stock Photo.

Charleston S.C. June 13, 1864

Maj.-Gen. John G. Foster,

Commanding U.S. Forces, Coast of South Carolina.

General:

Five general officers and forty-five field officers of the United States Army, all of them prisoners of war, have been sent to this city. They have been turned over to Brigadier-General Ripley, commanding First Military District of this department, who will see they are provided with commodious quarters in a part of the city occupied by noncombatants, the majority of whom are women and children. It is proper, however, that I should inform you that it is part of the city which has been for many months exposed day and night to the fire of your guns.

Very respectfully your obedient servant,
Sam Jones
Maj.-Gen. Commanding.[3]

The decision to use prisoners of war as human shields—a term explicitly codified in the laws of armed conflict only after the Second World War—to deter Union forces from bombing Charleston followed the abandonment of many Confederate positions along the Atlantic coast.[4] A last resort by Major General Jones in an effort to arrest the assaults of the North's much more robust military, which was set to vanquish the South, the human shield entered the battlefield as a weapon of the weak and only later emerged as one of the most contested legal figures of international law.[5] And even though Major General Jones was surely not the first to deploy human shields in the history of warfare, his decision to use shields is chronicled in the records of the American Civil War, where we find early traces of the kind of discussions that would later characterize political struggles over the use and definition of human shields. This was also one of the first times in history that human shielding triggered debates about the deployment of humane and inhumane violence in armed conflicts.

SHARED VALUES

Three and a half years earlier, on December 20, 1860, the representatives of the people of South Carolina had passed an ordinance of secession dissolving the state's connection with the government of the United States.[6] South Carolina had thus become the first state to secede from the Union, and Charleston became a flash point of discontent.

The Civil War's first full battle began in Charleston. On April 12, 1861, shore batteries under the command of a Confederate general opened fire on the US Army–held Fort Sumter in Charleston harbor.[7] No one could have imagined the extent of the horrors that would follow. Most people believed that this war would be very different from the Mexican-American War of 1846–1848, where the customs of warfare accepted by "civilized people," as Andrew Jackson had been keen to claim, "did not apply."[8] The moral customs of armed conflict, it was assumed, simply had no currency in a war with the Mexicans, who were regarded as "savages," because savages, to cite Thomas Jefferson, carried out "indiscriminate butchery of men, women and children," and therefore the whole enemy population could and should ultimately be "exterminated."[9]

By contrast, it was assumed that the war between the North and the South would be a humane war: one fought by "civilized people" who had gone to the same colleges, belonged to the same political parties, sat in Congress together, and jointly run the federal government. Consequently, the general presumption was that the warring parties would understand and respect certain rules of engagement, since both sides came from similar backgrounds and shared certain moral convictions and ethical standards. However, the Civil War, with its estimated 620,000 casualties, confirmed that even when "civilized people" fight each other, extensive acts of inhumanity are not precluded.[10] Attacks directed against civilian populations, extrajudicial executions, and rape were par for the game. Thus, the way Major General Jones concludes his threatening letter to Major General Foster—"Very respectfully your obedient servant"—underscores that inhumane violence can easily be draped in an etiquette of civility.

THE LIEBER CODE

Three days after Major General Jones dispatched his letter of warning, Major General Foster sent an elaborate response:

> GENERAL: I have to acknowledge the receipt this day of your communication of the 13th instant, informing me that 5 generals and 45 field officers of the U.S. Army, prisoners of war, have been sent to Charleston for safe-keeping.... Many months since Major General Gillmore, U.S. Army, notified General Beauregard, then commanding at Charleston, that the city would be bombarded. This notice was given that noncombatants might be removed and thus women and children be spared from harm. General Beauregard, in a communication to General Gillmore, dated August 22, 1863, informed him that the noncombatant population of Charleston would be removed with all possible celerity. That women and children have been since retained by you in a part of the city which has been for many months exposed to fire is a matter decided by *your own sense of humanity*. I must, however, protest against your action in thus placing defenseless prisoners of war in a position exposed to constant bombardment. It is an indefensible act of cruelty, and can be designed only to prevent the continuance of our fire of Charleston. That city is a depot of military supplies. It contains not merely arsenals but also foundries and factories for the manufacture of munitions of war.... To destroy these means of continuing the war is therefore our object and duty. You seek to defeat this effort, not by means known to honorable warfare, but by placing unarmed and helpless prisoners under our fire.[11]

By questioning Jones's "sense of humanity," Foster was in effect criticizing his response to the violence meted out by the North, suggesting that the way Jones had been defending Charleston was inhumane. The idea that a certain sense of humanity should be preserved while carrying out violence may seem self-evident to the contemporary reader, but, at the time, it was part of a relatively new vocabulary that reflected the emergence of a new system of norms aimed at regulating warfare.

The worldview that violence during armed conflict could be deployed in humane ways was also one of the key assumptions informing the Lieber Code, the newly drafted instructions for the conduct of federal soldiers in the battlefield. Formulated by the German-American legal scholar Francis Lieber in April 1863—the same year Henry Dunant founded the International Committee of the Red Cross, the leading humanitarian organization concerned with the preservation of humane standards in armed conflicts—the Code was essentially a law-of-war manual written for the military. Yet, it ended up heralding the branch of international law that governs the conduct of hostilities.[12] Lieber, a professor at Columbia College in New York, was also propelled by the fact that three of his sons participated in the war, two on the Union side, while the third fought for the South and was eventually killed in combat.[13]

Major General Foster's effort to balance military necessity with some form of common humanity echoed the newly drafted Lieber Code. In his letter to Major General Jones, the Union general justified bombing Charleston because it housed factories that manufactured munitions and served as a depot for military supplies. He thus implied that his forces were operating in accordance with the definition of "military necessity" developed by Lieber, and that Major General Jones was the one who would bear responsibility for harming the protected persons because he had not evacuated them from the city.[14] So even though Foster distinguished between combatants and noncombatants in the letter—framing Charleston's civilian population, specifically the women and children who were living in the besieged town, as protected noncombatants—the existence of a military target within urban space consequently legitimated the resignification of the entire civic area as hostile, opening it to indiscriminate attacks.

Lieber's legal conception of humane violence was grounded in two apparently contradictory beliefs. On the one hand, Lieber was in favor of sparing civilians from the violence of war. On the other hand, he thought that military efforts to distinguish between combatants and civilians could enhance the acceptability of war and thus prolong the fighting and its brutal effects.[15] "The more vigorously wars are pursued," he wrote in the Code, "the better it is for humanity. Sharp wars are brief."[16]

For Lieber, wars that adopted less brutal practices but extended over a long period were often the most ruthless, while fierce wars that were speedy often ended up being the most humane. Indeed, the Code highlights not only how war was beginning to coalesce as a legal institution, but also how humanitarian concerns have, at times, been invoked to justify forms of indiscriminate violence.[17] Thus, it is not surprising that even though the distinction between combatants and noncombatants was invoked in both Foster's letter and in the Code itself, the assumption was that military necessity overrides this distinction and at times even undoes its significance. The bombing of Charleston thus became a necessary act of humane violence.

WEAPON OF THE STRONG

Foster's letter goes on to intimate that Jones's use of human shields would not succeed as a deterrence strategy, stating that "I have forwarded your communication to the President, with the request that he will place in my custody an equal number of prisoners of like grades, to be kept by me in positions exposed to the fire of your guns so long as you continue the course stated in your communication."[18] And indeed, on June 27, Foster received a response from Washington D.C. noting that "The Secretary of War has directed an equal number of Rebel generals and field officers to be sent to you [...] to be treated in precisely the same manner as the enemy treats ours; that is, to be placed in a position where they will be most exposed to the fire of the Rebels."[19] Human shielding was thus countered with human shielding.

Here, in one of the first historical records of a debate about the deployment of human shields, we witness how shields can be used not only as a weapon of the weak but also as a weapon of the strong, a fact that has been either ignored or overlooked by many contemporary commentators.[20] Moreover, Foster was not the only Union officer to deploy shields. General Rousseau, who was the northern commander in Alabama in 1862, was outraged by the "killing of loyal citizens by lawless persons firing into railway trains," and consequently ordered "that the preachers and leading men of the churches, (not exceeding twelve in number) in and about Huntsville, who have been acting secessionists, be arrested and kept in custody, and that one of them be detailed each day and placed on board the train on the road running by way of Athens and taken to Elk River and back...."[21] The use of human shields, it turns out, was not entirely uncommon during the American Civil War.

Interestingly, in his letter accusing Jones of scattering high ranking prisoners of war in different sites within Charleston in an effort to deter the north from attacking the city, Foster's underlying assumption is that holding women and children within the city and in close proximity to the areas where bombings took place did not constitute a shielding practice, but was, rather, an act of negligence, denoting a lack of humanity.[22] As we will see, the use of *civilians* as shields became a crime only following the post-World War II legal codification process, even though denunciations about the use of women and children as human shields already began to emerge during the First World War.

Completely missing from Jones's and Foster's script are African Americans, who comprised about half of Charleston's population at the time. "Negroes are to this country what raw materials are to another country," a Charleston planter had exclaimed several decades earlier.[23] In the minds of most white southerners and many northerners, African Americans were private property.[24] Their elision from the correspondence suggests that the value ascribed to these human beings was negligible; their vulnerable condition in the midst of war was not considered as deserving any consideration, let alone legal protection.

The correspondence between the two generals and the criteria they adopted for defining who can and cannot be deployed as a shield reveals that the figure of the human shield is predicated on a hierarchy of humanity, where some lives are worth more than others. Women and children were not used as human shields, although they were entitled to certain forms of protection during war. Soldiers from the rank and file were not deployed as shields due, it seems, to their relatively low social class and their expendability in war, while non-whites were not used as human shields because they were considered the white man's property and therefore did not even warrant mention in Jones' and Foster's epistolary exchanges.

Lieber's Code offers protections to all noncombatants, but in the American Civil War the only "protected persons" explicitly depicted as human shields are captured high-ranking officers, and in General Rousseau's case, "preachers and the leading men of the churches." Human shielding thus reveals the hierarchy of value ascribed to different members of society, underscoring the different political gradations of "humans, not-quite-humans, and nonhumans," to borrow the categorization used by cultural critic Alexander Weheliye.[25] In contrast to all the other people present in Charleston at the time, only those senior officers captured as prisoners of war were considered to have enough value to render them transformable into shields—namely, people whose vulnerability could, at least potentially, generate deterrence. According to this logic, not all humans are valuable enough to become shields.

In some respects, the generals' correspondence echoes the ancient practice—since Greek and Roman times—of giving or taking hostages as a guarantee for the fulfillment of promises, contracts, or treaties between two parties.[26] Indeed, it was an accepted and, one might even say, universal practice among the social elites to send hostages—often people who were members of a noble family—as a surety that their contractual obligations would be fulfilled.[27] Similar uses of hostages continued well into the nineteenth and twentieth century, with the British colonial government in India routinely taking captives from noble families in order to guarantee agreements it had reached with different "tribes."[28] Crucially, mutual recognition by the contracting parties that the person who served as hostage was valuable in the eyes of those who handed him or her over was a precondition for such agreements.[29] Indeed, the value ascribed to hostages served as deterrence against failure to fulfill the contract.[30]

A similar schema operates in the case of human shielding. While the Lieber Code does not mention human shields, it does briefly discuss hostages. The Code begins with the medieval definition, noting that "A hostage is a person accepted as a pledge for the fulfillment of an agreement concluded between belligerents during the war, or in consequence of a war," while adding that "Hostages are rare in the present age." The Code then draws a link between hostages and prisoners of war. "If a hostage is accepted, he is treated like a prisoner of war, according to rank and condition, as circumstances may admit. A prisoner of war is subject to no punishment for being a public enemy, nor is any revenge wreaked upon him by the intentional infliction of any suffering, or disgrace, by cruel imprisonment, want of food, by mutilation, death, or any other barbarity."[31] Framing prisoners of war as hostages allowed Lieber to offer them a series of protections, not unlike the protections offered to hostages of old.

As the Lieber Code underscores, recognition of the person's value is crucial for the humane treatment of imprisoned enemy troops. The same is true for the deployment of prisoners of war as human shields. And, as the American Civil War highlights, for a person to be able to become a shield, he or she has first to be recognized as having a certain social status and political value that at least in theory transforms his or her vulnerability into a tool of a deterrence.[32] Within the context of war, high-ranking officers possess more value than other human beings. Moreover, during the Civil War, such officers were most often members of the upper class. Precisely the combination of their civil and military status rendered them suitable to be used as shields.

DISAVOWING THE HUMAN

The mutual charges and allegations did not prevent the two generals from continuing to correspond. At a certain point, Major General Jones delivered a letter written to Major General Foster from five captive Union generals.

> GENERAL: The journals of this morning inform us, for the first time, that 5 general officers of the Confederate service have arrived at Hilton Head, with a view to their being subjected to the same treatment that we are receiving here. We think it is just to ask for these officers very kindness and courtesy that you can extend to them, in acknowledgment of the fact that we, at this time, are as pleasantly and comfortably situated as is possible for prisoners of war, receiving from the Confederate authorities every privilege that we could desire or expect, nor are we unnecessarily exposed to fire.[33]

While Jones used the prisoners' letter to convey a threat, intimating that the conditions they were being held in could potentially get much worse, Foster ignored the insinuation and quickly replied:

> My Dear friends, I have received your letter of the 1st instant, and will observe your wishes in the treatment of the prisoners now placed in my hands. We all regret very much the circumstances of your being placed under our fire in Charleston, and everyone feels justly indignant at this barbarous treatment of prisoners of war . . . .[34]

This eerie exchange highlights two inherent features informing the practice of human shielding. The first is that human shielding is part of a politics of vulnerability, whereby the assailant is entreated to respond to human frailty rather than to military might. Indeed, in instances of human shielding the target is defended not through mobilizing armed forces, but rather by exploiting the defenseless status of people in conflict zones, in the hope that this will influence the opponent's moral sensibilities and propel the enemy to change its course of action.[35] Human precariousness replaces military might as the deterrent.[36]

The correspondence also exposes a central paradox informing the practice of human shielding.[37] On the one hand, both commanders share a similar view about the human value of high-ranking prisoners of war, probably because they also identify with them, given that they, too, were generals. This is the reason why the benevolent, courteous, and one could even say liberal treatment of the prisoners is continuously emphasized. At least in the generals' minds, this treatment must have stood in sharp contrast to the deplorable conditions in the prison camps, where an estimated 56,000 Union and Confederate soldiers perished in what is now considered one the most horrifying chapters of the Civil War.[38] Precisely because they were considered to belong to the top echelons within the hierarchy of humanity, Jones and Foster believed that these prisoners of war deserved humane treatment.[39]

On the other hand, unlike the low-ranking prisoners who were held under dreadful conditions in the camps but ultimately protected from the violence of the fight, the high-ranking officers were used as a buffer against the enemy's projectiles. They were deployed as fodder for the fire, people who were killable in the eyes of their captors. Paradoxically, due to the high value ascribed to them, they also became expendable.

This correspondence in the waning days of the Civil War lays bare very clearly that human shielding depends on the recognition of the shield's value by the attacking side. Yet, it also reveals how this recognition both reflects and reproduces racialized, gendered, and class hierarchies among humans, which helps explain why women, children, slaves, freed blacks and rank and file soldiers could not serve as shields. Concurrently, the high-ranking officers, who were recognized as the most valuable humans, lost the protections the Lieber Code bestowed upon prisoners of war and were literally transformed into weapons even though they were no longer participating in the hostilities. The recognition of their high value led to their conversion into killable subjects, revealing how humanism paradoxically avows the sanctity of human life only to disavow it. It is precisely this uncanny paradox that lies at the heart of the history of human shielding and the ethics of humane violence.

TWO

———

Irregulars

*The Franco-German War and the
Legal Use of Human Shields*

A FEW YEARS AFTER THE AMERICAN CIVIL WAR ENDED, another brutal conflict involving practices of human shielding erupted, this time an international armed conflict on European soil. Fearing that the planned unification of four southern Prussian states with the North German Confederation would alter the regional balance of power, Napoleon III declared war against Germany in July 1870, instructing the French military to assemble on the northeastern front.[1] It quickly became clear, however, that the French emperor had not done his homework. The German military was better prepared, better equipped, and better organized, enabling Field Marshal Helmuth von Moltke, who served as the military's chief of staff, to initiate a series of swift attacks across the French border, culminating in the Siege of Metz and the Battle of Sedan, where Napoleon was ultimately captured.

The French statesman Léon Gambetta did not wait long before dissolving the French monarchy and establishing, together with a number of political allies, the Third Republic, as he took on the role of interior and war minister. Gambetta's national defense government managed to function for several months, while the French army attempted to hold its ground in the countryside. Yet these efforts were unsuccessful, and the German military continued to ransack French villages and towns before laying siege to Paris. In the meantime, French citizens from both the occupied regions and southern France began organizing in small companies, attacking the German occupying forces' lines of transport and communications.[2]

The increasing availability of small weapons alongside the rise of nationalism clearly facilitated the mobilization of these French civilians, who embarked on a people's war to drive the German military out of their

FIGURE 4. *Francs-tireurs* in the Vosges Mountains in northeast France. Credit: *L'Illustration Européenne,* 1870.

country.[3] Composed of partisans from different classes, the various bands of French fighters took on specific names, such as the Wild Boars of Ardennes and the Railway Destroyers. Their generic name, however, was *francs-tireurs,* or free shooters, because the first groups to organize were made up of members of rifle clubs and unofficial military societies.

The French partisans wore either civilian clothes or an assortment of uniforms and emblems they had haphazardly assembled. One notorious group dressed as the seventeenth-century Musketeers made famous by Alexander Dumas's novel.[4] Some of these fighters had guns, while others carried hatchets, crowbars, mining tools, or picks. By mid-September 1870, they were carrying out attacks on the outskirts of Paris, ambushing German patrols in the woods and shooting at them from villages (figure 4).[5] Focusing on sabotage, they destroyed train tracks, blew up bridges, and felled trees and laid them across roads to block the advance of German troops and supplies.[6]

Anticipating the warfare techniques used a century later by the Chinese Communist insurgents led by Mao Tse-tung and later adopted by the Viet Cong, the French francs-tireurs fought in the regions from which they hailed and hid among fellow civilians.[7] By the end of the war, German intelligence had estimated that they numbered 37,000 fighters.[8] Thus, on one side of the conflict were the partisans who knew the terrain and were able to detect the German army's most vulnerable positions. On the other side was a state army occupying France and trying to counter the French insurgency with methods of warfare that included the systematic use of human shields.

HUMAN SHIELDING AS COUNTERINSURGENCY

Field Marshal von Moltke, who had adapted Lieber's Code into the regulations he issued to the armed forces, decided to introduce new techniques to quell French resistance, noting that good warfare practices require creativity, innovation, and flexibility.[9] He was particularly outraged by the attacks carried out by nonconscripted soldiers, or irregulars, as they were referred to at the time; he considered their warfare practices both immoral and in contravention to the laws of war.[10] He feared that if his military did not react harshly, the popular support already enjoyed by the francs-tireurs would broaden and ultimately produce a series of taxing challenges. Hence, at the beginning of the campaign he ordered his subordinates to distinguish between the regular French army, who were to be "treated as bona-fide belligerents," and the francs-tireurs, who "had no belligerent rights and were liable to be summarily shot."[11]

Later, Moltke expanded his instructions: when individual insurgent attackers could not be caught, the entire community was to be held responsible and harshly punished. "Experience has established that the most effective way of dealing with this situation," the field marshal wrote, "is to destroy the premises concerned—or, where participation has been more general, the entire village."[12] As the occupation continued, he instructed whole regiments or divisions to participate in "pacifying actions," and reprisals as well as collective punishment soon became common practices.

When a German patrol took fire from Héricourt, for example, a squadron charged into the village and burned it to the ground, while Châteaudun, a market town of seven thousand, disappeared into smoking ashes under similar circumstances.[13] As part of their counterinsurgency strategies, high-ranking German commanders began using human shields against the francs-tireurs, instructing their officers to protect the trains transporting German soldiers and supplies with French "inhabitants who are well known and generally respected, and who shall be placed on the locomotive."[14]

Chronicling the war, Scottish captain Henry Montague Hozier, who accompanied the German army as an assistant military attaché, recounted how different dignitaries were tied to train engines. In Nancy, "the first hostage was Monsieur Leclair, the venerable president of the court of appeal. On another occasion, Procureur-General Israd was 'invited' to make an involuntary journey. Escorted by two Prussian gendarmes, he had to mount the tender and travel to Luneville, where his colleague in that town took his place. The president of the Chamber of Commerce, a judge, and a barrister also occupied in turn the post of danger."[15]

Just as only high-ranking Union officers were used as shields by the Confederate General Jones, in the Franco-German War only people of a certain social class and status were forced to serve as human shields. The assumption was that these dignitaries embodied a higher human value than "regular civilians" and therefore, if tied to the train engine, could deter the francs-tireurs from sabotaging the supply lines. But in sharp contrast to the American Civil War, in occupied France it appears that human shielding worked as an effective form of deterrence. When confronted with a human shielding situation, the francs-tireurs refrained from attacking the trains. This might explain why in France the deployment of human shields became standard policy and was not merely a spontaneous initiative introduced by a number of generals in the midst of the conflict, as it had been during the American Civil War.[16]

In order to institutionalize the practice, the German civil governor of Rheims, for example, published this written decree: "The trains shall be accompanied by well-known and respected [French] persons inhabiting the towns or other localities in the neighborhood of the lines. These persons shall be placed upon the engine, so that it may be understood that in every accident caused by the hostility of the inhabitants, their compatriots will be the first to suffer. The competent civil and military authorities together with the railway companies and the *etappen* commandants will organize a service of hostages to accompany the trains."[17]

Such orders did not sit well with the nascent body of international law. By intentionally subjecting civilians to imminent danger in order to prevent the attacks by French irregulars, the German occupying forces undermined the principle of distinction between combatants, who are permissible targets, and noncombatants, who are entitled to protection from hostilities. This principle, which had already begun to coalesce as one of the pillars of the laws of armed conflict, also serves to distinguish between humane and inhumane violence: only violence that aspires to discriminate between combatants and noncombatants is considered humane.

To justify the indiscriminate warfare practices, the German popular press vilified the resistance fighters as ruthless murderers and criminals, claiming that the French insurgency was barbaric. In an essay published ten years after the war, Moltke wrote that "even the disorder of the francs-tireurs did not delay our operations a single day. Their gruesome work had to be answered by bloody coercion. Because of this, our conduct of the war finally assumed a harshness that we deplored, but which we could not avoid. The francs-tireurs were the terror of all the villages; they brought on their own destruction."[18] The French resistance—and particularly the fact that it was led by insurgents who were not fighting at the behest of the state—was thus blamed for the use of civilian dignitaries as human shields.

IN THE SHADOW OF THE LAW

The Franco-German War is unique not only because it was the first war to systematize the use of human shields, but also because it was the first international armed conflict that took place after the signing of international conventions that explicitly invoked the notion of "humanity" as the ethical principle that should regulate the conduct of war. By the time conflict broke out, the Lieber Code was not the only document regulating the use of violence during war. Between the American Civil War and this war, the 1864 First Geneva Convention and the 1868 St. Petersburg Declaration had been drafted and ratified, making the Franco-German War the first conflict between two countries that were signatories to treaties aimed at regulating the permissible acts of war.[19] While both documents appealed to the notion of humanity, the St. Petersburg Declaration noted also that "the only legitimate object which States should endeavor to accomplish during war is to weaken the military forces of the enemy," thus drawing a distinction between military and civilian targets.[20]

By signing these treaties, states had for the first time agreed on a legal vocabulary for articulating what became known as the principle of distinction and what constitutes humane violence during armed conflict. And by the time the Franco-German War erupted, the new legal and ethical frameworks had become increasingly important in the eyes of politicians and high-ranking military officers.

The wartime incidents and the different conventions that had been drafted before the war as well as the treaties and military manuals that appeared in its immediate aftermath induced jurists from different countries to clarify whether human shielding is a legitimate practice according to the laws of armed conflict.[21] Indeed, the attacks carried out by French irregulars against the German occupying forces and the latter's indiscriminate response spurred conflicting legal interpretations from the most renowned judicial minds of the late nineteenth and early twentieth centuries.

PARADIGM SHIFT

The legal debate that followed the Franco-German War focused on the status of irregulars within the laws of war, and the use of human shields—referred to as hostages by the legal experts who participated in the discussions—emerged for the first time as a major issue of concern. The arguments took place on the pages of key legal textbooks over more than three decades, up to the outbreak of the First World War, and they reflected a major transformation in the underlying assumptions informing international law and the ethics of humane violence.

The founders of international law, among them Francisco de Vitoria (1480–1546), Alberico Gentili (1552–1608), and Hugo Grotius (1583–1645), had subscribed to the idea that all nations are bound by a universal natural law. Their writings were informed by medieval Christian conceptions of justice, norms of honor, and martial virtue, and they had inspired the French jurist Antoine Pillet, who following the Franco-German War had railed against the indiscriminate warfare practices deployed by the German occupiers.[22] Referring to the German deployment of human shields in several French towns, Pillet wrote that it "constitutes one of the most evident violations generated by recent practices of war.... There is no military virtue in using noncombatants as shields against the military operations of the enemy.... Noncombatant immunity is against this kind of practice."[23]

Pillet's invocation of "military virtue" assumes that modes of humane warfare derive from natural law. Following this line of thinking, the use of human shields is illegal because it is indiscriminate: it breaches the notion of "noncombatant immunity," which was, in turn, perceived as a manifestation of a universal dictate prescribing a certain humane deployment of violence.

Hence, Pillet judged the German use of French civilians as shields to be an egregious violation of the laws of war and an inhumane act.

On the other side of this debate were jurists who sought to reconstruct the entire system of international law under a new paradigm of state-centric jurisprudence. The legal scholars advocating this shift were positivists who believed in the centrality of the state, and their main claim was that international law is a reflection of "sovereign will rather than natural law."[24] Rejecting the natural-law idea that state action had to be guided by a higher morality, the positivists considered the sovereign state as the highest authority that is "bound only to that which it had agreed."[25] In their view, the international arena was created by sovereign authorities that allocated jurisdictions and built order by contract among independent sovereigns. Rules of international law were not codes to be discovered through inquiry into the nature of justice but were agreements formulated by states to regulate relations among them.[26]

Representing the positivist strain, the renowned German jurist Lassa Oppenheim followed by the British jurist James Spaight defended the use of human shields during the Franco-German War, but they did so in a roundabout way. They actually agreed with Pillet that the deployment of French dignitaries as human shields was a violation of international law since it undermined the principle of distinction, but they framed the German practice as an act of legitimate reprisal that rendered the shielding practice legal.[27]

The purpose of a reprisal is to induce compliance with international law.[28] A legitimate reprisal is defined as an intentional violation of a given rule within the law of armed conflict with the aim of making the adverse party discontinue a policy of violation of the same or another rule of that body of law.[29] A reprisal is, in other words, a form of derogation of the laws of armed conflict but is, somewhat paradoxically, used "to ensure compliance with those same laws."[30] Put simply, the law is violated in order to preserve the law.

While modern treaties have limited the scope of legitimate reprisals to operations carried out against armed forces, in the nineteenth century reprisals could be legally directed against civilians.[31] Indeed, until the mid-twentieth century a punitive approach towards civilian populations was both commonplace and regarded as legally sanctioned.[32] Oppenheim and Spaight accordingly argued that the use of civilians as human shields was part of a legitimate form of reprisal.

The debate becomes particularly interesting once one considers the reason why these legal scholars perceived the French assaults on the German supply trains as illegal. Given Spaight's claim that destroying railways is a "perfectly legitimate act of war," the violation they are referring to has nothing to do with the nature of the French attacks, but rather with the identity of those perpetrating them.[33] For any belligerent assault to be legal, it must, according to Spaight, "be carried out by the enemy's proper agents of war," and since the francs-tireurs were not part of the regular combatant troops, they were not proper agents of war.[34] Or as Oppenheim claimed, "there is no doubt that a belligerent is justified in resorting to reprisals in each case of train-wrecking by *private enemy individuals.*"[35]

Furthermore, since the French were fighting a people's war, whereby civilians served as combatants, violence that had been rendered illegal because it was considered to be inhumane, including the use of human shields, could legitimately be used both against the irregulars and against the civilian population that helped them hide. Insofar as the goal was to repress and destroy irregular combatants who blurred the distinction between civilians and combatants, the state's army could legitimately violate the laws of war and inflict forms of indiscriminate punishment that "ensure compliance with those same laws." In this way, these legal scholars justified the coercive use of French dignitaries as shields and, in effect, the dehumanization of civilians.

IRREGULAR SHIELDING

This legal debate took place in what years later cultural theorist Stuart Hall would call a "conjunctural moment."[36] Precisely because international law center-staged the state as the supreme authority, the irregular emerged as an important legal figure, albeit an illegitimate one. Positivist jurists believed that if the state's monopoly over the means of legitimate violence were secured, interstate violence would be circumscribed and limited.[37] However, because irregulars—today's insurgents, partisans, resistance fighters, and terrorists—do not operate at the behest of the state, these legal thinkers thought that they would destabilize the international order aimed at regulating the humane conduct of war and thus end up increasing the levels of violence. According to this worldview, the sovereign's role is to engender stability and reduce violence at all costs, and therefore in the fight against irregulars, the protections conferred on civilian populations can be forfeited.[38] In other words, inhumane violence can legally be deployed in a war against irregulars.

This logic first emerged in Thomas Hobbes's mid-seventeenth-century

Leviathan, where he lays out the social contract between citizens and their sovereign. Hobbes's general idea was extended from the local to the international sphere with the development of the laws of war, but the logic remained similar: irregulars threaten the political and legal order, and in order to secure their eradication, civilian protections can be sacrificed by sovereign states.[39] The irregular thus emerges as a threat to the international legal order, surfacing as a prominent legal figure precisely because it is incompatible with the ascendancy of positivist jurisprudence, which center-stages the state and therefore the regular army. Since it challenges the statist paradigm, positivist jurists believe it is necessary to repress and ultimately annihilate the irregular at all costs.

The fact that the human shield emerges as an urgent topic at the same time as the irregular is not coincidental. Both challenge the laws of war's attempt to draw clear distinctions. Human shields are legally protected persons—either civilians or prisoners of war—who are meant to deter attacks by occupying the space between a belligerent and a legitimate military target and are thus transformed into weapons of war. Irregulars are civilians who might spend their time plowing the fields or selling fruits at the market but, a short time later, might shoot at a supply train or ambush a military convoy, immediately thereafter returning to the fold of their community to hide. Even when they participate in hostilities, they are not considered lawful combatants because they are not fighting at the behest of the state.[40] Therefore, the violence they deploy is by definition illegal and was considered in the fledgling international legal order as inhumane. Both figures occupy a threshold position that does not adapt to the rigid legal distinction between combatants and noncombatants. That is why they both become a threat to international law.[41]

As we see in the case of the Franco- German War, the regular military can and does use—or one should say "produce"—one threshold figure, the human shield, to fight against the other threshold figure, the irregular. Indeed, to this very day, human shielding practices continue to be intricately tied to the irregular, where the figure of the irregular and the figure of the human shield are part and parcel of the same conundrum. Neither is reducible to civilian or to full-fledged combatant—both lie somewhere in between.

THREE

———

Settlers

The Second Boer War and the Limits of
Liberal Humanitarianism

THE GERMANS WERE NOT THE ONLY ONES to use human shields to protect their trains from attacks waged by irregulars. The same practice was adopted in 1900 on the African continent, this time by the British against Dutch settlers, who were called Boers. Following the British government's refusal to withdraw its troops from territories where numerous gold and diamond mines had been discovered, the Boers declared war against the imperial army. The context was unusual. It was a colonial setting, but the fighting parties were white. Consequently, the rules of engagement and the implementation of the laws of armed conflict, which in other colonial wars were deemed inapplicable, were regarded as pertinent and were closely scrutinized by the British press and debated in the House of Commons.[1]

During the days preceding what would become the Second Boer War, Winston Churchill, who at the time was an ambitious war correspondent, received a lucrative offer from the *Morning Post* to travel to South Africa and report on the new colonial conflict. Whether out of fear of solitude or simply a taste for alcohol, Churchill packed six bottles of champagne, eighteen bottles of wine, six bottles of light port, six bottles of French vermouth, and eighteen bottles of ten-year-old Scotch whisky to take to the African continent. A few days later, he left Southampton on a steamer packed with soldiers for a two-week trip to Cape Town's harbor.[2]

It was clear that Great Britain had a score to settle with the Boers, particularly after the 1881 defeat at the Battle of Majuba, where hundreds of British soldiers had been humiliated and forced to raise the white flag.[3] Indeed, in his unpublished imperialist pamphlet *Our Account with the Boers,* Churchill had called for revenge following this debacle. "Imperial aid must redress the wrongs of the Outlanders," he wrote, adding that "Imperial troops must curb

FIGURE 5. The wrecked British armored train on which Winston Churchill was travelling after the Boers captured him, 1899. Credit: The Australian War Memorial.

the insolence of the Boers. There must be no half-measures. The forces employed must be strong enough to bear down all opposition."[4]

A month and a half after his arrival in Cape Town, Churchill went missing while travelling by train with more than a hundred British soldiers.[5] As it turned out, the Boer resistance had attacked the armored railcars while they were crossing the Republic of Natal (figure 5). In his ecstatic account of the incident, Churchill wrote that, in his young career, nothing had been as exciting as being trapped in the clanging of "rending iron boxes, with the repeated explosions of the shells and the artillery, the noise of the projectiles striking the cars, the hiss as they passed in the air, the grunting and puffing of the engine."[6] After surrendering along with a group of soldiers, Churchill was transferred to a prisoner of war camp in Pretoria, from which he managed to escape a few months later.

As Churchill's account of the Boer attack underscored, the armor protecting the trains was insufficient for shielding the travelling soldiers. This, in turn, encouraged the Boers to continue targeting the railway network, causing significant losses to the imperial troops. The royal forces responded by adopting a series of new counterinsurgency measures—among them the use of human shields. This triggered a heated debate within Parliament and among journalists, legal experts, and humanitarians, some of whom denounced the practice as inhumane. British liberals were outraged, but not because they rejected imperial violence, which they thought was, at times, a necessary tool for extending universal humanity across the empire.[7] Their criticism of using Boer settlers as human shields was that the violence was directed at whites, thus revealing the racial underpinnings of their conception of humanity. Human shielding would have probably passed unnoticed if the people used as shields had been black.

COUNTERINSURGENCY DILEMMAS

Significantly, only a few months before the outbreak of the war, Britain had signed the 1899 Hague Convention, which contained a series of "general rules of conduct for belligerents in their relations with each other" as well as the way they should treat civilian populations.[8] The Hague Convention did not prohibit the use of human shields but did stipulate that forms of collective punishment could not be inflicted on civilian populations. According to the great powers, such articles were considered irrelevant to colonial wars because these wars were framed as internal conflicts and the laws of war were deemed applicable only to conflicts between two or more sovereign states. After all, these articles were formulated, as Noura Erakat reminds us, by colonial states and therefore are "structurally detrimental to people still under colonial domination."[9] But as the British officer Charles Edward Callwell—who decided to revise his famous 1896 manual, *Small Wars,* to include the lessons learnt from the Second Boer War—noted, when confronting the Boer settlers the Royal Army faced a thorny dilemma, one that did not exist in other colonial wars where British soldiers faced mainly nonwhite enemies.[10]

Precisely because the hostilities in South Africa were between whites, Callwell believed that the laws of war might be applicable and that the counterinsurgency strategies in such a context need to be amended. Underscoring the exceptionality of the situation, he noted that the unusual enemy "presented all the features of rebels in a civilized country," although actually, Boer settlers were fighting for national independence in a black territory that had been colonized since the seventeenth century.[11] The racial lens through which Callwell saw the war raised a series of dilemmas about the counterinsurgency techniques that should be adopted. The enemy's race, as it turns out, determined which methods of warfare were perceived to be legitimate and humane.

In January 1900, two months after Churchill had been captured, Field Marshal Lord Frederick Sleigh Roberts of Kandahar was tasked with defeating the Boer guerrillas. The man had considerable experience quelling revolts in India, Abyssinia, and Afghanistan, yet he had never had to confront groups of white irregulars in an imperial war. A month before assuming command of the troops, his son had been killed by Boer fighters in one of the most humiliating defeats for British forces. Roberts was therefore anxious to suppress the resistance. He established his headquarters on a luxurious train before launching the onslaught into Boer territory.

Meanwhile, the rebels started digging trenches along key natural defense lines, while dynamiting bridges and railway culverts in order to prevent the British forces from advancing. The attacks slowed the British troops' progress, and the field hospitals began to fill with wounded men.[12] Notwithstanding fierce Boer resistance, Roberts managed to conquer Pretoria, liberating British prisoners of war who, unlike Churchill, had not managed to escape. Just as the warring parties seemed ready to sign a peace agreement ending the hostilities, the Boer guerrillas reorganized and dealt the imperial battalions a series of heavy blows. Several trains and stations were attacked, and weapons, ammunition, and food supplies destined for Roberts's troops were seized by the resistance fighters.[13]

In response, Roberts decided to introduce punitive counterinsurgency measures directly targeting the Boer civilian population. Echoing the directives Field Marshal von Moltke had published thirty years earlier during the Franco-German War, he issued two infamous proclamations. The first proclamation, from June 16, 1900, reads as follows:

> Whereas small parties of raiders have recently been doing wanton damage to public property in the Orange River Colony and South African Republic by destroying railway bridges and culverts and cutting the telegraph wires; and whereas such damage cannot be done without the knowledge and connivance of the neighboring inhabitants and principal civil residents in the districts concerned ... I warn the said inhabitants and principal residents that, whenever public property is destroyed or injured in the manner specified above, they will be held responsible for aiding and abetting the offenders. The houses in the vicinity of the place where the damage is done will be burnt and the principal civil residents will be made prisoners of war.[14]

Roberts thus transformed all noncombatants living in those areas where Boer guerrillas carried out raids into accomplices, while rounding up civilians in concentration camps and instituting retaliatory practices against anyone who supported the rebels. A man of his word, he went on to authorize the incineration of Boer farms in areas where rebel attacks had increased. That proclamation was, however, only the preamble to the one published three days later, which included a new "prophylactic method" that had never before been used by the British military in South Africa: "As a further precautionary method, the Director of the Military Railways has been authorized to order that one or more of the residents, who will be selected by him from each district, shall from time to time personally accompany the trains while travelling through their district."[15]

SELECTIVE HUMANITARIANISM

The practice of forcing Boer civilians to serve as human shields on the trains was systematized in the following months, triggering heated debates in Britain. Many British liberals were outraged by the fact that the imperial army had decided to adopt counterinsurgency techniques usually reserved for nonwhite populations. For the first time in recorded history, human shielding became a popular topic in the Western press, so much so that even Arthur Conan Doyle—the famous novelist who wrote about the adventures of Sherlock Holmes—intervened in the debate. Writing a letter to *The Times* about how to deal with train wreckages, he called upon the military to "put a truck full of Boer irreconcilables behind every engine which passes through a dangerous part of the country."[16] Later, in a book he published about the Boer War, Doyle claimed that his proposal had been too lenient, writing that "in the case of the train hostages, we have gone too far in the direction of clemency. Had the first six khaki-clad burghers been shot, the lives of many of our soldiers would have been saved."[17]

In a similar vein, the secretary of the Army League and Imperial Defense Association wrote a letter to *The Times* entitled "Guerrillas and Derailing: A Protest," in which he attacked the "misplaced humanitarianism" of the government in dealing with the Boer rebels. Supporting Roberts's proclamations, he cited the "effective measures" taken by the Germans in the 1870–71 war with France and by the federal forces in the American Civil War, arguing that only such methods could stop guerrilla warfare.[18]

In spite of the support Roberts received in certain circles, his proclamations were never officially sanctioned by the British administration in South Africa; the colonial bureaucrats, it appears, did not want in any way to suggest that the practice had been approved from the top, particularly after humanitarian activists began criticizing in the British press and in Parliament the use of hostages as shields.[19] Impassioned discussions about the use of human shields were further fueled by revelations about the treatment of Boer civilians in the concentration camps Roberts had set up. The two issues were connected in the eyes of the humanitarians because both were considered dehumanizing practices.

Leading the campaign against the concentration camps, which housed over a hundred thousand Boer civilians, was humanitarian activist Emily Hobhouse, who had returned from South Africa after having spent several months chronicling the conditions of the internees. Measles, typhoid, diphtheria, and dysentery had resulted in the death of an estimated one in every five people in the camps. Describing the appalling circumstances in a damning report, she called upon the British government to alleviate the detainees' dire living conditions.[20]

In response, the government set up the Committee of Ladies to investigate the situation in the camps. This was the first official investigation commission composed of only women, and it was led by the famous suffragist Millicent Fawcett.[21] The committee corroborated some of Hobhouse's findings, but even as both the independent and the governmental reports discussed in detail the dreadful conditions of white Boers, they almost completely ignored the plight of black South Africans, of whom over a hundred thousand had also been detained in concentration camps. And like their white counterparts, several thousand of the black internees had also perished in the camps.

Notwithstanding the fact that both whites and blacks were subjected to inhumane conditions by the imperial forces, the humanitarians restricted their criticism to the way the Boers were treated. The ethical imperative introduced by the humanitarians was progressive only in the sense that it was concerned for the well-being of people from other countries and not only the plight of their British compatriots. Like the conservatives with whom they debated, the humanitarians ignored the suffering of nonwhites. The new humanism operated along racial lines, excluding certain racial groups from the fold of humanity.

Reinforcing this racial conception of the human, whereby only the vulnerability of some deserves humane treatment, other humanitarians penned articles focusing on the use of human shields. One of the pioneers of investigative journalism in Britain, William Thomas Stead, wrote a series of articles as well as *Methods of Barbarism: The Case for Intervention,* a book in which he called for international humanitarian intervention on behalf of the Boers.[22] In a similar vein, renowned liberal jurist Frederic Mackarness attacked the support for human shielding as "wholly inconsistent with the principles recognized by civilized nations as applicable to the treatment of hostages."[23]

In an article published in *The Speaker,* Mackarness condemned the British use of human "screens" as an inhumane method of warfare prohibited by the 1874 Brussels Declaration, according to which the population of an occupied territory cannot be forced to fight against their own country. By way of conclusion, he noted that in "modern regular war of Europeans and their descendants in other portions of the globe, protection of the inoffensive citizens of the hostile country is the rule."[24]

For the British humanitarians, international law was a question of white blood. Native populations were routinely subjected to the indiscriminate use of inhumane violence without protest, not to mention public outcry. But because in this case the enemies in the colony were white, these humanitarians believed that their use as human shields was illegal and that the laws of war were pertinent to the conflict. This highlights how the applicability or inapplicability of the laws of war was influenced just as much by the skin color of rebelling populations as by the colonial setting.

Meanwhile in the House of Commons, liberals denounced Lord Roberts's proclamations as an egregious violation of "civilized" norms. Labor MP Thomas Shaw argued that "men of the same race will not be treated contrary to every rule that should prevail among civilized mankind . . . . It is said that we want to extinguish a nationality. I fear that these practices have gone far to create a nationality. Lord Roberts was entirely mistaken as to the effect that was going to be produced by his proclamations."[25] Shaw considered human shielding a supreme form of cruelty, adding that the use of civilians on trains was a barbarous practice that put Great Britain in bad company with the Germans, who had utilized the same counterinsurgency technique in 1870–71. Conservative MPs responded to Shaw, invoking the German and American deployment of human shields to argue that it had been sanctioned by some of the highest authorities of international law as a legitimate form of reprisal.[26]

FIRST-CLASS HUMAN SHIELDS

John Brodrick, the secretary of state for war, immediately forwarded the exchange in the English press to Herbert Kitchener, who in November 1900 had replaced Lord Roberts as the commander of the British forces in South Africa.[27] Although he adopted Roberts's human shielding tactics in an effort to quell a new wave of attacks against trains, Kitchener was also aware of the growing criticism being voiced by liberal humanitarians back home. He consequently refined his predecessor's directive, instructing his subordinates to provide civilians used as human shields with "first class accommodation and rations for the journey," noting also that they "were to be under personal charge of the officer commanding the train escort."[28] From then on, Boer shields were to travel first class.

Notwithstanding this gesture, English humanitarians were not placated.[29] Among the fiercest opponents of human shielding was Viscount James Bryce, a Scottish lawyer and politician who fifteen years later, as we will see, would produce one of the first reports on the violations of international law committed by Germans during the occupation of Belgium in the First World War. A cosmopolitan antiwar politician, Bryce's opposition to the use of human shields and other crimes committed by the British against the Boers was grounded in the idea that Britons and Boers belonged to the same civilized race and religion and had nothing in common with the "savage tribes" of South Africa.[30] As a pro-Boer MP, Bryce asked the secretary of state for war which other "civilized countries" considered putting hostages on trains a legitimate counterinsurgency practice.[31] Initially, Brodrick refused to respond, but later he allusively declared that "it is well known that in one great war, at least, the practice was continually followed."[32]

Given the colonial context in which the British carried out their counterinsurgency campaign against the Boers, denunciations of human shielding focused on white-on-white barbarity, an affair of "Europeans and their descendants,"[33] while black Africans were elided from the majority of these discussions triggered by both the government and the humanitarians. Their elision underscores how even among liberal thinkers, political conceptions of humanness and thus human shields were inflected by and through race. In an imperial theatre of violence, the liberal critique of civilized warfare was grounded in racist assumptions about the way whites should fight whites, which were posited as oppositional to the way whites were allowed to fight blacks. The figure of the human shield produced among humanitarians a selective moral aversion to the deployment of white noncombatants to protect military targets, revealing how racial distinctions pervade the ethics of humane violence.

FOUR

Reports

World War I and the German Use of Human Screens

MORE THAN FOUR DECADES after the Franco-German War, human shields were once again deployed on European soil, this time during the First World War. In August 1914, immediately after Germany invaded Belgium, the German general Otto von Emmich, who commanded the forces responsible for securing the roads into the neighboring country, issued a proclamation that was handed to the civilian population by soldiers on the front lines. Perhaps because Germany had promised not to invade Belgium in previous political agreements, in the proclamation the general framed the occupation as an effort to create a corridor that would allow Germany to protect itself from French hostilities:

> It is with the greatest regret that the German troops find themselves forced to cross the frontier of Belgium. They are impelled by inevitable necessity, the neutrality of Belgium having already been violated by French officers who in disguise crossed Belgium in [vehicles in an effort] to enter Germany.
>
> Belgians! It is our greatest wish that there may yet be found a way of avoiding a combat between two nations who have hitherto been friendly and at one time even allies. Remember the glorious day of Waterloo, when the German armies helped to found and establish the independence and prosperity of your country. But we must have a free road. The destruction of bridges, tunnels, and railways will be regarded as hostile acts.
>
> Belgians! It is for you to choose. I therefore trust that the Army of the Meuse will not be compelled to fight you. All we wish is to have a free road to attack the enemy who wanted to attack us. I give a formal guarantee to the Belgian people that they will not suffer from the horrors of war; that we will pay in money for the provisions that must be taken in the country; that our soldiers will show themselves good friends of a people for whom we feel the utmost esteem and greatest sympathy. It depends on your discretion and wisely conceived patriotism to save your country from the horrors of war.[1]

Despite General Emmich's affable tone, a few months after the fighting began, a number of reports were published describing Germany's brutal treatment of the Belgian population, including its extensive use of civilians as "human screens."[2] These were among the first documents that relied on international law to denounce inhumane violence. And while the Belgian government published the first account of the war, as we will see, the different countries involved in the fighting also put out similar documents, ultimately leading to a battle of reports.

At first, Germany was blamed for violating *jus ad bellum,* the criteria that determine whether waging war is permissible, but swiftly the debate shifted to the infringement of *jus in bello,* the regulations determining legal conduct within the fray.[3] The cruelty of the German military was emphasized, including reference to a series of massacres carried out against Belgian civilians. Faced with armed resistance that included attacks against communication and transportation lines, the German troops apparently had not hesitated to bomb densely populated areas, burn houses and villages, execute civilian hostages, and use human shields.[4] A few months later, the German military occupied a strip of northern France bordering Belgium and subjected the French population to similar treatment.

The German use of human shields was quite systematic and was not confined to the occupied territories. When French airplanes bombed the German city of Freiburg, striking the civilian population, individuals and organizations started to send petitions to the local municipality, asking that a prisoner-of-war camp be created within the city that would serve as a shield against aerial attacks. Under public pressure, the municipality forwarded the petitions to the military, and after a few days the first prisoners of war were moved to the city center to form a protective shield.[5]

Across the English Channel, the British government used testimonies about German atrocities to galvanize public support for entering the war. Germany's violation of the 1839 Treaty of London, signed by Britain, Germany, and other leading European powers, was invoked. According to the treaty, Britain was obliged to defend Belgium if another country violated its neutrality, and this was used to convince the British public that intervention was not only the moral thing to do but also a legal obligation. British statesmen reiterated that the Treaty of London was a "cornerstone of European international law," while insisting that Germany had also violated the Hague Conventions.[6] Germany responded by trying to minimize the legal significance of Belgium's occupation; it described the sixty-five-year-old treaty as a "scrap of paper" and argued that many of the Hague articles regulating armed conflict did not apply to the current situation.[7] But most politicians and jurists across Europe were not convinced, arguing that Germany's belligerent act had destabilized Europe's legal order.

The governmental reports produced following the German occupation of Belgium, and later of France, focused extensively on the inhumane warfare methods adopted by the Germans. The figure of the human shield became a key lens through which European states debated the use of violence, advanced their legal and ethical arguments, and forged a distinction between civilized and uncivilized violence. For Britain, these reports about "German barbarism" also constituted a tool for justifying its military intervention.

DOCUMENTING GERMAN ATROCITIES

The First World War was different from previous European wars due to developments in logistics, infrastructure, and technologies supporting the war effort. The railway networks and other improvements in the means of transportation enabled the ongoing movement of armed forces, and the delivery of thousands of tons of supplies to the troops stationed at the front helped prolong the war.[8] Simultaneously, the aerial bombings of entire towns and the dramatic improvement in standardized weapons, such as mortars and assault rifles, increased the indiscriminate targeting of noncombatants—a practice regularly adopted in colonial wars—on a scale that had been unprecedented in Europe.

Perhaps not surprisingly, within days of Germany's invasion, stories of "atrocities" started to circulate in the European press, pushing Britain, France, and Russia to deepen their involvement in the war. Shortly thereafter, the Belgian government started to gather testimonies from Belgian and French civilians as well as German soldiers and set up a commission to investigate alleged war crimes committed against the seven million civilians living under occupation. The objective was to determine whether the German military had violated the laws of war.[9]

This was not the first time a government established a commission to assess possible human rights violations. Millicent Fawcett, as we noted in chapter 3, led a government commission charged with investigating the concentration camps set up by the British during the Second Boer War, and Roger Casement was appointed by the British Foreign Office to investigate alleged crimes carried out by King Leopold in the Congo. The Congo report exposed the horrific conduct by Belgians in the colony.[10] Casement went on to lead an investigation commission in Peru in 1910, charged with looking into the exploitation of indigenous rubber-gatherers by the Peruvian Amazon Company.

Yet, a key difference between those reports and the one on Germany's occupation of Belgium was that the latter relied heavily on the laws of war, using them as a reference point when assessing evidence of German atrocities. In this sense, it served as a precursor to the reports initially published by the International Committee of the Red Cross and from the 1970s onwards by scores of human rights and humanitarian nongovernmental organizations like Amnesty International and Human Rights Watch. Indeed, the Belgian commission was probably the first to systematically use the Hague Conventions as the primary lens to assess and judge the conduct of armed forces during war. Moreover, in an effort to reinforce the Belgian findings, the British and French governments followed suit and appointed their own commissions to investigate alleged German crimes.

The first in a series of Belgian reports, aptly named *Reports on the Violation of the Rights of Nations and the Laws and Customs of War,* was published in 1915, not long after the German invasion. Its objective was to expose the brutal tactics adopted by the Germans.[11] The report was immediately translated into English in an effort to reach an international audience. Significantly, five months before the First World War began, the Germans had relaxed the instructions protecting enemy civilians and institutionalized the use of human shields. Indeed, in March 1914, the German military had issued a new manual for the rear guard—the *Kriegs-Etappen-Ordnung*—where human shielding appeared as part of the official protocol regulating armed conflict. The manual noted that "enemy civilians are liable to collective punishment in case of sabotage and to serve as hostages on threatened railways."[12] Predictably, one crucial violation highlighted in the Belgian reports was the repeated use of tens, and at times hundreds, of civilians as human shields (figure 6), often in retaliation against attacks perpetrated by the Belgian resistance, which routinely targeted railways, stations, and bridges used by the Germans to transfer supplies for their troops.

Denouncing "the outrages committed by the German soldiery when opposed by the chivalrous and heroic resistance of the Belgian nation," the Belgian commission continued to gather evidence of war crimes in the "statements made by actual witnesses—persons who have seen with their own eyes

"FIRE ALL THE SAME!" HEROIC ZOUAVE PRISONERS MARCHED BEFORE GERMANS.
The left-hand drawing illustrates, according to a French paper, a cruel German ruse practised in attacking a bridge over the Yser Canal, at Dry-Grachten, defended by Zouaves. The Germans pushed in front of them a number of Zouave prisoners. As they approached, there arose from the Allies' lines shouts of "Cease fire! Cease fire! Zouaves!" and the rifles and machine-guns stopped.

FIGURE 6. Germans using Belgian prisoners of war as human shields. Credit: *The Illustrated War News,* December 1914.

the deeds to which they testify."[13] It accused the Germans of compelling "civilians, women and children" "in nearly all places" to walk in advance of their troops so as to render it impossible for the resistance to shoot at them.[14] The inclusion of women and children as human shields points to a crucial historical shift, since it suggests that the political value ascribed to them had increased and that they, too, could now serve as a deterrent. By emphasizing the use of "womenandchildren"—who have, as feminist political scientist Cynthia Enloe observed, historically been framed in international conflicts as innocent and vulnerable subjects par excellence—as shields, the report also intimates that the Germans were, in fact, uncivilized.[15] Not unlike modern-day human rights reports, it provides a series of examples: "On the

6th [of] August [1915] a number of soldiers were made prisoners by a German column. At Saive a company of Belgians were encountered. The prisoners were immediately placed at the head of the troops, so [as] to cover the column and make it impossible for the Belgians to fire upon them. On the 23rd [of] August the Germans forced women and children to walk in front of the troops ordered to take the bridge at Lives, opposite to Biez. A number of these women and children were wounded."[16]

In one of many references to the 1907 Hague Convention, the Belgian commission states that "if it be not permissible to compel a man to fire on his fellow citizens, neither can he be forced to protect the enemy and to serve as a living screen. In both cases the effect would be to compel him to engage in acts of warfare against his own countrymen, to expose him to danger, and to inflict upon him the most painful moral violence."[17] Maintaining that some "German officers have little regard for such considerations," the authors condemn the employment of warfare strategies that "affect and injure neutrals and noncombatants more than the belligerent troops."[18]

They go on to lament the vague and insufficient protections international law confers on civilian hostages.[19] Although they comment that the law does not offer sufficient tools to adequately assess German warfare practices, the report's authors conclude that, according to the evidence gathered, the Germans committed a series of war crimes, with human shielding as one of the offenses appearing on the list.

THE GERMAN RESPONSE

The Germans did not hesitate to shoot back, publishing reports that countered the Belgian allegations. Despite its perceived deficiencies in the eyes of the Belgian commissioners, the 1907 Hague Convention on Laws and Customs of War on Land actually contains some important forms of protection for noncombatants. Article 2 permits spontaneous revolts against an occupying power but obliges resistance fighters to carry their arms openly.[20] In this way, the article calls upon warring parties to distinguish between noncombatants and combatants, while determining the conditions under which popular civilian participation in conflicts is legitimate. Specifically, the clause stresses the prohibition on targeting civilians who do not carry weapons.

Using this article to counter the Belgian accusations, the German government published a report entitled *The Belgian's People War: A Violation of*

International Law, also known as "the German White Book." Providing numerous excerpts from prominent German and Belgian newspapers and testimonies of German soldiers, this report suggested that the civilian population violated the Hague Convention because the local *franc-tireurs,* as the Germans also called the Belgian partisans, did not wear distinctive badges and adopted perfidious warfare methods.[21] They "regularly carried weapons in a concealed fashion,"[22] the White Book charged, adding that the German Army "is accustomed to make war only against hostile armies, and not against peaceful inhabitants."[23] Finally, following Lassa Oppenheim, the renowned positivist jurist who had justified the use of human shields during the Franco-German War, the Germans defended the harsh measures adopted against the civilian population as a form of legitimate reprisal against illegal guerrilla warfare.[24] Once again, military necessity took priority over civilian immunity.

The Belgian government issued a formal response, reiterating that the use of civilians as shields was the most barbarous violation committed by the Germans. "Nothing," the government said, "can surpass in dastardly cruelty the system inaugurated by the German troops as soon as they came in contact with the Belgian Army, the system of protecting themselves by driving men, women and children in front of them."[25] The government went on to deny the presence of franc-tireurs, claiming that Belgian resistance was carried out by its regular army, while simultaneously rejecting the German argument that in instances of irregular warfare, reprisals against civilian populations were legitimate.

The debate on human shielding did not remain confined to the Belgian and German reports. Shortly after those reports were published, the methods of warfare used by the Germans were investigated by other countries, and for the first time in history the deployment of human shields was discussed in the international political arena.

CHRONICLING THE USE OF HUMAN SCREENS

Joining the war over information and its legal interpretation, the French and British governments also published a number of reports concluding that the repertoires of violence deployed by the Germans were inhumane. The French assembled testimonies of occupied civilians and French soldiers, excerpts from notebooks left behind by German soldiers, and letters of soldiers to German newspapers were amassed together with translations of German military orders and leaflets distributed by the German army to the French civilian population. To these the commission also added forensic evidence, including images of prohibited ammunition.

Every section of the report offered an explanation and interpretation of the clauses of international law breached by the occupying army. The investigative team denounced the German violation of Belgium's neutrality and accused the Germans of several crimes, among them the use of civilians and prisoners of war as "human screens," as human shields were called at the time. These screens, the report asserted, were lined up in front of German troops who shot over their heads, thus exposing them to the fire of the French army.[26]

In Britain, Viscount James Bryce, the MP who had condemned the use of Boer hostages as shields during the Second Boer War, was appointed by the Liberal government to lead the Committee on Alleged German Outrages in Belgium. This committee interviewed mainly Belgian witnesses, among them many refugees who had fled to England, but it also interviewed British soldiers who had joined the Belgian resistance immediately after the German invasion. Based on the evidence they gathered, Bryce and his team concluded that the German military had systematically violated the laws of war.[27] The major crimes committed against civilians included indiscriminate killing, cruel treatment, and the deployment of civilians as human screens.

Concerning the use of human screens, the Bryce report conceded that not all forms of human screening are illegal and that in some instances, "when terrified civilians were rushing about to seek safety, . . . groups of them might be used as a screen by either side of the combatants without any intention of inhumanity or of any breach of the rules of civilized warfare." However, it concluded that "the rules and usages of war were frequently broken, particularly by the use of civilians, including women and children, as a shield for advancing forces."[28] The Bryce report was translated into over thirty languages, covered widely by the international press, and distributed among diplomats through British embassies and "propaganda headquarters," in particular in the United States where Bryce had served as British ambassador.[29] The report helped bolster widespread anger against German atrocities among European officials, US representatives, and an array of intellectuals.

In their White Book, the Germans rushed to refute the allegations made in the Bryce report, stating that the refugees interviewed by the Bryce Commission were unreliable, given the mental conditions under which they had provided their testimonies, conditions not "conducive to the presentation of accurate and veridical evidence."[30] Not unlike the Belgians and their allies, the Germans understood that the way warfare practices are framed determines the legitimacy of the violence that had been deployed. The struggle over the presentation of evidence and the definition of what constitutes humane and inhumane violence was not only about the conditions under which evidence was procured but also about the way violence was portrayed.

RATIONALIZING VIOLENCE

The appearance of reports, where evidence is gathered and war crimes are systematically recorded and subsequently interpreted in relation to international laws, constituted a watershed that helped transform how the ethics of humane violence is understood. These reports helped enhance the distinction between civilized and uncivilized warfare, between enlightened and barbaric actors, and thus shaped the ethical perception of conflicts. After the end of World War I, the Belgian, French, and British reports—including the passages on human shielding—were used as incriminating evidence in the Report of the Commission on Responsibilities instituted by the victors at the 1919 Paris Peace Conference in order to prosecute the German emperor Wilhelm II for his violations of the "laws of humanity."[31]

Indeed, in the eyes of many Europeans, the German occupation of Belgium constituted a moral turning point in the history of war. After reading the different reports about Belgium's occupation, the eminent international jurist Antoine Pillet, who had written about the use of human shields during the Franco-German War, claimed that the practices adopted by the Germans amounted to a "war of savages." According to Pillet, the use of human shields constituted a crime that helped implement a policy of ethnic cleansing, and the evidence gathered in the governmental reports signaled the death of international law.[32]

But if during the Second Boer War, debates about human shields exposed the racial dimension of the ethics of humane violence, during the First World War the "atrocious" German deployment of Belgian human shields and the battle of reports that framed the Germans as barbaric became one of the tools to justify British military intervention. Ironically, the documentation of barbarism in the reports became the means to justify more barbarism, rather than to restrain war. In fact, Britain's invocation of human shielding to rationalize the use of violence was not an isolated phenomenon limited to the First World War, but rather it is a widespread strategy employed throughout the entire legal and political history of human shielding, and even more today than in the past.

The difference between then and now is that today reports denouncing human rights violations and infringements of international law are no longer a state prerogative and have become key tools in the hands of nonstate actors and civil society organizations, such as Amnesty International and Human Rights Watch, which use them to critique state violence.[33] As we will see, several decades after the First World War, these organizations also started to cite the deployment of human shields in order to draw a distinction between humane and inhumane warfare. Indeed, almost every conflict is now accompanied by a battle of reports in which human shields often serve as markers symbolizing the exercise of barbaric violence.

FIVE

Peace Army

*International Pacifism and Voluntary Shielding
during the Sino-Japanese War*

BETWEEN THE FIRST AND SECOND WORLD WARS, Agnes Maude
Royden, a pacifist and a prominent peace organizer, formulated a concrete
antiwar strategy based on the deployment of voluntary human shields in
conflict zones.[1] One generation younger than Millicent Fawcett and Emily
Hobhouse—who had written the humanitarian reports about the treatment
of Boer prisoners during the Second Boer War (see chapter 3)—she, too, was
a suffragist. Royden was also the first female preacher in the United Kingdom,
and in 1921 she founded a nondenominational church in London called the
Guildhouse. The church's one-thousand-strong congregation regularly
assembled to hear her sermons about women's and workers' rights, decolonization, and Gandhian principles of nonviolent civil disobedience.[2] Over the
years, Royden acquired a name as a leading feminist and antiwar campaigner,
and when she traveled to the United States, Australia, New Zealand, India,
and China—as she frequently did—it was not uncommon for crowds of several thousand people to gather to hear her speak.[3]

During the 1915 invasion of Belgium, while the German military was forcing civilians to serve as involuntary shields, Royden published a pamphlet
called *The Great Adventure: The Way to Peace,* where she first mentioned
the idea of mobilizing masses of people who would be willing to risk their
lives for peace. "If millions of men will go out to offer their lives up in war,
surely there are those who would die for peace!" she wrote. And then she
asserted: "And if not men, we could have called out women. . . . There are
those who are ready to die for peace as any of the millions who with such
generous courage go to war. And had they been organized and ready, there
would have been no war. . . . In this way only, could we really have saved
Belgium."[4]

Indeed, in this tract Royden describes war as a great adventure and says that those who go to war know that they not only risk defeat but also "rightly glory in their willingness to take that risk in a good cause." She adds, "I, too, would have risked something—everything indeed—to win, not a devastated and ruined Belgium, but Belgium unscathed, untouched." She concedes that since the British had made a pledge to Belgium, it was their responsibility to intervene after German forces invaded the country. But, in her view, it would have been better if the British soldiers had crossed the channel unarmed; they could, she says, have "saved Belgium intact or suffered with her." Instead, the thousands of British soldiers who were sent to Belgium to fight against Germany ultimately helped perpetuate the same militarist ideal as the one espoused by the invaders: the notion that "might is right, and that the strongest nation has the right to force its government and its ideals on the less powerful."[5]

The objective of antiwar activism, in Royden's opinion, is not only to stop a particular war but also to dismantle the underlying social norms that sustain militarism. The idea of making war in order to make peace—an idea that haunts the proliferation of humanitarian wars that we know today—is, she claimed, a contradiction in terms, yet "this is what we set out to do when we 'fight German militarism' with the weapons of militarism." Royden maintains that one "cannot kill a wrong idea except with a right idea," and even though peace is often framed as "a dull, drab, sordid, selfish thing," it is actually guided by a far mightier heroism than the one that informs military reason. Peace is actually a great adventure, and when people begin to conceive it as such, they will "be drawn after it again."[6]

A LIVING WALL

Royden's views were influenced by many thinkers, and Mahatma Gandhi was among the most important.[7] In her mind, Gandhi revealed the political significance of Jesus's teachings within a contemporary context, so much so that in her eulogy to him she wrote that "The best Christian in the world and the man most like Christ was a Hindu. He was Mahatma Gandhi."[8] Royden was particularly taken by Gandhi's idea of satyagraha—literally "holding on to truth." Although he first translated *satyagraha* as "passive resistance," over the years he continuously developed the idea, emphasizing that resistance must also be active.[9] This included putting one's body on the front line to resist injustice, an element that has inspired many voluntary human shields in conflict zones and civil protests to this day. Royden travelled to India several times to meet the Indian resistance leader, and when he visited London in 1929, he delivered a speech at Royden's church.

In December 1931, Gandhi attended a conference convened in Geneva by the Women's International League for Peace and Freedom, an organization created in 1915 to advocate for peace beyond the framework of treaties between great powers. Several British feminists were involved in the organization, including Royden. After his speech, one of the participants asked Gandhi: "How could a disarmed neutral country allow other nations to be destroyed?" There are, he replied, two ways that a neutral country could prevent such destruction. If he had been the president of Switzerland, he would have refused passage to the invading army by preventing all supplies from entering his country. Alternatively, he said, people could take the initiative and create "a living wall of men and women and children ... inviting the invaders to walk over your corpses."[10]

We do not know if Royden was present to hear this exchange, but it seems likely that Gandhi's idea of creating a living wall of people to resist war influenced her political imagination.[11] Indeed, a few months later the suffragist came up with a strikingly similar proposal in order to try to stop the Japanese occupation of China. Gandhi's claim that nonviolent resistance has an active element seems to have motivated her to try to come up with forms of pacifism that were not limited to antiwar declarations and included active opposition to war.[12] In addition, Gandhi's idea of satyagraha as a soul force driven by love in opposition to brute force was also picked up by Royden, who juxtaposed spiritual power against military might. Both these ideas figured prominently in her attempt to mobilize a living wall of human shields to stop the Second Sino-Japanese War.

A SHIELDING ARMY

Japan's invasion of China in 1931, followed by the occupation of Shanghai in late January 1932, motivated Royden to publish a letter in the *Daily Express*—together with the Scottish minister Herbert Gray and the Anglican reformer Richard (Dick) Sheppard—urging civilians to volunteer as human shields so as to create a buffer between the warring parties.[13]

A few days later, on February 28, Royden gave what would become one of her most famous sermons at the Guildhouse called "The Peace Army." In that sermon, after insisting that the League of Nations should have employed all possible means short of killing and withholding food to enforce constraint between the Japanese and Chinese, Royden told her congregation that since the League had failed to adopt a plan to stop the fighting, "men and women who believe it to be their duty should volunteer to place themselves unarmed between the combatants."[14]

A decade later, Royden explained the rationale informing her idea:

> The position in 1931 was a difficult one for pacifists. We felt it was an outrage that Japan should be allowed to attack China and get away with it. We also felt that it would be little less than grotesque if we pacifists began to clamor for war! Yet what was the alternative? The dilemma perplexed us so much that the three of us, Dr. Dick Sheppard, Dr. Herbert Gray and myself, went into a little retreat to seek light on our difficulty. It was then that it dawned upon us that the pacifist should be prepared to put his own body between the contending forces, as long ago, a Christian monk, Telemachus, had done. He stepped down into the arena between the gladiators, and by his death put an end forever to gladiatorial shows in Rome.[15]

By organizing a group of transnational activists who were willing to enter the conflict zone voluntarily, Royden hoped to create a "living wall" against war itself.[16] Initially, she thought the biggest obstacle was the practicality of sending an army of human shields from Europe to China. In her sermon, she recounted how this had preoccupied her for several days but then the "light came to me." She would ask the League of Nations to transport the peace army from Europe to China. Let us, she wrote, "ask the League to send us, unarmed to secure the scene of the conflict. This is not a national thing; it is international. It is not one country against another; it is those who believe in spiritual power against those who believe in material force."[17]

An internationalist in outlook, Royden believed that it was in the interest of humanity to resolve strife among countries and that without a proactive peace strategy, the League of Nations was in danger of unravelling.[18] Almost twenty years before the international community institutionalized the use of peacekeeping forces as an instrument for preventing armed conflicts, she suggested that the only way to stop the war was by sending "an unarmed body of soldiers of peace" to serve as a barricade between the two sides. Military might could be surmounted only by mobilizing spiritual power. "We expect," she wrote in 1933, that the appearance between opposing forces of a number of people willing to sacrifice their lives in the endeavor to prevent fighting and bloodshed—to die rather than to kill or allow others to kill—would generate a spiritual force strong enough to stop war. This is our answer to those who say that hundreds of thousands of noncombatants have been sacrificed in past wars without the slightest effect on the fighting. . . . The point is not whether people are killed, but why they are killed and in what spirit they die. The spirit in which they die is the spirit released into the world at their death, and perhaps only by their death it can be released.[19]

NONVIOLENT ETHICS

Royden's ideas challenged the dominant ways of thinking about war in two ways. First, she introduced a completely new understanding of human shielding in war zones. Until then, shielding had been a coercive act, whereby civilians or prisoners of war were forced to serve as shields to protect military targets, and therefore shielding was conceived as an inhumane practice that undermined the principle of distinction between civilians and combatants. Prefiguring the emergence of an international antiwar movement, Royden proposed that civilians themselves could choose to risk their lives in order to stop wars.

In this radical departure from the conception of civilians as passive agents, she underscored the ability of civilians to become politically engaged actors who can use their own vulnerability as a form of spiritual power aimed at ending the fighting. Thus, against the increasingly frequent military practice of using the precarity of civilian life to gain military advantage, this feminist preacher proposed transforming that same fragility into a strategic tool against war, showing how human shielding can be used not only to facilitate war but also to prevent it. Indeed, Royden's nonviolent ethics led her to revolutionize the dominant conceptions of human shielding and radically depart from the discussion of humane and inhumane violence that had characterized the debates of the previous decades. The notion of humane violence was for her not only completely foreign but also a contradiction in terms.

Second, in contrast to the way governments, militaries, and legal experts discussed the ethics of violence, Royden did not invoke the law of armed conflict. As a suffragist she understood that domestic English law had disenfranchised women, and as an internationalist she knew that the laws of war often facilitated colonial conquest. She realized that no legal framework could protect voluntary human shields who wanted to stop war, since law, as

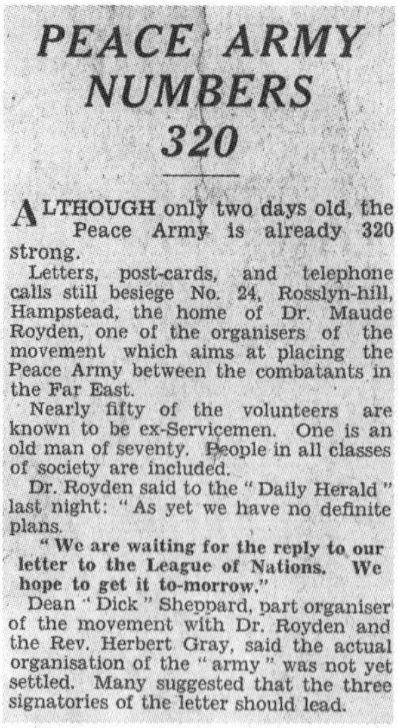

PEACE ARMY NUMBERS 320

ALTHOUGH only two days old, the Peace Army is already 320 strong.

Letters, post-cards, and telephone calls still besiege No. 24, Rosslyn-hill, Hampstead, the home of Dr. Maude Royden, one of the organisers of the movement which aims at placing the Peace Army between the combatants in the Far East.

Nearly fifty of the volunteers are known to be ex-Servicemen. One is an old man of seventy. People in all classes of society are included.

Dr. Royden said to the "Daily Herald" last night: "As yet we have no definite plans.

"We are waiting for the reply to our letter to the League of Nations. We hope to get it to-morrow."

Dean "Dick" Sheppard, part organiser of the movement with Dr. Royden and the Rev. Herbert Gray, said the actual organisation of the "army" was not yet settled. Many suggested that the three signatories of the letter should lead.

FIGURE 7. Article about the growing number of people willing to volunteer as shields, 1932. Credit: London School of Economics Women's Library Archive.

she intimated in her writing, often facilitates and legitimizes domination. For Royden, law establishes which wars are just and unjust (*jus ad bellum*) and which warfare methods are legal (*jus in bello*). She wanted to find a way to eradicate wars *tout court.* She saw not law but spiritual power—generated by the willingness of human beings to place their bodies on the line and, if need be, sacrifice their lives—as the only way to achieve her goal.

In response to Royden's appeal, about a thousand people wrote back to say they were willing to travel to Shanghai to serve as voluntary shields. Royden was disappointed, thinking that the number was insufficient. Her proposal to send human shields to Shanghai did not, however, materialize for an entirely different reason. Immediately after publishing their appeal in the *Daily Express,* Royden and the two other agitators had written a letter to the League of Nations asking the organization to provide transportation to China for the volunteers (figure 7). Secretary General Eric Drummond had promptly replied, saying that "it would be very far from my thought to 'dismiss such an offer [of sending voluntary shields] as fantastic,' but I fear that it is not constitutionally open to me to lay these offers before the Council of the League of Nations otherwise than on the formal demand of one of the States which are Members of the League."[20]

Royden and her partners had assumed that the states composing the League of Nations would be willing to help them solve their practical difficulty of getting the volunteers to China, but not a single state picked up the gauntlet. Their plan had challenged the state-centric paradigm informing the international legal order, a legal system that does not allow civilians and other nonstate actors to intervene in international armed conflicts. Perhaps surprisingly, her suspicion of the law had not translated into a suspicion of the state. Nevertheless, while she had failed to build a peace army, her appeal to fellow citizens to voluntarily put their lives on the line helped introduce a form of human shielding that could serve as a weapon of peace rather than as a weapon of war.

SIX

Emblem

The Italo-Ethiopian War and Red Cross Medical Facilities

NOT LONG AFTER BENITO MUSSOLINI'S SON, Vittorio, returned from the 1935–1936 Italo-Ethiopian War, where he had served as an air force pilot and military photographer, he published a memoir about his incursions into the Abyssinian skies. *Flights over the Amba Mountains* tells the story of the war in Ethiopia, combining a patriotic narrative with pictures immortalizing "little black faces" in their daily lives alongside aerial images of the wreckage caused by Italy's bombing campaign. The memoir aimed to educate a young generation of fascist readers about "the beauty of war," while conveying Vittorio Mussolini's personal experience "at the threshold of life."[1]

The war began in 1935, when Italy attempted to colonize Ethiopia. Mussolini the father wanted to vindicate the 1896 debacle of Adwa, in which Italy had been defeated by Ethiopian troops.[2] Yet, during the four decades separating the two wars, both Ethiopia and the global order had undergone crucial political transformations. Following the First World War, Ethiopia had become an independent sovereign state and a member in the League of Nations. Also, during this period, transnational black anticolonial consciousness had grown. So, when Italy attacked Ethiopia, it encountered widespread international condemnation. As the pan-Africanist American historian and sociologist W. E. B. Du Bois put it, "The black world knows" that "this is the last great effort of white Europe to secure the subjection of black men."[3]

During its invasion and subsequent occupation of Ethiopia, the Italian military did not hesitate to use mustard gas, execute captured prisoners, and systematically target civilian sites—crimes that violated the laws of war.[4] The fascists also systematically bombarded medical facilities operated by different Red Cross societies, especially from Sweden, Austria, Britain, Egypt, and Switzerland.[5] The 1907 Hague Regulations affirmed that "hospitals and places where the sick and wounded are collected" should be spared "as far as possible" from sieges and bombardments, "provided they are not being used at the time for military purposes" and are marked by an emblem to alert the enemy that the facilities are protected.[6]

The Ethiopian government denounced the Italian bombardments as inhumane and as a violation of the legal prohibition to target medical facilities. In response, the Italians claimed that the Ethiopians were duplicitous, using field hospitals marked by the emblem to shield combatants and military supplies. Therefore, they argued, bombing the hospitals was legitimate reprisal for the enemy's illegal use of the emblem to shield legitimate military targets.[7] Thus it was during the Italo-Ethiopian War that the accusation of illegal shielding was extended from human beings to medical facilities.

WHITE NEGROES

Although the public debate was about the legality of using medical facilities as shields, the argument really turned on the issue of race.[8] While Ethiopia was a League of Nations member (alongside two other African countries, Liberia and South Africa),[9] it occupied a unique position in the international order in the era between the two world wars. On the one hand, Ethiopia was portrayed as a sovereign state with independent political institutions. It had passed all the admission criteria necessary for membership in the League of Nations: most prominently, having a stable government and having control of its borders. It had also satisfied the two conditions specifically imposed upon it prior to its inclusion: "pledging to abolish slavery and to relinquish its right to import arms."[10]

On the other hand, Ethiopia was perceived as different from other League members. It was considered a civilized country, but not quite.[11] Ethiopians were regarded as "white negroes," where whiteness denoted their sovereignty and acceptance into the League of Nations, while *negro* gestured to the population's "uncivilized" nature.[12] An Austrian anthropologist described Ethiopia as "the only [nation] that is civilized without wearing trousers and shoes."[13] Hence, the country occupied a liminal position in the League: it was accepted as a member state, enjoying all the privileges and protections bestowed on the League's members, including the right to be supported militarily by other members in case of aggression by another state. But because its population was black, it was perceived as not having fully shed its "residual barbarism" and therefore as failing to fully enter the fold of humanity.

Ironically, Italy, which was among the four permanent members of the League's executive council, had supported Ethiopia's 1923 application to the League, hoping that this would facilitate its own hegemony over the African country. However, immediately after the application was accepted, the fascist regime had a change of heart and began sidelining Ethiopia. In the years leading up to the 1935–36 war, Italian politicians and jurists tried to undermine the African country's status within the League. In a 1932 letter to Benito Mussolini, Emilio De Bono, the Italian minister of colonies, wrote, "Ethiopia, in spite of its membership at the League of Nations and its effort to assume the attitude of a civilized people, is nothing but a semi-barbarous State."[14] In a similar vein, Carlo Cereti, an eminent Italian jurist, maintained that given its ambiguous status, Ethiopia should be removed from the League, since its inclusion in the family of nations "obstructed the development of civilization."[15] As it turned out, Italy would use such characterizations of the African country to legitimize its imminent invasion.

BLACK PERFIDY

In his memoir, Vittorio Mussolini offers a detailed account of the Italian forces' bombing of Red Cross facilities during the Italo-Ethiopian War. Recounting his experience during several reconnaissance flights between February and March 1936 over Red Cross encampments, he writes, "While we are still descending, I tell the Colonel that I can see something white and red [the Red Cross emblem]. He answers that I should be patient [before bombing it]."[16]

Mussolini continues by portraying the Ethiopian resistance as ubiquitous and as camouflaging itself by hiding within civilian sites and medical facilities, making it impossible for the Italians to abide by international law's principle of distinction, which calls on warring parties to distinguish between combatants and noncombatants. He describes how the Italian air force took precautions to protect civilians—including distributing leaflets in Amharic and French warning the combatants to refrain from opening fire on Italian forces while hiding within civilian and medical structures. At one point he declares that he was "expecting to see the blonde hair of some Swedish [Red Cross nurses] waving a white handkerchief as a sign of cordial camaraderie. Instead, we almost lost our lives" due to the shots fired by the resistance groups from the medical encampment.[17] He then explains that because the Ethiopian resistance had transformed the medical organization's emblem into a shield, "the red cross was destroyed."

The younger Mussolini's depiction of the war—juxtaposing a treacherous and brutal armed resistance that illegally used medical facilities as a shield against an honest, law-abiding, brave fascist military—was compatible with its portrayal in Italy. Indeed, a crucial element in the Italian media's coverage of Ethiopia's conquest was the accusation that the Ethiopian army systematically used civilian sites to hide, adopting, as it were, perfidious strategies against the fascist military. Perfidy was an egregious violation of the laws of armed conflict, and shielding behind medical facilities served as the prime example of such duplicitous and inhumane warfare practices used by the black fighters.

The Red Cross emblem assumed a key role in the Italian propaganda campaign. Several Italian newspapers decried the Red Cross's "pseudo medical units" as they pondered "what hides in Ethiopia behind the inviolable Red Cross."[18] Citing the testimony of a European advisor to the Ethiopian emperor, the influential paper *La Stampa* claimed that the misuse of the Red Cross emblem was so widespread that Ethiopians even used the insignia to mark deposits where beer was stored.[19]

The struggle over the ethics of humane violence also migrated to the realm of images. Drawings portraying the Ethiopian army abusing the Red Cross emblem decorated the covers of some of the most-read Italian magazines and newspapers. On one cover, a few armed Ethiopian men are portrayed assaulting and robbing a Dutch Red Cross medical unit (figure 8). The caption "Ethiopian Civilization," intended as ironic, highlights the Ethiopians' failure to understand that medical facilities and services are protected under international law, a lack of understanding that is rendered synonymous with being uncivilized.

A second magazine cover portrays a huge Red Cross tent under which Ethiopian armed men are taking refuge (figure 9). The caption translated into English reads: "One among the many episodes of abuse of the Red Cross emblem by the Abyssinians. During a reconnaissance in the area of Quoram, our aircraft saw and photographed a huge cloth with a red cross. . . . When our airplanes got closer, hundreds of armed soldiers, fearing we would bomb them, rushed from every direction, hiding under the tent" that was marked by the Red Cross emblem.

LA TRIBUNA ILLUSTRATA

Supplemento illustrato de "La Tribuna,,

Anno XLIV – N. 13   29 Marzo 1936 – Anno XIV   Cent. 30 il numero

Civiltà etiopica. — *La carovana inviata verso Quoram dalla Commissione sanitaria olandese che intendeva prestare la propria opera di soccorso ai soldati del Negus, è stata assalita e svaligiata tra Ualdia e Colfo da una banda di predoni abissini, che ha pure ferito il medico capo della missione.*

(Disegno di VITTORIO PISANI)

FIGURE 8. "Ethiopian Civilization," front page during Italo-Ethiopian War. Credit: *La Tribuna Illustrata,* March 1936.

In a similar vein, the national newspaper *Il popolo di Roma* published a cartoon entitled "Pro-Negro Red Cross" in which a white doctor and his assistant are nursing a black patient in a Red Cross encampment (figure 10). One of the two oxygen cylinders in the cartoon looks like a warhead, though it has a red cross on it. In the caption, the assistant tells the doctor: "This oxygen tank doesn't have a tube fitting," implying that it really is a warhead. The message was clear: The Red Cross encampments harbor Ethiopian combatants and serve as arms depots. Therefore, its medical units should be treated as legitimate military targets. (As we will see in chapter 17, "Info-

LA TRIBUNA ILLUSTRATA

Supplemento illustrato de "La Tribuna,,

Anno XLIV — N. 3   19 gennaio 1936 — Anno XIV —   Cent. 30 il numero.

Uno dei tanti episodi dell'abuso, da parte degli abissini, dell'emblema della Croce Rossa. Nella zona del Quoram, alcuni nostri apparecchi in ricognizione hanno visto e fotografato un enorme telo rosso-crociato, disteso su di un prato alla periferia del paese e sostenuto da arbusti. All'avvicinarsi dei nostri aeroplani, nel timore di essere bombardati, centinaia di soldati armati accorrevano d'ogni parte nascondendosi sotto il telo o raccogliendovisi intorno.

(Disegno di VITTORIO PISANI.)

FIGURE 9. "One among the many episodes of abuse of the Red Cross emblem." Credit: *La Tribuna Illustrata,* January 1936.

War," eighty years later, Israel adopted strikingly similar imagery in the infographics it produced to justify the bombardment of hospitals and other civilian infrastructures in Gaza.)

Newspapers were not the only platform used to justify the bombing of Red Cross health facilities. A prominent illustrator and cartoonist produced a postcard depicting armed Ethiopian children dressed partially in military uniform and partially in Red Cross attire who are fleeing from armed Italian children wearing military clothes (figure 11). One of the black children is carrying a Red Cross umbrella embroidered with Ethiopian motifs. On the

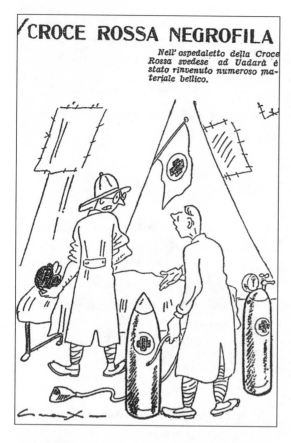

FIGURE 10. "This oxygen tank doesn't have a tube fitting." Credit: *Il popolo di Roma,* January 1936.

FIGURE 11. Postcard by Aurelio Bertiglia, Italo-Ethiopian War.

ground, an ammunition chest with British-made dum-dum bullets—prohibited by the 1899 Hague Declaration on expanding bullets—is marked with the Red Cross emblem. At the center of the image is a white child prodding the red-crossed rear end of a black child with a bayonet. This postcard combines Italy's accusation that the Red Cross was shielding Ethiopian fighters with its allegation that other League member states were supporting the Ethiopian government in its perfidious practice.

ITALY AND THE LEAGUE OF NATIONS

To be sure, Italy was not the only country to bomb medical units that belonged to the International Committee of the Red Cross. Since the First Geneva Convention in 1864, which set up the legal protections provided to medical facilities and staff, Red Cross hospitals had been targeted. Beginning in the 1870–1871 Franco-German War, which had been waged just a few years after the convention was signed, and continuing through World War I, the breach of medical immunity was widespread.[20] However, the Italo-Ethiopian War was different because the fascist regime used race to shift the focus away from its own breach of medical immunity and other violations of international law onto the Ethiopians.

In its communication with the League of Nations' commission dealing with the Italo-Ethiopian War, the Italian government reiterated its charges about the uncivilized character of Ethiopian warfare. Responding to a series of accusations made by the Ethiopian government at the League of Nations, including the charge of endangering international peace and the deliberate targeting of the International Red Cross—an accusation accompanied by the testimonies of personnel from Red Cross units attacked by the Italians during the war—the fascist government claimed that the "guerillas" were using the Red Cross emblem as a shield. In other words, Ethiopian "atrocities" and "war crimes" legitimized Italy's harsh methods of warfare.[21]

The Italians went on to argue that "the only clause of the Geneva Conventions which the Abyssinians regard as valid, and clamorously invoke on every occasion, is that which lays down that any persons taking refuge under the Red Cross sign should be secure from aerial bombardment."[22] As evidence of their position, the Italians submitted to the League of Nations a number of memorandums that included aerial pictures similar to those published by Vittorio Mussolini in his memoir, ostensibly showing Ethiopian efforts to shield themselves behind Red Cross medical units.[23]

WARRIORS WITHOUT WEAPONS

The Red Cross also took an active role in the debates about shielding and international law. In 1936, after the Italian air force had repeatedly bombarded medical units in Ethiopia, the head of the International Committee of the Red Cross, Max Huber, wrote a letter to Benito Mussolini asking him to take appropriate measures to stop targeting their facilities. In his response, Mussolini did not deny the bombings. He argued that "by reason of their own innate feelings of humanity, the Italian airmen, in their operations in East Africa, make it an obligation to respect the emblem of the Red Cross, even though they know that the enemy makes illegal use of this for war objectives." He added that "the standards laid down in the Geneva Conventions, however, require that there shall be no misuse of the Red Cross emblem for illegal purposes, especially those of war."[24] It was, he intimated, the Ethiopian fighters who were ignoring the laws of war and behaving unethically by seeking refuge in the medical units.

At about the same time, the official journal of the International Committee of the Red Cross featured articles by legal experts on the visibility of the Red Cross emblem and the dangers posed by aerial war to hospitals.[25] While practically all the contributors to the journal condemned Italy's bombardment of medical facilities, the president of the International Association of Hospitals, in his article, divided the blame between the Italians who bombed hospitals and the Ethiopians who were accused of using them as shields, asking the countries that sent medical staff to Ethiopia to take all necessary precautions to "assure the security of their hospitals."[26]

Along similar lines, in his 1951 memoir, *Warriors without Weapons,* Marcel Junod, who had served as the International Committee of the Red Cross delegate in Ethiopia during the war, referred to the Red Cross committee as a "third warrior"—namely, a humanitarian warrior without weapons. Junod defended the neutral position of the Red Cross in the conflict. But his memoir reveals his racial bias.

On the one hand, he criticized the Italians for deliberately targeting Red Cross facilities. "The repeated bombing," he claims, demonstrated that "the Red Cross insignia offered no protection."[27] Indeed, one could infer from his descriptions that the emblem itself had become a prime target. On the other hand, he depicts the Ethiopians as a backward people comprised of bellicose tribes unaware of the laws regulating war and the meaning of humane violence. Describing one of his meetings with the Ethiopian emperor, Junod suggests that the laws of armed conflict—which aimed to make war more humane by distinguishing between combatants and noncombatants—were completely incomprehensible to the black ruler.[28]

Junod was even critical of his own organization, which, in his words, "was only concerned with possible violations of the Red Cross emblem." The Red Cross, he claimed, rejected the Italian justifications only when the bombings endangered its own medical structures and staff. "The underlying question of whether it was legitimate to bomb largely civilian targets and what the International Committee of the Red Cross's reaction should be to that bombing was not raised. . . . Geneva simply did not appreciate" that the systematic targeting of the Red Cross was part of an extended Italian strategy of systematic and deliberate targeting of the black civilian population of Ethiopia.[29]

For the Geneva-based organization, international law did not apply to the black side of the war the same way that it did to the white side, and its denunciations of Italian aerial bombing focused on protecting itself and its emblem rather than on protecting civilians regardless of their race. The human shielding cases involving the bombing of hospitals in Ethiopia thus reveal the ethnocentric conception of humanity driving the Red Cross's humanitarian activities in the period between the two world wars.[30]

RACIALIZED LAW

The debate on the relationship between humane violence and human shielding that accompanied the Italo-Ethiopian War suggests that a population's race can shape Western interpretations of how international law should be applied to conflicts. Ethiopia was included within the family of nations as a sovereign state, but its society—and here *society* means "race"—was considered not fully civilized. The notion of sovereignty, as we have seen in the discussion about the status of irregulars among legal experts following the Franco-German War, informs the foundation of international law. It also serves as a gatekeeper, determining *when and where* international law can be applied. The fact that irregulars are not acting at the behest of a sovereign state and that colonized people are denied their own sovereignty implies, for example, that international law does not apply to them. Society, however, also plays a vital role in the application of international law. Positivist social theories about the varying "degrees of civilization" of different social groups have served as crucial tools in the construction of a hierarchical international order that benefits some and harms others.[31] In fact, a racialized notion of society regulates *how international law is applied,* almost always to the detriment of nonwhite societies.

While during most colonial wars, international law was not considered applicable due to the indigenous people's lack of sovereignty, in the Italo-Ethiopian War international law was relevant because Ethiopia was a sovereign state. Yet, as the Italian propaganda campaign and the opinions voiced by leading figures within the Red Cross reveal, the law was applied differently because Ethiopia's society was black.

The tacit agreement between the Italian government and the Red Cross about Ethiopia's incapacity to understand the laws of armed conflict underscores that even when a state's sovereignty offers it certain protections, the racist application of international law grounded in Darwinist social theories can erode those protections. Ultimately, the manner in which the Red Cross dealt with the bombardment of its hospitals in Ethiopia reveals how the inclusion of Ethiopia into the family of nations did not undo the imprint of colonialism in international law.

SEVEN

Nuremberg

Nazi Human Shielding and the Lack of Civilian Protections

NOTWITHSTANDING THE REPORTS PUBLISHED by the Belgian, British, and French governments denouncing the German military's use of civilians as human shields during the First World War, civilians were also deployed as human shields throughout the Second World War. Given the horrific crimes carried out against millions of noncombatants, the deployment of human shields was certainly not the most egregious or pressing offense. Nonetheless, two cases of shielding were discussed at the Nuremberg trials.

The first case involved the German use of British prisoners of war as human shields in Crete. After issuing a directive declaring that "the occupation of the island of Crete is to be prepared in order to have a base for conducting the air war against England in the Eastern Mediterranean," Adolf Hitler chose General Kurt Student for the job. Student flew to Berlin to receive instructions and then to Athens, where he set up his headquarters in the Hotel Grand Bretagne, which had been abandoned by fleeing British troops. He had at his disposal hundreds of transport airplanes packed with paratroopers and supported by heavy bombers and Stuka aircraft, known for their ability to dive and bomb.[1]

On May 20, 1941, Student's elite paratrooper division known as the Parachute Huntsmen invaded Crete, supported by some six thousand troops travelling in two fleets. While his forces accomplished their mission, they suffered heavy casualties, due to the vigorous defense put up by British troops and the popular Greek resistance. Meanwhile, rumors of civilians killing Nazi paratroopers caught in trees and of roving bands of Greek partisans torturing wounded German soldiers lying helpless in fields began circulating among the Nazi troops.[2] As soon as these accounts reached Berlin, Hermann Göring, the architect of the Nazi police state and founder of the Gestapo, ordered Student to initiate a judicial enquiry and carry out harsh reprisals.

In a preliminary report published on June 4, a Nazi judge charged Greek civilians with participating "in the fight as francs-tireurs," claiming that many German paratroopers had been subjected to inhuman treatment or had been mutilated.[3] The Germans were rehearsing, in a completely new historical and geopolitical context, the same accusation they had used in the 1871 war against France and in Belgium during the First World War. A few weeks later, another judge found evidence of twenty-five cases of mutilation, almost all of them having been inflicted after death. General Student, however, did not wait for the publication of these reports, and had already issued the following order on May 31:

> It is certain that the [Greek] civilian population including women and boys have taken part in the fighting, committed sabotage, mutilated and killed wounded soldiers. It is therefore high time to combat all cases of this kind, to undertake reprisals and punitive expeditions which must be carried through with exemplary terror. The harshest measures must indeed be taken and I order the following: shooting for all cases of proven cruelty, and I wish this to be done by the same units who have suffered such atrocities. The following reprisals will be taken:
> 1. Shooting
> 2. Fines
> 3. Total destruction of villages by burning
> 4. Extermination of the male population of the territory in question
> My authority will be necessary for measures under 3 and 4. All these measures must, however, be taken rapidly and omitting all formalities. In view of the circumstances the troops have a right to this and there is no need for military tribunals to judge beasts and assassins.[4]

Student's soldiers obediently complied. In the village of Prassas, a total of 698 alleged francs-tireurs were summarily executed. In another village approximately 60 civilians were shot dead, while in yet another reprisal, German troops executed an estimated 200 male civilians. And in a punitive drive south of Chanea, several villages were completely destroyed, and 145 men and 2 women were shot.

NO CRIME WITHOUT LAW

These are just a few of the many documented atrocities carried out against civilians by General Student's Nazi units.[5] Yet, after the war, when Allied forces captured Student and brought him to trial at Nuremberg, not a single charge regarding his brutal policies toward civilians was introduced, primarily because, at the time, the laws of armed conflict offered only limited protections to civilians. The judges focused instead on the German troops' violations of existing laws carried out against enemy combatants and protected medical sites under Student's command. Consequently, he was accused of bombing Red Cross hospitals and murdering and mistreating British prisoners of war—who were protected persons according to the 1929 Convention Relative to the Treatment of Prisoners of War—during the invasion of Crete. This mistreatment included using the prisoners of war as human shields.[6]

The allegation that Student had ordered the deployment of "British prisoners of war as a screen for the advance of German troops" was discussed at some length during his trial at Nuremberg. This was a historic moment, since it was the first time that the accusation of human shielding was put forward in an international court of law. According to one witness, at least six of the prisoners of war who had been forced to march in front of Student's soldiers had been killed by the fire of other British troops.[7] Notwithstanding the gravity of the allegations, the prosecution failed to produce evidence regarding the exact number of British human shields who had been killed, leading the judges to acquit General Student on this particular charge. He ended up spending a mere two years in jail.

General Hermann Hoth, another highly decorated Nazi officer who had commanded panzer groups on several fronts during the war, was similarly convicted at Nuremberg of using prisoners of war as shields. He deployed Soviet prisoners to detect and serve as buffers against booby traps placed in the buildings his forces intended to occupy and was incriminated by his own quartermaster, who had written in his war diary that "the billeting of POWs captured in the city and some of the inhabitants of the country in the buildings used by our own troops has proven to be a useful countermeasure against the time bombs put there by the enemy." As a result of these measures, the bombs "were found and rendered harmless in a very short time."[8] Although the tribunal sentenced Hoth to fifteen years in prison for this and several other crimes, he was released on parole in 1954.

Because the laws of armed conflict prohibited only the use of prisoners of war as human shields, these are the only two incidents of shielding mentioned in the thousands of pages comprising the fifteen volumes of the Nuremberg military tribunals, even though there is ample evidence that the practice of using civilians as shields had been widespread during the Second

World War.[9] Macabre testimonies from numerous witnesses across Poland describe Wehrmacht troops and SS units forcing civilians to march in front of tanks and infantry soldiers as the Nazi soldiers continuously shot over their heads in an effort to vanquish the Polish Home Army.[10] In April 1945, in a desperate attempt to resist the Allies' offensive, Hitler ordered the SS to round up the *prominenten*—VIP prisoners, who included European presidents, prime ministers, generals, and secret agents—in order to serve as human shields and protect his bunker from bombardment.[11] This might not be surprising, considering that the Germans were simply continuing a practice that they had instituted as far back as the 1870–71 Franco-German War and had introduced into military manuals on the eve of the First World War. But the Germans were not the only ones to employ human shields. Japanese soldiers in Okinawa had used civilians as shields against American troops who were set to capture the island, while in the struggle against partisans in Hungary, town mayors together with the Home Guard took civilian hostages and used them as shields before killing them.[12]

Notwithstanding overwhelming evidence that various military forces had used human shields during the Second World War, none of the officers involved in these other incidents were tried in either Nuremberg or the Tokyo war crimes trials. There are, no doubt, many political reasons for this, but at the time, international law was very limited in its protection of civilians. At least in relation to the use of civilians as human shields, in Nuremberg the principle of *nullum crimen sine lege* ("no crime without law") seems to have prevailed.

PRECARIOUS BALANCE

While the matter of different forms of civilian protection had punctuated discussions by philosophers, historians, jurists, and military experts for hundreds of years, the legal codes that began to take shape in the late nineteenth century had relatively little to say about civilians, and what they did say was often entangled in contradictions.[13] The 1863 Lieber Code instructs commanders to "inform the enemy of their intention to bombard a place, so that the noncombatants, and especially the women and children, may be removed before the bombardment commences." Yet, the Code immediately adds that "it is no infraction of the common law of war to omit thus to inform the enemy. Surprise may be a necessity."[14]

On the one hand, the Lieber Code underscores the principle of distinction between combatants and noncombatants and avows the latter's immunity. On the other hand, the Code immediately adds that in the face of military necessity, the protections conferred on civilians can be forfeited. Avowal and disavowal of civilian protections thus operate in tandem.[15] This double move is worth dwelling on, since it has animated practically all international conventions drafted since that time. Its persistence should not be too surprising considering that the Lieber Code was the blueprint for the conventions emanating from the two international peace conferences held in The Hague in 1899 and 1907.[16] The international conventions negotiated at these conferences include several articles prescribing civilian protections. Yet, like the Code that served as their predecessor, these documents' efforts to restrain violence against civilians are accompanied by exceptions in favor of the attackers. The ethics of humane violence protects civilians, but in certain circumstances governments and militaries exploit these exceptions in order to justify the deployment of lethal violence against them.[17]

In fact, the development of the laws of war from the mid-nineteenth century until today can be viewed as an effort to fine-tune the balance between civilian harm and the right to kill, vanquish, and destroy. As the weapons and technologies of destruction developed over time, the codes that aim to protect civilians have been expanded in an effort to maintain the precarious balance between civilian harm and the anticipated military advantage— namely, the principle of proportionality. Significantly, then, the laws of war, including the codes dealing specifically with civilians, do not aim to eliminate or even necessarily to subdue violence, but rather to direct its application so as to sustain an acceptable proportion between what militaries consider necessary to accomplish their objectives and the protections bestowed on civilian lives and infrastructures.[18]

Abidance by the principle of proportionality is one of the ways to determine whether the violence deployed was humane. When an act of war is disproportionate and produces "too many" civilian casualties, it is considered a war crime even though the laws of war do not actually specify what constitutes "too many," leaving it up to militaries and their governments to offer convincing interpretations. Therefore, the law expects the warring parties to anticipate the impact of their actions to ensure that military necessity does not override the immunity bestowed on protected persons and sites.

One of the guardians of proportionality has been the International Committee of the Red Cross, which, since its establishment in 1863, has assumed the role of drafting legal conventions and treaties. Historically, the organization has prepared proposals of conventions and then organized diplomatic conferences where it has presented them to officials representing the member states of the League of Nations (and later the United Nations) in order to convince them to ratify the conventions. Usually, humanitarian lawyers work together with government and military lawyers on the proposed drafts until they agree on the clauses and exact wording—and if they cannot agree, the draft is often left to wither on the vine.

In the late 1920s, the Geneva-based organization managed to secure the approval of the League of Nations' member states for a series of changes to the Hague Conventions dealing with the wounded and sick as well as with prisoners of war. Even though the original conventions that were up for revision did not include the term *human shield,* the lawyers addressed human shielding in the 1929 Convention Relative to the Treatment of Prisoners of War. This was the first convention to explicitly outlaw the deployment of prisoners of war as human shields, stating that "no prisoner may at any time . . . be employed to render by his presence certain points or areas immune from bombardment."[19] (At the same time, this Convention says nothing about whether belligerents are permitted to bomb a target that is protected by prisoners who are being used as shields. This silence can be—and has been—interpreted as providing a green light for such attacks.)

It was this unequivocal condemnation of deploying prisoners of war as shields in the 1929 convention that allowed the Nuremberg prosecutors to charge generals Kurt Student and Hermann Hoth. However, the lack at that time of a code explicitly outlawing the weaponization of *civilians* explains why the same prosecutors could not indict officers for exploiting civilians for the same purpose.

But why was the use of civilians for human shielding not codified as illegal before the Second World War? After all, accusations of belligerents using civilian shields abounded: from the Franco-German War and the Second Anglo-Boer War in South Africa through the First World War to the Italian conquest of Ethiopia. In fact, the omission of a legal clause prohibiting the use of civilians as shields merely reflects a much broader problem: namely, the relative absence of codification relating to civilians trapped in conflict zones.

The various efforts of the Red Cross to introduce a convention dealing specifically with civilians during the years leading up to the Second World War suggest that Red Cross staff were well aware that the existing legal system did not provide adequate protections to civilians.[20] According to the humanitarian organization, in the numerous conflicts that took place between the two world wars,[21] the "position of civilians and armed forces tends to become increasingly similar" due to the "blind effects of modern mass warfare, which have inflicted untold inhuman suffering on civilian populations of all nations."[22] To confront this horrific reality, the Red Cross adopted a dual strategy: it strove to dramatically expand international law so as to develop a convention dedicated to the protection of civilians and simultaneously to institute a policy to circumscribe the space in which war can be legally fought by creating safety zones for civilians.[23]

In 1934, the Red Cross convened a conference in Tokyo in an effort to draft a new convention dedicated to civilian protections.[24] The draft was handed to the Swiss government, which approached several European governments to see if they were interested in ratifying the document. Most governments simply did not respond, while the French, according to Swiss foreign minister Giuseppe Motta, made clear their "firm and definite refusal" to sign such a convention.[25] In 1938, the Red Cross convened yet another conference to discuss the codification of civilian protections in international law, but the looming Second World War brought the process to an abrupt end.

It was only in the aftermath of the Second World War, and particularly in light of the many horrific crimes carried out against civilian populations, that states agreed to introduce significant changes into international law with the hope of generating a more humane normative framework.[26] This required a recalibration of the balance between military necessity and civilian immunity.

EIGHT

Codification

The Geneva Conventions and the Passive Civilian

THE SECOND WORLD WAR and the annihilation of millions of civilians underscored that the ostensible proportionality between military advantage and civilian harm was out of joint. Although the extermination of indigenous populations over a span of several centuries in different European colonies from North and South America to the Congo and South West Africa had failed to generate moral upheaval in the metropoles, when genocide occurred on European soil, it propelled politicians and humanitarians to finally join forces and revolutionize international law.

The massive codification enterprise that followed World War II included the United Nations Charter, the Universal Declaration of Human Rights, the Convention on the Prevention and Punishment of Genocide, and the four Geneva Conventions of 1949 for the protection of victims of war. The field that had been called "the laws of war" or "laws of armed conflict" was renamed "international humanitarian law," and, at least ostensibly, the new conventions institutionalized the idea that all people are part of a global and universal humanity.[1]

These conventions introduced numerous new protections to civilians and by so doing increased the legal and political value ascribed to the lives of defenseless civilians trapped in the midst of war.[2] As part of this effort, the deployment of civilians as human shields was outlawed, and following decades of legal and political debates, the weaponization of the human body as a protective screen for military activities was rendered irreconcilable with the idea of humane violence.

Capitalizing upon the legal momentum produced by Europe's reckoning with the war's horrors, immediately after the fighting subsided the International Committee of the Red Cross began organizing the drafting of new conventions that took into account experiences gathered from the field.[3] In 1947, it convened a meeting of government experts to discuss the reformulation of the laws of war. The experts were divided into three working groups. The first was responsible for revising the 1929 Geneva Convention for the Amelioration of the Condition of the Wounded and Sick in Armies in the Field, the second was asked to modify the Convention Relative to the Treatment of Prisoners of War from the same year, and the third was charged with drafting the Fourth Geneva Convention, an entirely new convention relating to the treatment and protection of civilians.[4] Stressing that the dreadful suffering endured by civilians during the war had "brought to light the tragic insufficiency of international treaty law," the Geneva-based organization noted in a 1947 report that "public opinion in every land" was pressuring governments "to adopt treaty stipulations with the object of affording protection to civilians."[5]

For the first time in history, an entire convention was dedicated to outlining civilian protections, and the distinction between international law's two axiomatic figures—combatants and civilians—which had already been introduced in previous conventions, was further underscored and institutionalized as the bedrock of international humanitarian law. Unlike international human rights law that emerged at the same time and prohibits killing people, this body of law permits killing combatants, and killing noncombatants is also, at times, acceptable. The latter is crucial, since the way the civilian is categorized and the circumstances in which he or she is killed determine whether the use of violence is legal and ethically humane.[6]

The newly drafted Fourth Geneva Convention offered concrete protections to civilians. It stressed that "violence to life and person [of civilians], in particular murder of all kinds, mutilation, cruel treatment and torture; taking of hostages; outrages upon personal dignity, in particular humiliating and degrading treatment" are illegal forms of inhumane violence. In a similar vein, it added a series of other protections to civilians, such as to those "engaged in the operation and administration of civilian hospitals, including the personnel engaged in the search for, removal and transporting of and caring for wounded and sick civilians."[7]

By introducing new civilian protections, the legal code indicated that belligerents who violated these protections could be charged of perpetrating war crimes. In this way, the drafting of the Fourth Geneva Convention Relative to the Protection of Civilian Persons in Time of War constituted a progressive move that dramatically augmented the value attributed to civilian life.[8] This progressive move also included the introduction of a clause that criminalizes the use of civilians as human shields.[9]

EXTENDING CIVILIANHOOD

The effort to increase the value ascribed to the lives of civilians by introducing clauses that protect civilians was supplemented by a move to extend civilianhood to populations that had been excluded in the past.[10] Up until the Second World War, the meagre protections bestowed on noncombatants in international law had not been conferred on all civilians, but only on those who were nationals of one of the warring parties and only during the war.[11] Civilians who were not nationals of an enemy country or who remained in a territory occupied by a warring party lost all legal protections. They were treated like colonized populations who had never been protected by the laws of armed conflict.[12]

While there were numerous examples of the mistreatment of civilians during the war, the working group responsible for drafting the civilian convention was particularly interested in how the Nazi regime, after occupying Poland, had declared that the country "no longer existed" and then published a military order that the treatment of Polish nationals would no longer be regulated by the internationally accepted laws of war. Overnight all Polish civilians became subjects of the Third Reich rather than nationals of an enemy country upon whom certain legal protections are bestowed, and they were subjected to German military decrees instead of the laws of armed conflict. Polish Jews, communists, gays, Roma people, and recalcitrant Christians were sent to concentration camps and the gas chambers because the Führer had published a decree applicable to all Polish territories that Germany had occupied. The fact that the existing laws of war could not defend civilians whose country had been occupied by an enemy led the working group to expand the protections provided in the convention to civilians living under military occupation.[13]

Although the members of the working group were appalled by how easily millions of civilians had lost all protections in Europe, in their discussions they evidently failed to note that civilian populations in the European colonies had been subjected to genocidal violence for several centuries and had never been protected by international law. The annulment of the meagre civilian protections provided by international law before World War II and the use instead of emergency regulations and military decrees to control occupied populations generated outrage not because the practice was new but because Germany had introduced it on European soil.[14]

Despite the major achievements in modifying the global judicial field in the immediate aftermath of the Second World War by adding numerous protections for civilians and by extending civilianhood to populations living under military occupation, the majority of member states continued to consider international law inapplicable to colonial wars, and therefore civilianhood was not extended to indigenous populations still living under colonial rule.[15] This helps explain why it is difficult to find allegations of human shielding in the anticolonial liberation struggles that sprang up immediately after the war. Because colonized people were still not accepted as members of the family of nations, the vulnerability of indigenous people could not serve as a weapon of deterrence.

THE PASSIVE CIVILIAN

The drafters of the Fourth Geneva Convention Relative to the Protection of Civilian Persons in Time of War, initially called the Civilian Convention, did not define the term *civilian* in its own terms, but rather identified it in terms of the opposite of *combatant,* as *noncombatant.* The civilian is the combatant's other, a person who does not take an active role in the hostilities. Thus, within the limits of the convention, the term *civilian* applies in a relatively specific context: to noncombatants trapped in the midst of war or living under a belligerent occupation. Being defined in terms of what they are not doing, civilians are conceived of as passive individuals—a fact that would affect how the legal figure of the human shield took shape after World War II.

The restricted nature of the definition of *civilian* became apparent during the diplomatic conferences convened by the Swiss government in 1949 (a year after the working groups had formulated drafts of the conventions), where delegates representing the United Nations member states finalized the documents. A heated debate took place about the meaning of the term among the government experts who discussed the formulation of Article 3A of the

Civilian Convention's initial draft. The article declares that civilians in a conflict zone who are "suspected of or engaged in activities hostile to the security of the State" will "not be entitled to claim [the protections bestowed on civilians] under this Convention."[16]

The Soviet and Bulgarian representatives were extremely critical of the article's wording, the latter claiming that he did "not understand even now what is meant by 'activities hostile to the State.' I have already said and I still say: this might be interpreted to cover just anything."[17] He explained further:

> It is clear that a person definitely charged with espionage or sabotage will be prosecuted. There is no doubt on this point. It is possible, however, to imagine the case of a person who, in the territory of a belligerent Power or in occupied territory has formed a small group whose members exchange unofficial news, listen to the foreign radio in the evening or at night, spread this news abroad, and print as best they can a small underground newspaper which they distribute; other people will buy it, will read it or will, perhaps, make financial contributions towards its publication and distribution. We have here a very wide and elastic conception, an almost unlimited list of activities which might be regarded as hostile to State security. I question whether complete forfeiture of rights and privileges as stipulated at the end of the first paragraph, could really be imposed for all activities of this kind, on the grounds of suspicion against persons who are alleged to have taken part in such activities.[18]

The Bulgarian's point is that according to the article's proposed formulation, civilians can remain protected only so long as they remain politically inactive. As legal scholar Karma Nabulsi has highlighted, such depoliticization of civilians is intricately tied to the laws of military occupation, which fail to distinguish between "non-violent political behavior and violent resistance."[19] In a context of belligerent occupation and war, practically any political activity carried out by civilians can be interpreted as "hostile to the security of the state," placing civilians who do not fight but are nonetheless politically active on the combatant side of the combatant-noncombatant divide, thereby stripping them of the protections outlined in the Civilian Convention. Notwithstanding the argument's logic, the delegates of Australia, the United States, and the United Kingdom voiced their opposition to any changes, and the original formulation of the article was approved by an overwhelming majority.[20]

The new regime of civilian protection that emerged after the Second World War and the ethics of humane violence on which it was grounded were thus marked by a fundamental contradiction. The civilian was defined as a person who is passive in the political arena. Any political activity could be framed as contributing to the war effort of the opposing side, which would lead to the loss of protections that the convention bestows on civilians. Hence, at the very moment that civilians were given numerous protections and their lives were considered more valuable, the notion of civilianhood was deflated, potentially exposing politically active civilians to lethal violence.

FROM PRISONER SHIELDS TO CIVILIAN SHIELDS

It is in this context that we need to understand the article in the Fourth Geneva Convention that prohibited the use of civilians as human shields, along with the subsequent applications of that article to the present day. The clause explicitly rendering the deployment of civilians as human shields illegal was included as a result of concern about the treatment of hostages. According to the Lieber Code, armed forces are required to protect hostages. Nonetheless, these guidelines, which were considered part of customary international law, had not stopped the Germans from executing civilian hostages or deporting millions of civilians to concentration camps during World War II. Although existing legal clauses prohibited the execution of hostages, the members of the working group drafting the Civilian Convention noted that the prohibition was not categorical, while the rights of civilians who had been taken hostage and interned in camps were not clearly spelled out.

The government experts making up the working group concluded that it was necessary to introduce new stipulations prohibiting hostage-taking and that civilians interned by an occupying power must be treated according to the terms laid out in the 1929 Convention Relative to the Treatment of Prisoners of War, which was also being revised at the same time by another working group. Noting that according to the 1929 convention, prisoners of war should be "humanely treated and protected, particularly against acts of violence," the experts suggested that almost all of the articles in that convention could be "applied by analogy" to the new Civilian Convention, since the treatment of civilians should not be inferior to the treatment of prisoners of war.[21] The analogy was, in other words, considered apt because prisoners of war were deemed passive, similar to the way civilians were being conceptualized.

Thus, the members of the working group copied many of the articles from the 1929 Convention Relative to the Treatment of Prisoners of War into the newly drafted Fourth Geneva Convention Relative to the Protection of Civilian Persons in Time of War. Among these was Article 24, which declares: "No prisoner of war may at any time be sent to, or detained in areas where he may be exposed to the fire of the combat zone, nor may his presence be used to render certain points or areas immune from military operations."[22] The article's language is crucial. The prisoner shield is a person who is either "sent" to an area under attack or "detained" within an area under attack, thus framing human shielding as a form of coercion carried out by enemy combatants against prisoners of war who have no agency. Moreover, the prisoner shield does not render the area immune, implying indirectly that a military target defended by human shields can be legitimately attacked.

This article was copied by the working group and became Article 28 of the Fourth Geneva Convention. In this process, the civilian is also framed as passive, as a person who is forced to become a shield. That is why the 1949 Fourth Geneva Convention—as well as the 1977 Additional Protocol that supplemented it—deals only with involuntary shielding and says nothing about civilians who volunteer to become human shields. The figure of the voluntary human shield was and remains inconceivable in international law because it jeopardizes the notion of the civilian as essentially a passive victim of violence.

LETHAL PROTECTION

Prior to the approval of Article 28 of the Fourth Geneva Convention, the passivity of the civilian who is deployed as a shield became a point of discussion among the working group's members.[23] They agreed that it should be rendered illegal for a warring party to transfer civilians to a conflict zone in order to shield legitimate military targets. Yet they could not agree on the status of civilians who were already trapped in a conflict zone, and they debated whether in certain circumstances such civilians could be considered human shields.

Denmark's delegate referred to the secret instructions issued by the Danish government forbidding the evacuation of civilians from Jutland in the midst of World War II. "Sometimes," he said, "cases arose where, in the higher interest of the State, the population must, even in case of danger, forgo their right to benefit by measures taken ostensibly on humanitarian grounds."[24] He was afraid that when a state's military did not allow civilians trapped in a conflict zone and scattered among combatants from their own country to flee, the military could be charged with using these civilians as human shields. He argued that even if military commanders deem it necessary to prohibit the civilians from running away from the area, it would be wrong to blame the commanders for deploying the civilians as human shields. In other words, any form of civilian activity—even the effort to flee a conflict zone—could be overruled by military necessity as defined by military commanders.

Ultimately, the United States' representative suggested dividing the article in two, leaving intact the part prohibiting the coercive transfer of civilians to use them as shields, while cutting out the part about civilians who become shields because of their proximity to the battlefield and distributing it among other articles.[25] This solution resolved the impasse, yet it did nothing to protect civilians trapped in a war zone. As we will see in the chapters on Sri Lanka, Gaza, and Iraq, this decision would have enormous repercussions later on, allowing governments, military commanders, and legal experts to invoke human shielding to justify the use of violence against civilians trapped in proximity to hostilities.

The codification concerning human shielding reveals the paradoxical and even confounding way international humanitarian law conceptualizes not only human shields, but civilianhood more generally. On the one hand, the Fourth Geneva Convention forbids the use of civilians as human shields, thus avowing the value ascribed to the lives of civilians by defending them from belligerents who want to deploy them as weapons. On the other hand, according to the law, legitimate military targets do not become immune from attack even when human shields are deployed to protect them, meaning that belligerents can still attack targets that are protected by civilians used as human shields and ultimately kill them. While the value of civilian life is asserted in post–World War II international law, the notion of military advantage pushes back.

NINE

People's War

Casting Vietnamese Resistance as Human Shielding

NOT LONG AFTER THE SECOND SINO-JAPANESE WAR erupted in July 1937, Mao Tse-tung, who by that time was already the head of both China's Communist Party and the Red Army, began developing a theory of war that simultaneously combined methods of struggle against China's own internal feudal regime with strategies for expelling a foreign invader—in this case, the Japanese troops. This, he thought, could be accomplished by waging a very different kind of war from the one found in the "reactionary" manuals of the Chinese government, which were simply copies of Western military counter-insurgency manuals.[1] As it turned out, his theory of war also challenged—in a very peculiar way—the distinction between combatants and civilians as well as the notion that civilians can only be passive victims during war.

Mao searched for different sources of inspiration—from Chinese military thinkers such as Sun Wu Tzu to Lenin's theory of a people's insurrection—while also reflecting on the historical experiences of other national liberation struggles, particularly the Ethiopian anticolonial war against Italy. He wanted to find a way of producing a collective will among all members of the Chinese population,[2] and after much deliberation he concluded that a revolutionary war is a "mass undertaking" that necessitates tearing down the "Great Wall" between combatants and civilians. The goal was to transform small Red rural pockets of power into a national revolutionary force—a political objective that would culminate in the institution of a totalitarian regime in the 1950s.

Although the idea of a people's war as a form of warfare already had existed in several revolutionary struggles—from the American Revolution to the Italian Risorgimento—where combatants and civilians had fought in concert, Mao refined and deepened its meaning.[3] "By saying that civilians can very quickly become soldiers," he wrote, "we mean that it is not difficult to cross the threshold" between noncombatants and combatants.[4] If a people's war is to succeed in defeating both internal and external enemies, the civilian population has to commit itself to the war effort.

The logic was straightforward. Given the asymmetry of power between the revolutionary forces on the one hand and the feudal regime and the foreign invaders on the other, only revolutionary combatants who could strike their enemies and then swiftly blend into the local population could achieve military and political gains.[5] According to this strategy, the civilian population must support the war effort by feeding the fighters, caring for the wounded and sick, and providing them with intelligence. Crucially, the population was also expected to protect and conceal the guerrillas' movements.

Mao understood that his model of people's war could be successful only if the masses supported the struggle and were involved in the revolutionary effort. He consequently insisted that the Communist vanguard had to infiltrate society at every level so as to promote through political education the cooperation between soldiers and civilians. The success of the revolution depended on the capacity of the guerrillas to work together with the people.

Mao's ideas spread like wildfire. His writings were translated into several languages, inspiring multiple anticolonial and self-determination struggles across the globe in the 1950s, 1960s, and 1970s. Insurgents from Malaya, India, Sri Lanka, and Vietnam as well as Palestine, Algeria, and Angola, and all the way to Cuba adopted his principles and teachings. Over the years, intellectuals, students, and political activists in numerous Western capitals were also influenced by his writings and created local Maoist groups. Even Western militaries began reading his work in an effort to improve their counterinsurgency techniques.[6]

Given Mao's anti-imperialist ideology and his personal charisma, such developments are not particularly surprising. No one, however, predicted that the Maoist version of the people's war, which is a doctrine aimed at advancing political liberation, would be framed as an act of human shielding.

LIKE FISH IN THE WATER

Immediately after the Second World War, Mao's teachings found fertile ground in neighboring Vietnam. In 1945, Ho Chi Minh, the Vietnamese revolutionary leader who later became prime minister and president of North

Vietnam, founded the Democratic Republic of Vietnam. Adopting significant parts of Mao's theory of war, he, together with General Vo Nguyen Giap, the commander in chief and interior minister, established the Viet Minh, the national independence coalition, and launched a simultaneous assault against the Vietnamese feudal lords and the French colonial occupiers. A year later, he confronted French colonial forces in what became the First Indochina War—a conflict that would last until 1954, culminating in the French defeat at Dien Bien Phu.

General Giap was fascinated by Mao's writings. In one of his most influential formulations of a people's war as a unity between noncombatants and combatants, Mao had written that "the former may be likened to water and the latter to the fish who inhabit it."[7] Giap immediately adopted the metaphor in his insurrection manual *People's War, People's Army*, stressing how for the Vietnamese resistance fighters the water was mainly made up of rural people.[8] The rural people both screened and sheltered the Vietnamese combatants, allowing them to carry out decisive attacks against the French and immediately retreat into safe quarters where they would hide, be fed, treated when sick, train, and collect intelligence.

Even though the Vietnamese succeeded in driving out the French colonists, their independence was still under threat. After France's retreat, Ho Chi Minh decided to reject the 1954 Geneva Peace Accords that split Vietnam into North Vietnam and South Vietnam, aiming to unify the country under Communist rule. The United States, which feared the "domino effect" of a nonaligned state turning Communist at the height of the Cold War, chose to support the South Vietnamese government. The American military started training Southern Vietnamese security forces, thus transforming South Vietnam from a postcolony into an imperial proxy.

MIRRORING

Over the years, the war intensified. The Viet Cong—the National Liberation Front of South Vietnam, made up of troops from the south who operated under the central command of Ho Chi Minh's People's Army of Vietnam—adopted antigovernment guerrilla warfare and were slowly advancing towards Saigon, the southern capital. When the South Vietnamese military—which had been created with US funding and support—tried to engage the Viet Cong in the countryside, the guerrillas disappeared into a sea of rural people.

Ngo Dinh Nhu, the South Vietnamese president's brother and head of the secret police, declared that through their shielding practices the Viet Cong had become an invisible nightmare: "Since we did not know where the enemy was . . . , ten times we launched a military operation, nine times we missed the Viet Cong, and the tenth time, we struck right on the head of the population."[9]

The Saigon government and its American patron tried to address the Mao-inspired guerrilla warfare with a series of military-economic programs in the rural areas. Over the years a series of pacification plans were introduced, with the South Vietnamese army taking an active role in their implementation. As one US counterguerrilla advisor put it, only indigenous soldiers could accomplish the pacification mission, since the "guerrillas blend in with the people. They live with them, share the same poverty, tell them they are fighting for the people's future happiness. . . . Americans [can't blend in], our white faces are a handicap."[10]

Aiming to isolate the Viet Cong from their popular base, the first pacification program, named Agroville, lasted from 1959 to 1961. Building on counterinsurgency practices that had been developed by the British during the Boer Wars and had travelled to Algeria, where the French had tried to quell the anticolonial resistance,[11] Agroville created "secure zones" where three hundred to five hundred families were resettled in Rural Community Development Centers. The centers were designed to "afford the peasantry the social benefits of city life" by providing them with schools and medical services. But instead of enhancing the people's security and alienating them from the Viet Cong, the rural population continued to support the guerrilla fighters, not least because the US and South Vietnamese armies had forcibly uprooted them from their land and homes.[12]

Following the failure of the Agroville Program, in 1961 the US administration introduced a new plan executed by the South Vietnamese government in yet another effort to separate the fish from their water. President John F. Kennedy—himself a reader of Mao's works—decided to increase military aid to Vietnamese villages as a way to counter the guerrilla effort.[13] He instructed the military to launch the Strategic Hamlet Program, which ran from 1961 to 1963 and was devised by Robert Thompson, the newly appointed head of the British Advisory Mission to Saigon, who had previously been in charge of quelling resistance in Malaya. Thompson's aim was to mirror the strategies Mao had developed in his explication of a people's war, following the principle that counterguerrilla forces must adopt the same tactics as those used by the guerrilla himself.[14]

The program enjoyed the support of many advisors and most moderniza-tion theorists.[15] Harvard professor Samuel Huntington, who years later authored the notorious book *The Clash of Civilizations,* claimed at the time that the only way to deal with the Viet Cong fish was by draining the sea, using mass expulsions to deprive the people's war of its rural constituency.[16] In fact, the Strategic Hamlet Program operated very similarly to Agroville: it aimed to counter the insurgency by evicting the rural population from their homes and resettling them in new artificial hamlets surrounded by barbed wire.[17] Notwithstanding the initial enthusiasm for this program among the decision makers in Kennedy's administration, the transformation of the rural population in South Vietnam into internally displaced persons only increased the Viet Cong's political and military grip on the targeted areas.

OUTLAWING THE PEOPLE'S WAR

The practice of "taking a leaf from the insurgent book" and trying to develop a counterinsurgency strategy against a people's war simply didn't work.[18] The insurgency actually expanded during Strategic Hamlet, and the survival of the puppet government in South Vietnam was at further risk. When US president Lyndon Johnson and his new administration realized that the attempts to deprive the Viet Cong of its popular support were failing, they decided to launch a massive military operation.

The United States military again tried to confront Mao's people's war by mirroring the Viet Cong, but this time in a completely different way: by carrying out an offensive that disregarded the distinction between combat-ants and civilians.[19] In 1965, the CIA initiated the Phoenix Program in order to dismantle the "Viet Cong infrastructure," by which it meant Vietnamese civilians who were actively supporting the guerrilla fighters by feeding them and caring for their wounded while also offering them a place to hide. For seven years the rural population in South Vietnam was terrorized. Anyone suspected of being involved in the people's war, including Viet Cong opera-tives, informants, and supporters, became fair game as the CIA and the US and South Vietnamese militaries kidnapped, tortured, and ultimately killed more than twenty thousand civilians.[20]

During the same period, the US military launched Operation Rolling Thunder, a military campaign that began in 1965 and included the massive deployment of American troops in South Vietnam, reaching over half a million soldiers at the peak of the war in 1969.[21] Even as the US Air Force was dropping more than one million tons of bombs,[22] President Johnson claimed that the military was trying to avoid indiscriminate killing in "an effort that is unprecedented in the history of warfare."[23] However, every day the civilian "body count" increased, exacting a heavy toll on the Vietnamese population and amplifying the insurgents' popularity.[24] Simultaneously, heavy losses among American troops strengthened the opposition to the war at home.

Not only were the counterinsurgency tactics inadequate, but the existing international legal framework was not crafted to regulate conflicts between regular armies and guerrilla combatants fighting a people's war. The German jurist and political theorist Carl Schmitt noted that "the Geneva Conventions have European experiences in mind, but not the partisan wars of Mao Tse-tung and the later development of modern partisan warfare."[25] The rigid distinction and polarization between the active combatant and the passive civilian informing international humanitarian law did not address Mao's guerrilla techniques.[26] Nevertheless, in spite of its inadequacies in dealing with these forms of warfare, the US Department of Defense did use international law to claim that the Vietnamese tactics adopted in people's wars were criminal, especially the use of the civilian population as "human shields."

The Department of Defense reduced the people's war, a strategy of political struggle rather than military fighting, to an act of human shielding. Civilians were mobilized politically by the Maoist guerrillas in Vietnam, but in the eyes of the Americans, they were being forced to serve as shields. The American press amplified this charge, and in the midst of Operation Rolling Thunder, started publishing articles depicting the Viet Cong's deployment of noncombatants as shields. "Protected by Human Shields, Viet Cong Kill 33 Americans" was the title of one article, and "Viet Cong Use Human Shields, 10 Die, 16 Hurt" was the title of another.[27] The use of women and children as shields was continuously emphasized, serving as evidence of "the vicious nature of the Communist enemy . . . and its total disregard for human life."[28] The mounting number of civilian deaths was thus justified by invoking the human shielding accusation and producing a divide between the inhumane methods of warfare adopted by the Viet Cong and the "civilized" response of the American military.

In addition, the US military dropped twenty-three million leaflets from airplanes as part of its campaign to convince the rural population that support for the Vietnamese resistance was against their interests. Combining moral condemnation of shielding with accusations of Viet Cong cowardice, one leaflet called on the population to turn against the Viet Cong:

The [Viet Cong] claim that they are concerned for the welfare of the Vietnamese people. Why do they use your villages as a base to fight the forces of your government, the Republic of Vietnam? ... Why do the VC always hide in the midst of the people and refuse to meet the government's forces on the battlefield? The VC say they are strong, why must they continue to use defenseless women and children as shields and your villages for their protection? Refuse the VC demands and tell him to do battle in the fields, rice paddies, and woods away from your village and you.[29]

In addition to the leaflets that cast the civilian population who supported the war effort as human shields, the United States adopted a similar strategy at the diplomatic level. When the International Committee of the Red Cross asked the United States to uphold the four Geneva Conventions in Vietnam, Secretary of State Dean Rusk blamed the Viet Cong for violating the laws of armed conflict: "As you are aware, those involved in aggression against the Republic of Viet Nam [South Vietnam] rely heavily on disguise and disregard generally accepted principles of warfare."[30] In other exchanges between Lyndon Johnson's administration and several international humanitarian organizations, US officials followed the same script that had been used by the Italian Fascist regime in Ethiopia, portraying the Vietnamese insurgents as hiding behind human shields because they were uncivilized and ignorant of the principles of international law.

Similarly, in response to political pressures at home to stop certain targeting policies, the Department of Defense issued a report that expanded its interpretation of human shielding from the coercive use of a civilian or small groups of civilians to shield a military target to the use by insurgents of whole villages and towns as shields. Noting that the military was taking all possible precautions to "avoid civilian casualties," the report added that it was nonetheless "impossible to avoid all damage to civilian areas, especially when the North Vietnamese deliberately emplace their air defense sites, their dispersed POL [petroleum, oil, lubricants], their radar and other military facilities in the midst of populated areas, and, indeed, sometimes on the roofs of government buildings."[31]

Obviously, the Vietnamese resistance did deliberately intermingle with the people, leveraging their ability to hide like fish in the water for both military and political purposes. But in the administration's interpretation of this practice, virtually all civilian areas in North Vietnam and in the southern pockets controlled by the Viet Cong had become zones of illegal human shielding. The active participation of the civilian population in a people's war of resistance against a foreign occupier was not compatible with the existing framework of international law created by the Geneva Conventions, which ascribed the passive role of victim to civilians. Building on this concept of the civilian, Johnson's administration radically altered the meaning of Mao's complex notion of people's war by obscuring the political context informing the Vietnamese resistance and reconceptualizing the civilian population as hostages in the hands of the Viet Cong. The administration invoked the legal figure of the involuntary human shield, a passive figure who is exploited for military purposes, and it used the notion of shielding to interpret the violence in Vietnam. This became a way to convince the American public that their military was facing an inhumane and barbaric human-shielding enemy.

The American effort to outlaw the people's war by reducing it to an illegal act of involuntary shielding should be understood as part of an effort to outlaw the right to resist foreign invaders. This effort is paradoxical, given the way the American Revolution against the British has been framed as a people's war, a moral form of resistance that to this day is considered a source of national pride. Along similar lines, the contemporary liberal order in Europe casts the struggles that created European states during the nineteenth century as people's wars. The participation of European peoples in the liberation effort, including the partisan wars against the Nazis and Fascists, has been framed as courageous moral acts, and the notion of the people and the people's right to resist have been inscribed in the constitutions informing the political-legal order in countries like Italy and France. Yet when people's wars were adopted by liberation movements aiming to achieve self-determination in the global south, the concept acquired a completely negative valence aimed at generating moral and legal aversion.

VEGETATION SHIELDING

The American animosity towards shielding did not spare the environment. In 1957, the US Department of Defense began developing "tactical herbicides" as part of a program to introduce sophisticated techniques of warfare against the Viet Cong. After several years of testing, the Chemical Corps came up with a series of chemical agents, using the colors orange, blue, white, pink, green, and purple to label them according to their levels of toxicity.[32]

In 1962, the US launched in Vietnam the first systematic operation of herbicidal warfare in human history, extending the fight against a people's

FIGURE 12. Three US Air Force UC-123 Providers spraying herbicide
and defoliant chemicals. Credit: Underwood Archives, Getty Images.

war to the environment, which military commanders had also framed as an
illegal shield used for military objectives. Operation Ranch Hand lasted until
1971, dumping millions of gallons of herbicides and defoliants over Vietnam
(figure 12). The official objective was "to improve visibility in enemy controlled or contested jungle areas in order to expose infiltration routes, base
camps, weapon placements, and storage sites."[33] The idea was to defeat what
appeared to be an invisible enemy by pulverizing the jungles in which the
Viet Cong shielded themselves, while destroying the subsistence crops and
propelling massive displacement of civilian populations, who due to the air
strikes lost their source of livelihood.[34] In this way, the Vietnamese jungles
that shielded the resistance and enabled the fighters to carry out attacks were
also framed as part of Mao's sea. In Vietnam the specter of the shield tran-
scended the human realm to include the ecosphere.

When the hostilities finally ended, herbicidal warfare and its devastating impact on the environment were debated in the international conferences leading to the 1977 Additional Protocols to the Geneva Convention. The International Committee of the Red Cross insisted on completely prohibiting all forms of "ecological warfare." The US representative tried to convince the other international delegates to amend the new prohibition outlawing the widespread destruction of nature with a significant qualification: "unless [the environment serves] a direct military purpose, such as shielding the enemy from observation or attack." In response, the Vietnamese representative asked the other delegates to support the original Red Cross text without any amendments, arguing that the techniques used by the "imperialist aggressor" during the war on Vietnam "had led to the irremediable destruction of the soil and the micro-organisms of rivers and forests," constituting an ongoing crime against humanity.[35]

The United States was defeated in the diplomatic arena as it had been in its counterinsurgency efforts on the ground, and a new legal clause prohibiting the employment of "methods or means of warfare which are intended or may be expected to cause widespread, long-term, and severe damage to the natural environment" was adopted.[36] The international community concluded that the environment could not be punished for shielding.

TEN

Environment

Green Human Shielding

HUMAN SHIELDING FIRST EMERGED as a form of resistance in environmental struggles. While the Vietnam War was still raging, a small group of environmental activists in Vancouver, Canada, began meeting to establish an organization to protect the environment. As they deliberated about what to call the organization, one of the names they got excited about was "Green Panthers." The Black Panthers were making headlines across the globe at the time, and their relentless struggle against white supremacy and for social and economic justice in what some might call a homegrown people's war inspired the activists. But as police and FBI agents began gunning down the African American militants, the members of the fledgling environmental organization had a change of heart. "Anything short of non-violence," argued Robert Hunter, one of the founding members, "only gives the police an excuse to eradicate you." A few weeks later, while the group was thinking of ways to stop an imminent nuclear test that the United States was planning to carry out in the Aleutian Islands, southwest of Alaska, a reticent member suggested the name Greenpeace.[1] Less than two decades later, Greenpeace had become an icon, with a logo that is nearly as recognizable—at least in Western countries—as those of Coca-Cola and McDonalds.[2]

In 1970, however, it was not at all clear that a small group of activists, numbering no more than fifteen people at the time, could challenge the United States' military nuclear program, particularly at the height of the Cold War. Moreover, about four thousand kilometers of ocean waters separated the activists' hometown of Vancouver from the test site. A protest in front of a Canadian governmental building might have made them feel good, but they knew it would have no political effect. Some sort of direct action was required.

In one meeting, someone enthusiastically described a handbook recently published by the environmental organization Sierra Club called *Ecotactics,* noting that it offered numerous innovative ideas about how to mobilize the law and media, organize teach-ins, lobby, and use "guerrilla theatre"—spontaneous performances in unlikely public spaces aimed at surprising the audience and drawing attention to political issues.[3] At one point, someone else suggested that they "sail a boat up there and confront the bomb."[4]

In September 1971, twelve members set sail on a daring mission toward Amchitka, one of the Aleutian Islands where the Department of Defense was scheduled to test a five-megaton nuclear bomb, whose destructive capacity was 250 times that of the bomb that had been dropped on Nagasaki. Using a technical excuse, the Coast Guard arrested the activists before they reached the island. And although the bomb was detonated, further tests that had been scheduled were cancelled in the face of growing grassroots criticism that had been mobilized by the protest.

This strategy had already been used in 1958, when a group of advocates from the National Committee for a Sane Nuclear Policy (SANE) in the United States decided to sail a boat toward the Marshall Islands, where an atmospheric nuclear test was scheduled to take place. Albert Bigelow, one of the leaders, had attended Harvard before entering the Navy, where he had served with distinction as captain of a ship in the Second World War. Later he housed survivors of the Hiroshima blast who had been brought to Boston for reconstructive surgery. In the mid-1950s he joined the fledging antinuclear movement and in 1958, after a few years of advocacy, he set sail together with other members of the group to the restricted zone near the Marshall Islands.[5]

In his memoir, Bigelow explains that the ultimate horror was that in the face of a possible nuclear holocaust, people felt no horror. He concluded that the only way to arouse the public was by displaying a willingness to put one's body on the line and even sacrifice one's life.[6] The idea was to sail the boat to the nuclear test site, where the boat's crew could use their own bodies as environmental human shields to protect ocean life from the bomb's destructive impact. Although the US Coast Guard intercepted and detained the crew immediately after they set out from Honolulu, they did manage to propel the issue of nuclear testing onto the public agenda, which helped to spur the drafting of the Partial Nuclear Test Ban Treaty of 1963.[7] Their willingness to risk their lives by travelling to a nuclear test site served as an inspiration and model for not only Greenpeace but also the Sea Shepherds and other activists at the forefront of the environmental movement in the 1970s.[8]

The voluntary deployment of the human body in order to protect the environment from nuclear weapons marked a turning point in the history of human shielding. For the first time images of voluntary human shields circulated in the media, transforming this form of shielding, introduced by activists like Maude Royden between the two world wars, into a global spectacle. But even more crucially, environmental shielding added a new layer to voluntary shielding, combining the humane opposition to war with a sense of solidarity with the nonhuman environment.

ENVIRONMENTAL LIFE MATTERS

Environmental shielding was not, however, a modern Western invention. Bigelow, Greenpeace, and the others were inheritors of a venerable spiritual tradition of human shielding introduced centuries earlier in Asia by a Hindu sect called the Bishnoi. Indeed, this form of shielding was practiced in India in the eighteenth century by the followers of Guru Jambheshwar, the founder of Bishnoi (which means "twenty-nine" and refers to the number of its guiding principles).[9]

Guru Jambheshwar had formed the sect in the sixteenth century following the devastating effects of a long drought that had led to famine in the deserts of Rajasthan. Among the principles he developed were mercy to all living beings, a prohibition on cutting green trees, and a command to save the environment. Advocating a bodily politics of environmental protection, he claimed that "humans will have to sustain the environment around them in order for nature to sustain them." This, he thought, may have to include some form of sacrifice.[10]

Indeed, Bishnoi consolidated environmental shielding as a form of resistance. The most famous episode occurred in 1730, when Amrita Devi, a local woman belonging to the environmental conservation sect, hugged trees near Jodhpur, Rajasthan, to prevent soldiers from felling them in order to make room for the king's new palace. She was killed trying to shield the trees, as were 362 other Bishnois who followed her example.[11] Bishnoi ecotactics persisted over the centuries, and Mahatma Gandhi as well as other activists in India adopted their ideas. Indeed, at the same moment that Greenpeace emerged on the political scene, environmental shielding was also being adopted by the Chipko women's movement in northern India. Struggling against commercial deforestation, which threatened to flood the Himalayan

FIGURE 13. Women from the Chipko movement shielding trees in northern India, 1973. Credit: Bhawan Singh, Getty Images.

foothills, devastating the local population's subsistence agriculture, this group of women emulated Amrita Devi and hugged trees that were slated for felling (figure 13).[12]

Notwithstanding their different historical manifestations, from the Bishnoi and Chipko in India to SANE and Greenpeace in the United States and Canada, the diverse forms of environmental shielding mobilize the vulnerability of the human body in order to protect nature. In this sense, then, the politics of environmental shielding is also a politics of vulnerability, but it transcends solidarity with other humans, advancing an ethics in which the sacredness of human life is understood to be continuous with the sacredness of all biological life.[13] Both in its religious and its secular manifestations, this form of shielding can be considered part of what Rosi Braidotti has called the "posthuman turn"—which refers to a growing sense of relationship, collectivity, and solidarity between human and nonhuman beings.[14] This turn, however, is not as new as Braidotti argues—she situates its beginning in the 1970s—as it started well before the twentieth century, as the Indian tradition of tree hugging shows.

MURUROA

Contemporary environmental shielding has been inspired by the struggle against the nuclear threat. In 1959, France declared that it would begin carrying out atmospheric nuclear tests in the Sahara desert. Many African countries protested, highlighting the danger of nuclear fallout while also criticizing French colonialism and the use of Algeria as the testing ground.[15]

An international group of antinuclear activists from Ghana, the United States, and Britain gathered in Ghana's capital city of Accra to prepare for the 3,400-kilometer journey to the test site. They raised money, purchased several jeeps, and headed north, hoping to deter the French from dropping the bomb by serving as human shields. The activists tried to reach the testing ground three different times, and each time French forces stopped the convoys not long after they crossed Ghana's border with Burkina Faso.[16] Undeterred by the activists, the French undertook tests in the Sahara for a number of years. After Algeria gained independence in 1962, France looked for an alternative test site and decided to use the Mururoa atoll in French Polynesia. The ocean thus replaced the desert as the primary fallout zone (figure 14).[17]

When the United States cancelled the nuclear tests in Amchitka, Greenpeace decided to try to prevent the atmospheric testing carried out in French Polynesia. Since its establishment, the young organization had developed a two-pronged strategy. One group would sail within the perimeter of the nuclear fallout zone, thus enabling its crew members to serve as shields against the detonation of the bomb. A second group would create what they called a "mind bomb," an image so shocking that it would change political

FIGURE 14. The French nuclear test on the Mururoa atoll, 1970. Credit: Galerie Bilderwelt, Getty Image.

consciousness around the world and generate support for the organization's goals.[18] They did this by disseminating press releases and photographs of the shielding group's actions to the global media, framing environmental shielding as the ultimate human sacrifice against the apocalyptic effects of the nuclear bomb.

Calling themselves "warriors of the rainbow," a reference to a Native American prophecy that foretold the coming of a band of earth warriors who would save the world from environmental destruction, the organization's members drew a link between environmental shielding and sacrifice in war.[19] The fact that Greenpeace deployed human shielding practices on the high seas instead of on sovereign land or in territorial waters gave it a considerable amount of leeway that the activists who aimed to reach the nuclear test grounds in the Sahara did not have.

Greenpeace began looking for volunteers to make the 5,500-kilometer trip from New Zealand to the Mururoa atoll, after the French had announced that they were planning to test one of their bombs. David McTaggart, a Canadian citizen who had grown up in Vancouver and was a three-time national badminton champion, was, at the time, living in New Zealand. When he heard that Greenpeace was looking for a captain who would sail to Mururoa, he volunteered to lead the mission, called Greenpeace III. Although he was not an environmentalist at the time, he was a maverick and sailor and considered the task a challenge.[20] After numerous bureaucratic attempts on the part of the New Zealand government to ground the boat, he and three other men set sail toward the atoll.[21]

By the time the *Greenpeace III* vessel reached the Mururoa atoll in June 1972, the crew had shrunk to three and the transmission radio that enabled them to communicate with the outside world had broken. They were nonetheless determined to serve as human shields by staying within the perimeter of the nuclear fallout zone, thus not entering France's territorial waters—a belt of coastal waters extending about twelve nautical miles into the sea and regarded as part of the sovereign territory of the state—where the French military could legally apprehend them. For a couple of weeks, the French navy monitored their every move, instructing the environmentalists to leave the area while cruising extremely close to *Greenpeace III* in an effort to intimidate them. In his memoir, McTaggart recalls he had the distinct feeling of being hunted down.[22]

Nonetheless, he and the other crew members were unwilling to be bullied. Despite their inability to transmit messages to civilian ships or ports, they held fast, knowing that on the high seas they had right of passage and that if the French military tried to stop them, it would be violating international law. They managed to hear over the wireless that eight countries had just signed a treaty in Stockholm to ban atomic tests and that in New Zealand dock workers were refusing to service French ships. Consequently, they felt strengthened, knowing that their efforts had mobilized a global antinuclear movement.

Eventually, France decided that it must go ahead and run the test. It would no longer wait for *Greenpeace III*'s fuel, water, or food supplies to run out so the protesters would willingly leave the area. A French military ship began chasing the activists to force them out of the fallout zone. When it did not succeed, it rammed into the vessel, rendering *Greenpeace III* inoperable. The French then towed the Greenpeace boat to their military base and repaired it, on condition that the activists leave the area immediately after it was fixed.

During their stay on the island, not only were the activists not allowed to communicate with the outside world, but they unknowingly participated in military deception. McTaggart and his crew were invited to lunch with the French admiral, and as they were drinking wine and enjoying a healthy meal, a military photographer surreptitiously took photos. The images were sent to news agencies across the globe as evidence that there was no animosity between the environmental shielders and the nuclear nation. From the perspective of creating a "mind bomb," the protest appeared to be a complete failure. However, the news coverage *Greenpeace III* had generated as it was setting out to the Mururoa atoll had been sufficient to push the governments of New Zealand and Australia to file cases against France's atmospheric nuclear tests in the International Court of Justice.[23]

Following the French takeover of *Greenpeace III,* McTaggart flew to Canada. Less than two years later, however, in 1974, he set sail once again on a Greenpeace mission from New Zealand to try to stop another French nuclear test at Mururoa. Several other environmental groups had also launched vessels to serve as shields in the nuclear test site. Most of those boats did not reach the fallout zone due to harsh weather, and the one ship that did was boarded by French soldiers and towed away. *Greenpeace III* reached the area a couple of weeks later, just before the fourth planned blast, but French soldiers used a fast Zodiac to reach the Greenpeace boat. They took over the vessel after brutally beating McTaggart and another crew member.

Even though the protests against the French nuclear testing in the Pacific appeared to have failed, they nonetheless had an impact. A few months after *Greenpeace III* was taken over, the International Court of Justice delivered its ruling on the petitions filed by New Zealand and Australia. The court found that the claims made by the two countries had no legal foundation, since France had by then declared that it would stop conducting atmospheric nuclear tests in the South Pacific.

SAVING WHALES

Taking advantage of its growing success, Greenpeace decided to expand environmental shielding from direct action informed by the concerns of pacifists and the antiwar-antinuclear movement to shielding practices aimed at protecting the environment from corporate plunder.[24] The new goal was to save whales. Today whaling is carried out by eight-thousand-ton diesel-powered steel ships with harpoon guns mounted on the deck. Such ships kill, process, and package several whales per day. It is estimated that the multimillion-dollar business of harvesting whale meat has, over the years, reduced the whale population from a few million to several hundred thousand.[25] Gregory Peck, the actor who played Captain Ahab in the 1956 film version of Herman Melville's novel *Moby Dick,* spoke out against modern whaling practices in a 1981 advertisement for the Animal Welfare Institute: "A hundred years ago during whaling's romantic heyday, a three-year expedition netted an average of thirty-seven whales. Today a modern Japanese or Russian whaling fleet can eliminate thirty-seven whales a day with brutal military precision. There are cheap, plentiful substitutes for all whale products. Unfortunately, there are no substitutes for whales."[26]

Greenpeace activists had already reached a similar conclusion in the early 1970s. As Robert Hunter, a leading Greenpeace activist who persuaded the organization to launch a campaign to protect the whales, put it: "Instead of small boats and giant whales, giant boats and small whales; instead of courage killing whales, courage saving whales; David had become Goliath, Goliath was now David; if the mythology of Moby Dick and Captain Ahab had dominated human consciousness about Leviathan for over a century, a whole new age was in the making."[27] Not unlike Maude Royden, but in a context of environment protection instead of an antiwar movement, Hunter framed voluntary shielding as a heroic act of courage, calling the whaling campaign Project Ahab.[28]

Unlike nuclear testing, however, the mere presence of activists where whalers hunt for prey was insufficient to protect them, and a different strategy of shielding had to be concocted. The French use of Zodiacs to assault McTaggart's vessel during his second voyage to the Mururoa atoll provided the key. "We'd take a boat out to sea," Robert Hunter explained several years later, "find the whalers, put the high-speed rubber Zodiacs in the water, and race in front of the harpoons, making a clear shot at the whales impossible without a good chance of a human being getting blasted in the process. We would become living shields" (figure 15).[29]

It did not take long before Greenpeace's well-orchestrated antiwhaling campaign began to attract the media's interest. In one expedition, *Greenpeace V* followed the Russian harpoon boat *Vlasny,* whose sonar was powerful enough to track whales hundreds of fathoms below. The fishing boat followed the whales until they came up for air and then killed them. After several days, the activists noticed whale blows rising from the water not far from the *Vlasny* and detected harpooners preparing the cannons for the kill. Paul Watson and Robert Hunter each jumped into a Zodiac and steered

FIGURE 15. Greenpeace activists in a Zodiac shielding whales, 1988. Credit: Steve Morgan, Greenpeace.

their way towards *Vlasny* to position themselves between the hunters and their prey. Two other activists climbed into a third Zodiac to film the action. As the frantic and exhausted whales rose to get some air, one harpooner swung the green steel cannon from side to side, trying to aim the harpoon at a whale. Abruptly, Watson plunged his Zodiac in front of the cannon. "Looking past Watson's shoulder," Hunter recalls how he "saw the eyes of the harpooner. Then the steel bow rose and slashed down behind them" just missing both the Zodiac and the whale. Monitoring the harpooner, Hunter suddenly saw how "an officer on the *Vlasny* ran from the bridge to the harpoon mount, spoke some hurried words to the harpooner, and scrambled back to the metal catwalk. The harpooner stepped away from his weapon." "My God," Hunter thought, "he's been ordered not to fire. We've stopped them."[30] In this instance, Greenpeace was victorious.

However, a certain paradox informing environmental shielding becomes apparent here. To take a stand for the sacredness of all life, Greenpeace asks its activists to situate themselves between the environment and those out to destroy it, knowing that the assailants will be more hesitant to harm humans. Thus, while expressing solidarity with nonhuman lives, environmental shielding reaffirms the higher value of human life and reproduces the human-centric hierarchy by which humans are prioritized over animals and other organic life.

The fact that voluntary human shielding on the high seas is legal—and therefore very different from shielding on land or in territorial waters—helps explain Greenpeace's relative success. According to the Convention on the Law of the Sea, "no state may validly purport to subject any part of the high seas to its sovereignty."[31] While on sovereign land, people cannot be used as human shields to protect a legitimate military target, in international waters vessels and their crews can legally sail anywhere they want and can voluntarily use their presence to shield a target.[32] It is almost as if sovereignty, which, according to Thomas Hobbes, was passed from each individual to the state with the establishment of the social contract, reverts from the state back to the individual in the high seas.[33] Indeed, there is an inversion of the usual relations between the human shields and those attacking a target on land—whether they are states carrying out nuclear tests or commercial whaling ships deploying harpoon guns. On the high seas, attempts to obstruct the shielding boats' freedom to sail is a violation of the law; in other words, it is the prevention of shielding, rather than the practice of shielding, that is illegal.

During the first expedition to the Mururoa atoll, the French military ships waited a couple of weeks before they stopped *Greenpeace III* because they recognized that McTaggart and his crew had a right to sail in the fallout zone, and their actions to force the environmental shielders from the zone were illegal. Moreover, human shields on the high seas are protected by the flag of their boat and their citizen status, even if the country under which they sail disavows their action. The red-and-white maple leaf flag flying from the Greenpeace vessel's backstay meant that, legally speaking, Greenpeace's boat was a little part of Canada.[34] Even though the environmental group had no formal ties with the Canadian government and was, in a sense, a band of irregulars carrying out an insurgency operation against a foreign military, from the perspective of international law, for France to obstruct or take over the boat would be almost tantamount to launching an invasion against Canada itself. These particulars about engagement on the world's oceans allowed McTaggart to sue the French navy and government after the protest at Mururoa, and although the chances of a French court ruling against the state were highly unlikely from the outset, the judges did reprimand the navy for its provocative actions.[35]

Thus, human shields on the high seas can serve as the guardians of the law. For example, when Greenpeace first launched its shielding boats in the

Pacific Ocean, striving to stop nations from breaching the 1963 Partial Nuclear Test Ban Treaty, it was attempting to enforce the law. In the high seas, shielding is not only a legal form of resistance and protection but can be used by groups such as Greenpeace as a strategy to force states to apply existing treaties.[36] Ultimately, limitations to sovereign authority on the high seas render shielding a legitimate tool of political action, protection, and deterrence.

ELEVEN

Resistance

Antimilitary Activism in Iraq and Palestine

NOT LONG AFTER THE IRAQI MILITARY INVADED oil-rich Kuwait in August 1990, the United Nations Security Council called upon Iraq to withdraw its forces, threatening to punish Saddam Hussein for violating Kuwait's sovereignty if he did not comply.[1] While a US-led international coalition amassed its troops in nearby Saudi Arabia, the Iraqi dictator remained defiant and refused to pull out his troops. In response, civilians from different countries decided to follow in the footsteps of Maude Royden—who in the 1930s had attempted to create a peace army to serve as a buffer between Japanese and Chinese forces—and announced the creation of the Gulf Peace Team, whose goal was to travel to the front lines and serve as voluntary human shields in order to try to prevent the impending confrontation. They were, in the words of one of their leaders, "going to the area with the aim of setting up one or more international peace camps between the opposing armed forces. Our objective will be to withstand nonviolently any armed aggression by any party to the present Gulf dispute."[2]

The Gulf Peace Team was cofounded by Pat Arrowsmith, a long-standing civil disobedience and direct action advocate who in the 1950s had managed to mobilize thousands of people to march from London to the Atomic Weapons Research Establishment in Aldermaston to protest the development of nuclear weapons.[3] Later, in 1967, at the height of the United States' military involvement in Indochina, Arrowsmith was among the founders of a group whose aim was to promote nonviolent resistance to American aggression by sending voluntary human shields to "share the dangers of bombardment with the Vietnamese people."[4] The initiative failed not only due to lack of funding and public support but also because it was impossible to access the conflict zones. In 1990, Arrowsmith managed to convince army veterans,

108

pacifists, and other prominent antiwar and environmental activists to join the Gulf Peace Team.[5] In contrast to Royden's peace army, which had not reached the war zone, in the days leading to the First Gulf War Saudi Arabia permitted hundreds of peaceniks to establish a camp on its territory at a border crossing with Iraq, which was in a pilgrims' resting place on the road to Mecca.[6]

Notwithstanding the activists' efforts, their action did not protect Iraq from the ravages of Operation Desert Storm, in which 100,000 to 200,000 Iraqi civilians were killed.[7] Indeed, the activists were never allowed to cross the border and therefore did not have a chance to serve as shields. Yet, even as the Gulf Peace Team realized that their effort to prevent war was unsuccessful, their venture to the Middle East received widespread media attention and has since inspired activists across the globe to adopt voluntary human shielding as a form of direct resistance to political violence. Challenging the predominant ethics of humane violence, these activists understood that they did not have to be mere spectators of war and could use human shielding as a strategy for advancing a humane ethics of nonviolence.

THE GLUE UNITING ACTIVISTS

Following the First Gulf War, the United Nations Security Council imposed a series of harsh economic sanctions on Iraq with the aim of overthrowing Saddam Hussein. The measures remained in place for over a decade, and, in spite of numerous claims that the sanctions did not affect key humanitarian supplies, a leading medical journal characterized them as a "weapon of mass destruction" that caused the death of about 1.5 million people.[8] In 2002, the United States finally admitted that the sanctions had not undermined Saddam Hussein's regime and decided to launch a new military campaign. The attack was justified as part of the war on terror by highlighting Iraq's presumed links with the 9/11 terrorist attacks alongside the accusation that the regime was hiding weapons of mass destruction.

Concerned about the terrible humanitarian and political repercussions such a war would likely have for the entire region, citizens across the globe organized popular protests in an attempt to prevent the imminent invasion of a country already devastated by years of economic sanctions. Moreover, as it became clear that the United States intended to attack without the authorization of the United Nations Security Council, international solidarity

FIGURE 16. Two of the buses transporting voluntary human shields from London to Baghdad, 2002. Credit: Ali Kabas, Alamy.

activists concluded that any attempt to resist the war on terror necessitated direct action rather than traditional forms of democratic mobilization.

At the end of 2002, US military veteran Kenneth O'Keefe implored various activist groups to join forces in an effort to stop the war through pacifist intervention "from below."[9] Scores of people heeded his call and formed the Human Shield Action group. They bought three double-decker buses in London and drove across Europe and through Turkey and Syria all the way to Baghdad (figure 16). Meanwhile, groups ready to join the movement and serve as voluntary human shields in Iraq began mushrooming in Australia, India, South Africa, Mexico, Argentina, New Zealand, Korea, and Japan. At its peak, the movement numbered five hundred activists.

Among those who reached Iraq was the former director of Greenpeace Turkey, who in her memoir recounts that the volunteers came from different walks of life and included Buddhists, Islamists, Christian socialists, anarchists, social democrats, monarchists, and conscientious objectors.[10] Their commitment to human life united them, as well as their willingness to act in solidarity with those who were being put in danger's way. Ultimately, they believed that risking their lives was the best way to prevent the Western aerial bombing campaign and predictable civilian deaths. Thus, resistance through human shielding became the glue uniting activists from radically different political, ideological, and spiritual backgrounds.

HUMANITARIAN SHIELDING ACTION

Determined to reach the battlefield, the Human Shield Action group coordinated their entry into Iraq with Saddam Hussein's government—they had no other option if they wanted to enter the country—while simultaneously trying to preserve their political autonomy. Although they did not want to be manipulated by the Iraqi regime, they followed this route because they believed that their action could actually have a tangible impact on the impending war.

On the eve of the US attack, the Central Intelligence Agency (CIA) released a report entitled *Putting Noncombatants at Risk: Saddam's Use of "Human Shields,"* which denounced Saddam Hussein's use of *involuntary* shields—Iraqi and foreign civilians, as well as prisoners of war—to protect strategic installations during the 1990–1991 First Gulf War.[11] The CIA then went on to analyze the current crisis, claiming that "Baghdad is encouraging international peace groups to send members to Iraq to serve as voluntary human shields, and the Iraqi military continues its longstanding policy of placing military assets near civilian facilities and in densely populated areas."[12] Two months later, General Richard B. Meyers, chairman of the Joint Chiefs of Staff, added that all forms of shielding of military targets are illegal, even when civilians "volunteer for this purpose."[13] Legally speaking, there was, in his eyes, no difference between involuntary and voluntary shields.

Things on the ground were, however, more complicated than the CIA and General Meyers claimed. The shields repeatedly stressed their independence from Saddam Hussein's regime both in their press releases and in official exchanges with the Iraqi government. Donna Mulhearn—an Australian human shield in charge of media relations—explained the group's position in a journal entry from Baghdad: "The human shields value life, all life. We opposed the Iraqi regime and its crimes before it was trendy to do so. . . . To say that opponents to war are automatically Hussein supporters is just childish and implicates millions of people around the world who have expressed their opposition."[14]

In a letter to President George W. Bush, the activists further reiterated their autonomy from the Iraqi government and underscored that the locations they had selected for shielding were not military targets. "You," they wrote the president, "should be aware that each of these human shields has voluntarily installed him or herself on these sites in an effort to deter the aerial bombing of vital infrastructure without which normal civilian life cannot exist."[15]

Since their action was prompted by a nonviolent ethic of care by civilians for civilians, their aim was not to protect Iraqi military installations; they situated themselves, instead, at power plants, water treatment stations, and food silos that sustained millions of civilians, as well as in oil refineries located close to civilian areas, hospitals, and communication centers.[16] Their intervention represented a specific form of nongovernmental solidarity that could be characterized as a humanitarian shielding action—a form of human shielding driven by a sense of humanity and compassion for vulnerable civilians trapped in a war zone.

This type of direct action differs, however, from classical forms of humanitarian aid. Both humanitarian aid and humanitarian shielding actions are responses to real or potential humanitarian crises affecting civilian populations, yet humanitarian aid organizations like Oxfam or CARE rely on sophisticated bureaucratic mechanisms that aim to alleviate suffering while, at least ostensibly, excluding politics and political activists. By contrast, humanitarian shielding is political through and through and sets out to prevent the horrors of war rather than mitigate its devastating effects. If humanitarian organizations aspire to ease and relieve the suffering caused by war, humanitarian shields attempt to avert or stop it altogether.

Just as important, guaranteeing the staff's protection within the conflict zone is a key imperative that informs the way humanitarian aid organizations operate, while, for humanitarian shields, risk is the essential means for averting a humanitarian catastrophe.[17] They understand that resisting violence and shielding innocent lives might entail taking the ultimate risk, the risk of dying.

ACTIVE CIVILIANS

Contrary to their hopes, the Human Shield Action group did not manage to stop the war. Nonetheless, they did demonstrate that civilians willing to risk their lives in an effort to protect other civilians trapped in a war zone can, in fact, create a peaceful obstacle against the use of lethal violence. Significantly, none of the sites they occupied were hit by aerial strikes, except for a telecommunication building that was bombed the day after the human shields had abandoned it.[18] Those in the United States who supported the invasion argued that this clearly demonstrated the surgical and proportionate nature of the military's use of force and that the troops had never intended to target civilian sites.[19] From another perspective, this observation suggests that the shielding had actually worked. Precisely because human shielding altered the military and legal calculations in the battlefield, it served as a successful form of deterrence and resistance.

Irrespective of the reasons why the civilian sites were not bombed, the voluntary human shields in Iraq did present a legal challenge to the attacking forces. This became obvious when the US government decided to charge citizens who had served as human shields after they returned home. The activists were sued for up to $1 million on the grounds that their travel to Iraq was "unauthorized" and that their shielding actions comprised an "exportation of services" that violated the sanctions imposed on Saddam Hussein's regime. They were also accused of "shielding a Government of Iraq (GOI) infrastructure from possible U.S. military action."[20]

The courts, however, were unable to convict the citizens because the locations they stayed in were not legitimate military targets.[21] While military and legal experts have continued to frame voluntary human shielding as a form of direct participation in hostilities—which means that civilians who serve as shields lose the protections bestowed upon them by international law—civilian sites tend to be illegitimate targets. Therefore, it is difficult legally to characterize people protecting them as human shields and thus as participants in hostilities.[22]

Simultaneously, the voluntary shields challenged the laws of armed conflict because the legal articles dealing with human shielding are restricted to situations where civilians or prisoners of war are forced to become shields and do not, as one report stated, "cover an event where individuals acted knowingly and on their own initiative."[23] This, as we have seen, is due to the way international law construes civilians as passive actors. Thus, when civilians become active in a nonviolent and protective way, they challenge existing legal assumptions. Precisely because voluntary human shields in the case of Iraq were active civilians protecting civilian sites, the question of how to treat them remained unresolved. Accordingly, such shielding activities elude the law.

SUICIDE

Voluntary shields faced a completely different destiny in another area in the Middle East. One member of the Human Shield Action group, Tom Hurdnall, left Iraq at the end of the war but instead of returning home to Britain, he traveled to the occupied Palestinian territories. It was the midst of the second Palestinian uprising against Israel's military occupation, which erupted in September 2000, and Hurdnall joined the International Solidarity Movement, created by Palestinians, Israelis, and foreigners to provide assistance to the besieged Palestinian population through nonviolent protests and direct action such as voluntary shielding. After a brief period in the West Bank, he travelled to Rafah, a city on the southern tip of the Gaza Strip, where he and other activists tried to stop the demolition of houses.

In an interview, Hurdnall described how the Israelis "continually fired one- to two-second bursts from what I could see was a Bradley fighting vehicle. . . . It was strange that as we approached and the guns were firing, it sent shivers down my spine, but nothing more than that. We walked down the middle of the street, wearing bright orange, and one of us shouted through a loudspeaker, 'We are international volunteers. Don't shoot!' That was followed by another volley of fire, though I can't be sure where from."[24]

In January 2004, when a group of Palestinians came under heavy fire, Hurdnall noticed that three children were trapped in an area under attack. He picked up one little boy and brought him to safety. When he went back to shield the remaining two, he was shot in the head by an Israeli sniper.[25]

Hurdnall was not the only human shield who was killed by the Israeli military. A few months earlier, Rachel Corrie, a twenty-three-year-old American activist who had also joined the International Solidarity Movement, was run over in Rafah by an armored military bulldozer while shielding a Palestinian home from demolition. For several weeks, Corrie had gone to the demolition site, standing between the bulldozer and the Palestinian houses while wearing an orange fluorescent jacket and using a megaphone to call to the bulldozer operator to stop his work (figure 17). On March 16, 2003, she was crushed to death. The driver later insisted that he had not seen her.[26]

Like the activists of the Human Shields Action group, Corrie felt that participating in protests at home was not enough. In order to express her solidarity with the Palestinians resisting Israeli colonialism she also travelled to Rafah. She characterized her activity in the Gaza Strip as a form of "patriotic

FIGURE 17. Rachel Corrie protecting a Palestinian home before being killed by an Israeli bulldozer, 2003. Credit: Handout Getty Images.

dissent." "I am asking people who care about me—or just have some passing interest in me—to use my presence in occupied Palestine as a reason to actively search for information about the Israeli-Palestinian conflict, and of course particularly about the role of the United States in perpetuating it," she wrote in her diary just a few days before being killed.[27] Corrie was well aware of her "white-skin privilege" and noted that she was using it to protect non-white civilians and civilian infrastructures. But unlike the shields in Iraq, white privilege did not render her immune from lethal violence.[28]

The proceedings of the civil suit initiated by Corrie's family reveal the peculiar way in which the Israeli lawyers defending the military framed the presence of foreign human shields who had travelled to support the Palestinian struggle for liberation. In a sense, the defense lawyers became prosecutors and transformed the civil suit into a trial against Corrie and the shielding practices adopted by the International Solidarity Movement. In the defense they wrote:

> It was proven beyond reasonable doubt, that the ISM, among whose ranks was the deceased and the plaintiff's witnesses, is an anti-Israeli organization that carries out violent illegal acts, including barricading themselves in terrorist homes to prevent their demolition, harboring terrorists and terror

activists, taking part in confrontations with IDF [Israel Defense Forces] soldiers, and even standing as human shields for "wanted people" or houses of Palestinians. The organization's activists, under the organization's umbrella, are aware of the many risks that exist in the places they are active, but they are willing to endanger their lives for the agenda they wish to advance.[29]

The lawyers claimed that Corrie and other International Solidarity Movement activists were protecting legitimate military targets rather than civilians. In another passage, the lawyers depicted Corrie as "suicidal," since she and her fellow activists directly confronted "war machinery" and "went to firing zones where life-threatening live ammunition is fired."[30] Within the Israeli context—particularly during the second Palestinian uprising, known as the Second Intifada, when suicide bombers killed civilians in Tel Aviv, Jerusalem, and other Israeli cities—the lawyers' decision to characterize Corrie as a person who was carrying out a suicidal act was not coincidental. She, the lawyers intimated, was not really different from those who explode themselves in public buses and restaurants. The fact that Corrie was committed to nonviolent protection as a form of resistance rather than attack was beside the point. The rhetoric of the war on terror could transform any civilian into a terrorist, even a privileged one who had decided to embrace an active form of internationalist citizenship in solidarity with oppressed civilians.

In 2012, the Haifa district court accepted the Israeli military's interpretation of Corrie's actions and dismissed the civil lawsuit brought by Corrie's family. Her death, the judges ruled, was an "accident." Three years later, after the family filed an appeal, Israel's High Court of Justice upheld the Haifa verdict and reiterated the claim that the state is not responsible to compensate civilians injured or killed in a combat zone.[31] In this way the court effectively shielded the state and its executive arm from any charges filed by either international or local activists who shield Palestinian civilians. Unlike US courts, Israel's courts consider nonviolent direct action aimed at protecting civilians from a military occupation as part of combat.

TWELVE

Humanitarian Crimes

The International Criminal Tribunal
for the Former Yugoslavia

THE DISSOLUTION OF THE FEDERAL REPUBLIC of Yugoslavia was marked by the bloodiest inter-ethnic war on European soil since the Second World War. Following Slovenia's and Croatia's declaration of independence in 1991, Serbia mobilized its paramilitary forces to "protect" an estimated six hundred thousand Serbs living in Croatia. While Croatia's forces tried to prevent the expansion of "Greater Serbia" within its own territory, images on television screens around the globe depicted civilian populations fleeing their homes as their villages went up in smoke, abandoned patients who managed to escape hospitals that had been bombed from the air, and scared soldiers chained to military targets. Evening news commentators discussed the egregious violations carried out by the belligerents, the ongoing humiliations, and the utter contempt for the law. It was, as the judge advocate of the US Army put it, "war crimes at dinner."[1]

As the fighting escalated and reports of ethnic cleansing and even genocide began circulating, the United Nations decided to use military force to stop the crimes and aid the civilian populations fleeing the massacres in Croatia and Bosnia. The United Nations Security Council called for the establishment of the United Nations Protection Force (UNPROFOR), a contingent composed of troops from forty-two countries who were sent to serve as armed peacekeepers to defend the UN's humanitarian convoys. The war, however, did not subside, and in 1993 NATO was asked by the Security Council to provide military support to UNPROFOR and enforce a no-fly zone over Bosnia-Herzegovina in what came to be known as the first humanitarian war in history.

The ability to carry out a humanitarian war in Europe became politically possible only following the collapse of the USSR in 1991, which allowed the two major powers, the United States and Russia, to reach a consensus regarding military intervention in Bosnia. Indeed, not long after the 1989 fall of the Berlin Wall, the United States had announced the birth of a "new world order" based on multilateral cooperation between the two historic blocs.[2] For about a decade, this new order served as the central framework for upholding international peace and security and facilitated the emergence of humanitarian warfare. The war in Bosnia and the 1999 war in Kosovo, which broke out after the region with Albanian majority declared its independence from Serbia, became the first instances in which war and the ethical imperative of humanitarian protection of defenseless civilians converged.[3]

Humanitarian wars are ostensibly triggered by an ethical imperative that places responsibility on states to protect civilian populations that are subjected to lethal violence and war crimes. They are waged in the name of what later become known as the moral responsibility to protect (also known as R2P); codified in 2005, this principle calls upon UN member states to "protect populations from genocide, war crimes, [and] ethnic cleansing" using "peaceful means," but if need be also military intervention.[4] Its promoters usually portray military interventions of this kind as a form of violence driven by a universal sense of humanity. And since their objective is to protect civilians, humanitarian wars are purported to be "clean wars," and therefore their promoters claim to put special emphasis on distinguishing between legitimate military targets and civilians.[5] A humanitarian war is not a war that is necessarily less lethal, but one that according to its advocates abides by the principle of distinction and aims to avoid causing harm to protected persons or sites.

Although NATO presented both the war in Bosnia and the one in Kosovo as forms of armed humanitarian intervention, it adopted slightly different warfare strategies in each region. The way human shields were deployed in these two conflicts and the way they were debated in the international arena and the legal institutions created by the United Nations reveal how even within the context of a humanitarian war some people's lives are valued more highly than the lives of others, and therefore the same war crimes can count more in one context than in another. In spite of its presumed universality, the humanity on behalf of which humanitarian wars are waged can function as a mechanism of discrimination.

Although UNPROFOR was initially conceived as a peacekeeping mission, in 1992 it was given a green light to take "all necessary measures" to aid the displaced civilians in Bosnia.[6] After the Serbs intensified their efforts to ethnically cleanse the Muslim population in Bosnia, several UN member states, among them countries with majority Muslim populations, advocated for a more resolute intervention. The international response was initially moderate, but when the Serbs attacked the village of Srebrenica in 1993—the same village where two years later they would massacre over eight thousand civilians—and violated the ceasefire agreement they had signed with the UN negotiating team, NATO was asked to weigh in. Its task was to guarantee the warring parties' compliance with previous agreements and to protect UNPROFOR, which was providing humanitarian assistance to civilians. The UN Security Council condemned the targeting of civilians and the deliberate interdiction of humanitarian-assistance convoys by the Bosnian Serb paramilitary units, declaring that the Muslim village and its surroundings were a militarily protected "safe area . . . free from any armed attack or any other hostile act." This measure was later extended to other parts of Bosnian territory under Serbian attack.[7]

As it turned out, both sides criticized the creation of such zones. On the one hand, the Bosnian government accused the United Nations of complicity with Serbian ethnic cleansing practices because it had instructed Bosnian Muslims to leave their homes and gather in these safe areas—while UNPROFOR considered the Bosnian government's decision not to evacuate its civilians as an act of human shielding.[8] On the other hand, the Serbs accused the United Nations of providing a humanitarian shield for Bosnian forces, which then launched military operations from within the safe zones. In response, the Serbs obstructed the delivery of humanitarian aid to these refugee areas, while using these zones as a trap to capture UN peacekeepers and other civilians—who would later be used as shields.[9]

Human shielding in the Bosnian conflict reached its peak in 1994 and 1995, after NATO intervened more directly by enforcing a no-fly zone over Bosnia-Herzegovina and after it began bombing Serbian military targets more systematically. As the investigations of the International Criminal Tribunal for the former Yugoslavia later revealed, the commanders of the Serbian Bosnian forces responded by ordering "the prevention of all

FIGURE 18. United Nations Peacekeeper handcuffed to a Serbian arms depot and used as a human shield, 1995. Credit: Serbian Patriotic League.

movement of UNPROFOR vehicles and of all other international organizations in the area [controlled by the Serbs] and to fire on UNPROFOR if fired upon."[10] After clashing with and disarming soldiers of the UNPROFOR Ukrainian battalion close to Sarajevo, the Serbs led the Ukrainians to a nearby police station and then to barracks near an airfield. It was there that "their flak jackets, shoulder straps, and shoe laces were taken away" and they were deployed as human shields "in order to force NATO to stop the air strikes against Bosnian Serb military positions."[11]

As the fighting raged, hundreds of UN soldiers of different nationalities were captured in the safe zones—by both sides, mainly by Bosnian Serbs but also by Bosnian Muslim forces.[12] Serbian forces placed the UN hostages close to their military installations and distributed to the international press humiliating images and videos of these peacekeepers handcuffed to key NATO targets (figure 18). The deployment of peacekeepers as shields even pushed French president Jacques Chirac to create a Rapid Reaction Force of French, British, and Dutch troops, whose mission was to provide additional protection to UN personnel.[13]

In his military treatise *The Utility of Force,* General Rupert Smith, the head of UNPROFOR, whose testimony at the tribunal served to incriminate Serbian commanders, highlighted the intricate ways his men were deployed as human shields in Bosnia by the Serbs. Noting that although their task was characterized as a humanitarian mission, the multinational troops were caught in what he defined as "the first . . . hostage or shield situations" in the history of UN peacekeeping.

As a result, NATO increased its efforts to protect UNPROFOR personnel stationed close to the safe zones. The Serbs, however, could not be easily controlled, and as Smith points out, "The shield and hostage trap could be equally applied to NATO."[14] In other words, the deployment of peacekeepers as defensive weapons tied NATO's hands, forcing it to refrain from striking Serbian targets protected by shields because it was fighting a so-called clean war and did not want to risk killing captured UN peacekeepers. This was one of the few historical instances where involuntary shielding actually succeeded in deterring a military attack, ultimately limiting the sites NATO was willing to bomb.

REFUGEE SHIELDS

The situation in the Kosovo war nearly a decade later, at least at first blush, seems to have been very similar to that in Bosnia. After Kosovo voted for national independence in a clandestine referendum, the leader of the Albanian Democratic League of Kosovo, Ibrahim Rugova, tried to achieve a peaceful separation from Serbia. But when his Gandhi-style diplomacy failed, the newly formed Kosovo Liberation Army stepped in, attacking Serbian forces. The Serbs responded with an offensive, forcefully displacing thousands of Kosovar civilians from their homes.

Observing these developments with grave concern, Western leaders were adamant about preventing massacres and avoiding the mistakes they had made in Bosnia in 1991. "The international community stood by and watched ethnic cleansing," Secretary of State Madeleine Albright commented in 1998, as images of displaced Kosovar refugees kept appearing on television screens. She added that "we don't want that to happen again this time."[15] In 1999, NATO launched its second humanitarian war in the former Yugoslavia, in the name of preventing further egregious violations of human rights and alleged crimes against humanity perpetrated by the Serbian military and paramilitary forces.

The second intervention was a military operation completely orchestrated by the North Atlantic alliance. Whereas in Bosnia United Nations peace-keepers had intervened first and then NATO's armed forces had completed the job, in Kosovo NATO led a war from March to June 1999, and the United Nations peacekeepers intervened later to maintain the status quo. For the first time since the United Nations was established, an armed intervention led by NATO against a member state was justified on humanitarian grounds without the Security Council's authorization.[16]

Once again, Serbian forces used human shields to deter NATO's bomb-ings. Instead of international peacekeepers, however, this time the shields were Kosovar refugees. NATO immediately denounced the Serbians' use of internally displaced persons as human shields, warning that this practice would increase the number of civilian casualties. Moreover, after Serbian president Slobodan Milosevic sealed off Kosovo's borders, ensuring that refu-gees would be unable to escape from the areas targeted by the North Atlantic alliance, NATO accused the Serbian regime of turning the whole of Kosovo into a shielding area.

Several refugee testimonies published at the time by the US State Department confirmed that "Serb forces . . . removed young ethnic Albanian men from refu-gee columns and forced them to form a buffer around Serb convoys,"[17] and the mainstream media in the US framed the displaced Kosovars as a "refugee shield."[18] Denying these accusations, Serbia's official government media claimed that the Kosovars voluntarily returned to the territories bombed by NATO, blaming the alliance for the increasing number of civilian casualties.

Whereas in Bosnia in the early 1990s NATO had been dragged into a prolonged war, this time troops fighting on behalf of the North Atlantic alliance seem to have followed Lieber's observation that the more vigorously wars are pursued, "the better it is for humanity."[19] The goal was to take out the enemy as quickly as possible; although the war might not be as clean as NATO hoped for, a fast war would ultimately save innocent lives. The media reported that NATO was running out of targets due to the widespread use of civilians as shields, and if it "continue[d] to bomb alternative targets out-side Kosovo, such as economic and industrial centers [in Serbia], it is likely to face increasing criticism from the international community."[20] Then, a few weeks into the campaign, eighty-seven Kosovar civilians in the village of Koriša were killed in one of NATO's deadliest bombings.

Following the Koriša incident, human shielding became a prominent feature in the debate surrounding NATO's air campaign. The alliance's spokesperson identified three forms of shielding used by the Serbs: hundreds of Kosovar civilians were deployed to escort military forces; shields were positioned in proximity to military facilities; and in some instances the bodies of Kosovar civilians were placed by Serbs in areas bombed by NATO to cover up the ethnic cleansing that had been carried out before the bombing and to blame NATO for targeting civilians—a strategy of postmortem human shielding.[21]

NATO went on to claim that shielding in Kosovo was more complicated and pernicious than it had been in Bosnia. In Bosnia, the UN peacekeepers were clearly identifiable and were positioned in front of visible targets. By contrast, in Kosovo, Serbian forces blended among Kosovar noncombatants in an effort to compel NATO to kill civilians and then pay a heavy price in the court of public opinion. A Pentagon spokesman went so far as to claim that unintended civilian casualties had been caused by Serbian human shielding in "one-third to one-half" of the cases.[22]

HUMANITARIAN LAWFARE

In addition to UN peacekeepers and NATO airpower, the international community utilized another weapon in Bosnia and Kosovo: criminal justice. In 1993, not long after UNPROFOR was deployed, the United Nations Security Council established the International Criminal Tribunal for the former Yugoslavia. In the new post–Cold War global context, the creation of a tribunal to investigate crimes helped underscore that armed humanitarian intervention had been necessary and that universal justice would be meted out against war criminals.

When it instituted the tribunal in 1993, the Security Council believed that "the prosecution of persons responsible for serious violations of international humanitarian law . . . would contribute to the restoration and maintenance of peace."[23] It therefore conceived the International Criminal Tribunal as the continuation of war by legal means, which experts later defined as a form of *lawfare*.[24] This term usually refers to instances where nonstate actors such as rebel groups accuse their much stronger opponents—namely, governments and their militaries—of violating the laws of armed conflict during their attacks. The governments and militaries typically respond by claiming that the rebels purposefully put civilians in harm's way, and if civilians are killed, they turn to the law as part of their warfare strategy to blame the government's troops of egregious violations. But in Bosnia and Kosovo, lawfare became a weapon used not only by the Serbs but also by NATO.[25] NATO insisted that Serbian generals and leaders were responsible for the perpetration of war crimes, and it used the court as a mechanism to reiterate the humanitarian nature of its armed interventions.

Lawfare is intricately tied to the creation of international courts that exercise universal jurisdiction.[26] Within a year after the establishment of the tribunal for the former Yugoslavia, the International Criminal Tribunal for Rwanda was set up, and by 1998 the United Nations had adopted the Rome Statute, which led to the 2002 establishment of the International Criminal Court.[27] For the first time since the Nuremberg trials, international courts had a mandate to deal with war crimes—a mandate that led to several convictions, including that of Ratko Mladic, the "butcher of Bosnia," in 2017.

The tribunal for the former Yugoslavia was the first international court to investigate and convict military commanders for the crime of using civilians as human shields. During the Nuremberg trials a Nazi commander was convicted for using prisoners of war as shields, but no legal framework existed prohibiting the use of civilians to render military targets immune, not to mention peacekeepers. By the time the tribunal for the former Yugoslavia was established, legal clauses prohibiting the use of civilians as human shields had already been inscribed in the 1949 Fourth Geneva Convention and the 1977 Additional Protocols, and the chief prosecutor mobilized these conventions against Serbian military commanders.

IMMUNITY

Since the main objective of humanitarian wars is civilian protection, humanitarian warriors maintain that they respect the principle of distinction between legally killable combatants and protected noncombatants, as well as the principle of proportionality, making sure that in situations of military necessity civilian harm is proportionate to the anticipated military advantage. If a humanitarian war ends up killing many civilians, it defeats its own purpose. Hence, as mentioned, humanitarian wars present themselves as clean wars. Militaries that launch them usually claim to use humane forms of violence such as "surgical weapons"—weapons that are purportedly precise and can strike individual targets without hitting the surrounding area—and are concerned about abiding by international law.

When the International Criminal Tribunal for the former Yugoslavia had to deal with the use of lethal violence in Bosnia and Kosovo, the complexity of a humanitarian war waged on behalf of universal ethical values emerged. Although the tribunal presented itself as a model of transparent, fair, and impartial justice, and although it claimed to treat all the parties in the war equally, its political character was difficult to conceal.

After NATO killed scores of innocent civilians in Kosovo, its spokesperson, Jamie Shea, was asked if NATO recognized the tribunal's jurisdiction over NATO's military activities. He replied that the tribunal's chief prosecutor, Louise Arbour, would be allowed to start her work only when NATO granted her access to Kosovo. "NATO," continued Shea, "are the people who have been detaining indicted war criminals for the Tribunal in Bosnia." They were "those [who] have provided the finance to set up the Tribunal, . . . and I am certain that when Justice Arbour goes to Kosovo and looks at the facts she will be indicting people of Yugoslav nationality and I don't anticipate any other [indictments] at this stage."[28] Shea made it clear that the tribunal was expected to shield NATO.

Interestingly, however, the tribunal meticulously investigated allegations of human shielding in Bosnia and ended up incriminating several Serbian and Croatian commanders, while the use of human shields by the Serbian military in Kosovo received much less attention. It was the different bombing strategies NATO used in Bosnia and Kosovo that determined the different ways the international tribunal tackled the issue of human shielding in the two wars.

In Bosnia, NATO often refrained from bombing targets protected by human shields, and the court ended up handing out indictments to the Serbian officers who had deployed them. Indeed, the widespread documentation of the deployment of civilians as shields, alongside the testimonies of UN peacekeepers who had been taken hostage and the incriminating videos showing their use as human shields, made the investigations quite straightforward. The court deliberations involving the use of the UN peacekeepers as shields in Bosnia are particularly meticulous, detailing how they were captured, the military targets to which they had been chained, and the constant threat that they would be executed. Many of the defendants justified their use of peacekeepers as shields by claiming that these individuals had lost their status as protected persons. This defense actually constituted an admission of guilt, leading to the defendants' conviction.

Low- and high-ranking officers were incriminated in multiple war crimes, with the judges dedicating several passages in their rulings to condemning human shielding practices. Serb commander Radovan Karadzic was sentenced to forty years, while Ratko Mladic received a life sentence. Karadzic's crimes included the use of prisoners of war and civilian detainees as human shields "with discriminatory intent . . . in areas where they may be exposed to combat operations, for the purpose of rendering certain areas or activities immune from military operations or armed attack."[29] Mladic was convicted for chaining UN peacekeeping soldiers to radar stations and other "particularly important facilities which were possible targets of NATO attacks."[30] Such convictions served as a compensation for the humiliating failure of UN peacekeepers to prevent ethnic cleansing in Bosnia.

While the international tribunal had a relatively easy job convicting Serbian officers for their war crimes in Bosnia, investigating Kosovo was more complicated. During the Kosovo campaign, NATO had not limited its strikes to isolated military targets but had bombed areas in which civilians and combatants intermingled. The alliance argued that applying the principles of distinction and proportionality in Kosovo was much more difficult than it had been in Bosnia, given the complexity of the shielding situation; however, it did not admit that civilians had been killed as a result of its mistakes. Moreover, it insisted that it had fought a clean war. As the US State Department's ambassador-at-large for war crimes stated: "In no other conflict in military history had there been a greater effort made by one side, NATO, to comply with the laws of war. . . . Human shields were paramount reasons why NATO restrained its use of air power in scores of situations."[31]

However, even before the bombing campaign ended and the Serbian forces withdrew from Kosovo, prominent human rights organizations such as Human Rights Watch and Amnesty International portrayed a different picture. Using evidence they had gathered about several NATO bombings in which hundreds of civilians were killed, they questioned NATO's repeated claims that it had used precision munitions and that its military and legal offices worked together to ensure that NATO's forces abided by international law.[32] In one report, Human Rights Watch concluded that almost five hundred civilians had been killed in "nine incidents" as a result of NATO bombing "non-military targets" that "were illegitimate."[33]

Initially, NATO had attempted to prevent the international tribunal from taking into account the evidence provided by human rights organizations into its war conduct. After some deliberation, Prosecutor Carla Del

Ponte decided to consider the human rights organizations' accusations, but in the end her judgment leaned heavily in support of NATO's defense. Her final report on NATO's bombing campaign in the Kosovo war, issued in 2000, was based "essentially upon public documents, including statements made by NATO and NATO countries at press conferences," while refraining from using evidence from human rights organizations and from questioning the conduct of the alliance's commanders.

In the section of the report dealing with the killing of scores of civilians in Koriša—the most severe incident—the prosecutor merely reiterated NATO's claims, maintaining that the civilians who were killed during the attacks "were either returning refugees or persons gathered as human shields" unbeknown to NATO forces.[34] Amnesty International had investigated the same incident carefully and had reached a very different conclusion. It had argued that insofar as Serbian forces had used human shields to protect military targets in Koriša, they had violated international law. However, NATO's attack had been "disproportionate and therefore also unlawful."[35] Amnesty intimated, in other words, that if the court had closely examined the use of human shields at Koriša, it would have seen that NATO's aerial campaign was not "clean"—that the humanitarian war yielded *humanitarian war crimes:* violations of international law carried out while fighting on behalf of humanity. The court was not persuaded by Amnesty's claims and concluded instead that "the credible information available is not sufficient to show that a crime had been committed by the aircrew or by superiors in the NATO chain of command."[36]

Significantly, allegations of human shielding did not figure in the investigations of other incidents that took place during the Kosovo war. The final version of the indictment submitted against one commander of the NATO-supported Kosovo Liberation Army was amended by Prosecutor Del Ponte and the accusation of human shielding was deleted, as the Track Changes version made available by the tribunal reveals (figure 19).

Even though human shields were deployed in both Bosnia and Kosovo, the tribunal convicted only officers who deployed shields in Bosnia. In the first tribunal, the prosecutor used the figure of the human shield—particularly the UN peacemakers' being used as shields—as a tool for demonstrating how the court implements international criminal justice. By contrast, in the trials dealing with crimes perpetrated in Kosovo, human shielding was not part of the prosecutor's script. In Kosovo, NATO had

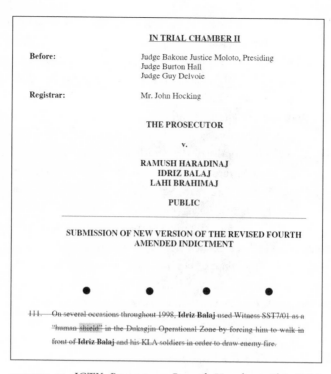

FIGURE 19. ICTY, *Prosecutor v. Ramush Haradinaj, Idriz Balaj, Lahi Brahimaj,* Revised Fourth Amended Indictment, pages 1 and 38. Credit: International Tribunal for the Prosecution of Persons Responsible for Serious Violations of International Humanitarian Law Committed in the Territory of the former Yugoslavia since 1991.

exerted less restraint, targeting the Serb forces in situations where it was difficult to distinguish between civilians and combatants. Dwelling on the exact circumstances in which human shielding took place could have potentially exposed NATO to a series of charges and perhaps even led to the incrimination of the alliance's humanitarian warriors. It would have revealed, in court, that those waging humanitarian wars also perpetrate war crimes.

THIRTEEN

Manuals

Military Handbooks as Lawmaking Tools

LAW OF WAR MANUALS ARE HANDBOOKS that have the complex task of merging the rules governing military operations with international law in order to produce a common vocabulary among legal and military communities for assessing warfare strategies and providing guidance for the troops, including specifying the tactics that can be legally adopted in the battlefield.[1] While these manuals aim to regulate the fighting according to the provisions outlined in international law, military commanders also assume that good manuals can actually facilitate effective combat operations. Thus, law of war manuals tend to have a dual function.[2] First, they are prescriptive devices for the armed forces waging combat: namely, they serve as operational tools for troops, providing guidance on how to fight the war in accordance with the law. Moreover, they incorporate and interpret international law in order to legally codify acceptable warfare practices. In this sense, international law helps define the boundaries of legitimate military action.

Second, military manuals, especially those drafted by a superpower, can become hegemonic tools that influence the forms and levels of acceptable violence in international armed conflicts and, in turn, the laws of war.[3] Indeed, manuals often influence the way international law is interpreted as well as its application on a global scale.[4] Consequently, law of war manuals not only instruct a state's own military about which practices coincide with international law, they also function as an international *lawmaking* device.

Colonel Daniel Reisner, who headed the International Law Department within the Israeli military between 1995 and 2004, was very candid about the process. As military legal advisors, he once said, "our goal is not to fetter the army, but to give it the tools to win in a lawful manner." This, he continued, can be accomplished by "a revision of international law. If you do something for long enough, the world will accept it. The whole of international law is now based on the notion that an act that is forbidden today becomes permissible if executed by enough countries."[5] Warmaking and lawmaking processes are thus deeply intertwined. Together they shape the common perceptions of what constitutes humane and inhumane violence.

This dual function—whereby the manuals adopt international law while also helping to shape it—is part of what Harvard law professor Duncan Kennedy calls "legal work."[6] Manuals interpret what the legal norms convey in a way that is compatible with the military's objectives, and this interpretation often becomes the dominant way the laws of war are construed more generally. This can be seen quite clearly in the law of war manuals issued by the United States, from the publication of the 1863 Lieber Code until the present day. Written during the American Civil War, the Code served as a law of war manual that aimed to provide "instructions for the government of armies in the field." In so doing, it also codified which practices were deemed lawful "according to the modern law and usages of war."[7] Years later the Code was utilized by the drafters of the 1899 Hague Conventions as a key point of reference.[8] From the outset, then, the Code was conceived as both an operational manual and an international instrument for defining the legitimate and illegitimate use of violence for "civilized nations" well beyond the borders of the country where it had been drafted.[9]

The next US law of war manual, *Rules of Land Warfare,* was not issued until 1914, right before the beginning of the First World War. It, too, incorporated the rules of international law accepted by the "civilized powers of the world,"[10] while being used by the US military to define the legitimate forms of fighting in both world wars. The third manual of this kind, *The Law of Land Warfare,* was published in 1956. Like its predecessors it instructed soldiers on how wars should be fought "among the civilized peoples." It had a major influence on US warfare strategies in several wars, especially in Vietnam.[11]

The latest law of war manual to date, the *Department of Defense Law of War Manual,* was issued in 2015 in an effort to influence the legal principles regulating the war on terror. Like its precursors, it frequently refers to the norms of war among civilized peoples as both its source and as something that it aims to shape and promulgate.[12] One of the experts who took part in the drafting of the 2015 manual noted that the document aspires to "have an effect beyond US shores," meaning that it aims to influence the way other militaries involved in armed conflicts interpret the application of international law and legitimate warfare strategies.[13] This handbook is also the first manual published after the two 1977 Additional Protocols to the 1949 Geneva Conventions, which underscored the legitimacy of irregulars fighting to liberate their countries from colonial domination, racist regimes, and alien occupation.[14] The manual can actually be read as a direct response to Additional Protocol I, which, as we will see, the US political and military establishments have often interpreted as legitimizing the deployment of violence by insurgents and terrorists as well as facilitating the use of inhumane techniques of warfare—including human shielding.

US MANUALS AND HUMAN SHIELDING

Significantly, until the publication of the 2015 manual, the question of how to deal practically with situations of human shielding was almost entirely absent from the American law of war manuals. However, the previous manuals did consider different kinds of incidents that today we would classify as acts of shielding. Article 117 of the Lieber Code prohibits carrying out military activities behind flags and emblems that mark protected people and sites such as medical facilities—an act characterized as "bad faith, . . . infamy or fiendishness."[15] While the 1914 manual does not mention human shields, it does contain a clause against using hospitals and medical personnel as shields, warning against the use of the Red Cross emblem to cover "wagons containing ammunitions or nonmedical stores," the use of a "hospital train" to "facilitate the escape of combatants," and firing "from a tent or building flying a Red Cross flag."[16]

In contrast to the American manuals, shielding was discussed in law of war manuals published by other countries. As we have seen, human shielding was introduced as a legitimate military strategy in the 1914 German manual. By contrast, the British *Manual on Military Law,* which also appeared that year, forbids the use of human shields. It states that the use of civilians to protect legitimate military objectives (such as trains) would necessarily expose them to both lawful and unlawful attacks and "cannot be considered a commendable practice."[17]

The 1956 US manual, issued seven years after the 1949 Geneva Conventions, incorporates the conventions' clauses on human shielding, prohibiting US soldiers from using either prisoners of war or civilians to make certain areas immune from attack. And like the Convention Relative to the Protection of

Civilian Persons in Time of War and the Convention Relative to the Treatment of Prisoners of War, the 1956 manual does not explain how soldiers should respond when enemies deploy human shields, except for one provision allowing for the use of tear gas instead of lethal weapons in situations "in which civilians are used to mask or screen attacks," in the hope that this would reduce civilian casualties.[18] The US military did not formulate its official stand on human shielding until 2015—one hundred and fifty years after human shields were deployed in the Civil War, sixty-six years after human shielding was first codified in the 1949 Geneva Conventions, and thirty-five years after its appearance in the Additional Protocols.[19]

In order to understand why human shielding received a prominent place only in the 2015 Law of War Manual and what led the manual's drafters to explicitly allow troops to strike targets protected by human shields, it is necessary to situate this manual in the context of the development of international law emanating from the post–World War II global order and the war on terror.

THE ADDITIONAL PROTOCOLS

Following the Second World War, the anticolonial struggles taking place around the world propelled major institutional and legal transformations in the global arena. While many populations still lived under colonial rule before the war, by the late 1970s the number of colonized people had been reduced significantly.[20] Due to the establishment of new nation-states in many former colonies, during this period the United Nations expanded dramatically from 51 members in 1945 to 149 members in 1977, a change that influenced the formulation of the Additional Protocols.[21] International law, after all, is a consent-based legal order, whereby those countries that are part of the family of nations participate in the drafting of the laws, sign the conventions so that they can come into effect, and, finally, ratify the laws to indicate consent to be bound by them.[22] Consequently, the identity, interests, and composition of the states taking part in the process shape international law's content.

More than two decades before the drafting of the Additional Protocols, representatives from the Global South had already asserted that international law did not protect the colonized population from imperial aggression.[23] Thinking of ways to introduce changes to the existing legal order, experts from twenty-nine African and Asian countries gathered in Bandung,

Indonesia, in 1955 to demand that they be included in the institutions and processes through which the global legal order is shaped and to legitimize anticolonial struggles.[24] Capturing both issues, Mohammed Bedjaoui, one of the legal advisers to the Algerian National Liberation Front, noted that indigenous people wanted anticolonialism to become a legitimate part of a "universal legal expression."[25]

It was not, however, until 1977, with the publication of the Additional Protocols, that people who had participated in anticolonial struggles finally had input into the formulation of international law. The process was incremental. A few years after the Bandung Conference, the right of colonized peoples to self-determination and independence from colonial powers was recognized by the majority of United Nations member states, thus securing the 1960 Declaration on the Granting of Independence to Colonial Countries and Peoples. This led to the creation of a Special Committee on Decolonization tasked with implementing the declaration. Then came the 1977 Additional Protocols.

There are two Additional Protocols. Protocol I refers to international armed conflicts, and Protocol II to noninternational ones, including civil wars. Member states decided to differentiate between the two situations, since they were not prepared to grant the same degree of legal protection to civilians and combatants in noninternational wars. Protocol I reaffirms the articles of the original Geneva Conventions of 1949, while adding new provisions to accommodate the changing configuration of United Nations member states, the anticolonial sentiments, and the developments in modern warfare that had taken place since the Second World War.

Two crucial changes are worth noting. First, the definition of civilianhood was broadened to include the populations of ex-colonies because the colonial subjects of old had become citizens of new sovereign states. This meant that international law was now applicable to them and that they could enjoy the legal protections it offered. Extending international law to the ex-colonized also marked a symbolic change, since it suggested that the "uncivilized populations" had finally entered the fold of humanity. If the 1949 conventions increased the value ascribed to civilian life, the 1977 Additional Protocols extended civilianhood to millions of people who had been perceived as rightless colonial subjects who were not part of global humanity and therefore did not deserve international legal protections.

Second, Protocol I stipulated, in paragraph 4 of Article 1, that it was legal to resist "colonial domination and alien occupation and [to struggle] against racist regimes in the exercise of their right of self-determination,"[26] thereby legitimizing the means through which these countries had achieved self-determination, while also altering the way the law relates to insurgents and guerrilla fighters—the irregulars of old. For the first time in history, anticolonial struggles like those carried out in Algeria and Vietnam—which involved insurgency as well as the direct participation of civilians in the hostilities, with shielding an integral part of certain warfare strategies—acquired a degree of global legitimacy.

Not surprisingly, the debates leading to the formulation of the Additional Protocols served as a site of contestation between former colonial powers and the newly established states about the legitimacy of people's wars.[27] On the one hand, Third World and socialist countries exerted pressure to expand the protections bestowed on civilian populations that had participated in the resistance to imperial aggressions.[28] On the other hand, several countries, not least the United States, Britain, and France, were uneasy with the recognition suddenly bestowed upon anticolonial liberation movements, and for many years afterward expressed their reservations—with Britain and France ratifying the Additional Protocols only in 1998 and 2001, respectively, and the United States failing to do so to this day.[29] Ten years after its publication, President Ronald Reagan explained his refusal to ratify Protocol I, evidently having Vietnam in his mind when he claimed that the legal document was "flawed," "vague," and "politicized":

> Protocol I . . . contains provisions that would undermine humanitarian law and endanger civilians in war. One of its provisions, for example, would automatically treat as an international conflict any so-called "war of national liberation." Whether such wars are international or non-international should turn exclusively on objective reality, not on one's view of the moral qualities of each conflict. To rest on such subjective distinctions based on a war's alleged purposes would politicize humanitarian law and eliminate the distinction between international and non-international conflicts. It would give special status to "wars of national liberation," an ill-defined concept expressed in vague, subjective, politicized terminology. Another provision would grant combatant status to irregular forces even if they do not satisfy the traditional requirements to distinguish themselves from the civilian population and otherwise comply with the laws of war.[30]

Reagan went on to justify his opposition to Additional Protocol I as an effort on the part of the United States to protect civilians "among whom terrorists and other irregulars attempt to conceal themselves."[31] The United

States thus presented its rejection in humanitarian terms, as a form of preventing irregulars from shielding themselves behind noncombatants and thereby putting them at risk.

LAWFARE AT WORK

According to consultants who participated in drafting the 2015 manual, its publication was initially delayed because of the US government's unwillingness to accept certain articles in Protocol I.[32] Matters became even more complicated in the wake of the 9/11 terrorist attacks and the ensuing war on terror launched by the US government under President George W. Bush. The opinion in certain circles in the Pentagon was that the legal quandaries precipitated by this war epitomized how the Additional Protocol legitimized "rogue states," insurgents and terrorists that often used unscrupulous warfare practices such as deploying civilians as shields.[33]

Yet another reason for the delay in publication was that US warfare strategies were rapidly being modified in an effort to confront insurgents fighting in Afghanistan, Iraq, Somalia, and Pakistan. In the eyes of Pentagon officials, the post-9/11 conflicts also created an opportunity to write guidelines based on new warfare technologies and actual experiences from the battlefield.[34] The prominent legal consultant Hays Parks explained: "We enjoyed a level of experience that did not exist during the Reagan Administration."[35]

One of the lessons learned, according to Parks, was that "if you wish to assume responsibility for each civilian casualty incidental to a lawful attack, your enemy and others will let you."[36] This idea—which suggests that responsibility for civilian casualties should be denied—has become prominent in the new millennium. This era is often characterized as one dominated by "lawfare," whereby powerful high-tech militaries and states blame insurgents and other nonstate actors for deploying international law as a technique of warfare against their troops. In the eyes of the US military, insurgents frequently provoke liberal militaries to use violence against civilians by deploying them as human shields, and when civilians die during the fighting, these insurgents can then accuse the militaries of war crimes.[37] This is why human shields have become prominent in US explanations of the increase in collateral damage within an array of conflict zones—and one of the reasons why human shielding was included in the 2015 *Law of War Manual.*

Both Presidents George W. Bush and Barack Obama pointed to human shielding as one of the main challenges to the application of the principles of distinction and proportionality in the war on terror, noting that the high price civilians have had to pay is due to the increasing use of human shields.[38] They thus echo military and legal experts who for several years have claimed that the goal of those who deploy human shields is to reduce the ability of the attacking party to discriminate among combatants and civilians, and therefore serves either as a deterrent or as a cynical form of lawfare used to blame belligerents who decide to strike targets protected by shields of killing civilians.[39] Human shielding is consequently considered by the United States and most state militaries to be a perfidious weapon used by the weak to make the strong take the blame for civilian casualties.[40]

Yet, when looking carefully at how the 2015 *Law of War Manual* has codified the question of human shielding, it becomes clear that the legal phrase *human shield* is not merely a weapon of the weak and can also be mobilized by strong states in their favor in order to legitimize the increasing number of civilian deaths on the battlefield. The main clause dealing with human shields states the following:

> In some cases, a party to a conflict may attempt to use the presence or movement of the civilian population or individual civilians in order to shield military objectives from seizure or attack. When enemy persons engage in such behavior, commanders should continue to seek to discriminate in conducting attacks and to take feasible precautions to reduce the risk of harm to the civilian population and civilian objects. However, the ability to discriminate and to reduce the risk of harm to the civilian population likely will be diminished by such enemy conduct. In addition, such conduct by the adversary does not increase the legal obligations of the attacking party to discriminate in conducting attacks against the enemy.[41]

In other words, insofar as human shielding limits the ability of the US military to discriminate between combatants and noncombatants, it enables militaries to modify their proportionality calculations and thus to legitimize the anticipated increase of harm to civilians. In a different clause, titled "Harm to Human Shields," the manual adds: "The party that employs human shields in an attempt to shield military objectives from attack assumes responsibility for their injury, provided that the attacker takes feasible precautions in conducting its attack."[42]

With regard to human shields, the manual's lawmaking effort is twofold: first, it aims to adjust the way the balance between the anticipated military advantage and civilian harm is computed so as to legitimize greater civilian casualties, and second, it strives to shift the responsibility for civilian deaths onto the shoulders of those who deploy them, rendering the attacking party legally immune from violating the principle of distinction.[43] Political theorist Judith Butler calls this twofold legal articulation of human shielding extortion through killing: "We can kill your people until you submit to our will, and you will be seen not only as presiding over this killing, but making it happen. The responsibility for those deaths will be yours."[44]

Ultimately, the manual provides the strong with a tool for justifying collateral damage during warfare and a legal defense for soldiers who kill civilians. It is in this sense that the human shield clauses in the manual can be understood as a pushback to the protections offered by Additional Protocol I to guerrillas taking part in people's wars. Initially, the United States decided not to ratify Protocol I so as not to lend it legitimacy. But with the commencement of the war on terror, it took a more proactive stance, aiming to influence the application of international law by using the 2015 *Law of War Manual* to reinterpret the clauses pertaining to civilian protection in Protocol I in a way more favorable to its military forces.

Unsurprisingly, the new manual was subjected to considerable criticism immediately following its publication. Adil Ahmad Haque, a professor of international law from Rutgers University, described the manual's position on human shielding as legally and ethically "indefensible," because it does not draw a distinction between voluntary and involuntary human shields, thereby ignoring the principle of proportionality and thus permitting the killing of defenseless civilians who are used as involuntary shields. He added that killing involuntary shields would not deter their use because the people who deploy them think a shield's death will lead to public criticism against the attacking party.[45]

Responding to Haque's critique, former deputy judge advocate general of the US Air Force Charles Dunlap claimed that American troops have a right to attack targets protected by human shields in order to discourage the proliferation of shielding by insurgent groups against militaries that try to abide by international law. The manual's "common-sense view," he says, is "that allowing unscrupulous defenders to succeed in deterring attacks through the use of human shields" would "perversely encourage the use of human shields."[46]

Notwithstanding Dunlap's arguments, in response to the criticism the manual received, the Department of Defense decided to revise the manual's human shielding clauses. The 2016 revised manual intimates that the principle of proportionality does apply to shielding situations, and it softens the language referring to the difficulties of discriminating between combatants and noncombatants.[47] The title of the second clause was changed from "Harm to Human Shields"—a phrase that explicitly acknowledges the harming of noncombatants who have been turned into shields—to the more prudent "Enemy Use of Human Shields" and thus shifts the focus from the strong to the weak. The 2016 version also admits that human shielding situations produce "complex moral, ethical, legal, and policy considerations" and acknowledges that the attacker should take feasible precautions "to reduce the risk of harm" to civilians used as human shields.[48]

In spite of these changes, the revised version makes it clear that when used as shields, civilians lose some of the protections international laws bestows on them. As long as the attacking party is taking feasible measures to protect civilians, an increase in the level of harm it inflicts on civilians who act or are forced to act as shields is justified because the defending party is the one violating international law. In other words, killing human shields is legally not the same as killing civilians.

The logic of reprisal that was used by the German jurist Lassa Oppenheim to justify the use of civilians as human shields during the 1870–71 Franco-German War reemerges in the manual, which notes that military forces are allowed to breach international law in order to induce their enemies to discontinue a warfare strategy that violates the law.[49] The legal term *reprisal* is not mentioned in the manual's clauses on human shields, but the idea that shielding could result in more casualties among enemy civilians is apparent. This can be interpreted as a pushback against the 1949 Geneva Conventions that circumscribed the scope of what counts as a legitimate reprisal, outlawing reprisals directed against civilians.[50]

The manual assumes that insurgents will continue exploiting the illegal use of shields as a defensive tool if the military refrains from attacking the insurgents. This assumption has two components. First, it suggests that the military must disincentivize the illegal act of shielding on the part of its enemies by attacking them anyway; therefore an increase in the permissible level of "collateral damage" is legitimate.[51] Second, it intimates that in cases of human shielding, reprisals are legitimate—in which case, legally speaking, either those who are deployed as human shields are no longer regarded as civilians or the lives of civilians who become shields are considered less valuable.

Lassa Oppenheim invoked a similar reasoning when he justified the Germans' use of human shields in the Franco-German War, arguing that it was a form of reprisal against the illegal assaults waged by irregular forces.[52] However, at that time reprisals against civilian populations were still deemed legal in international law. Moreover, his justification served a different purpose: during the Franco-German War, reprisals were invoked to rationalize the illegal use of human shields, whereas today the same logic is introduced to legitimize killing them.

FOURTEEN

Scale

Human Shielding in Sri Lanka and the Principle of Proportionality

AS WE CAN SEE FROM THE HISTORICAL OVERVIEW provided thus far, the status of the civilian has followed the trajectory of a pendulum. After the Second World War, there was a progressive movement that included an increase in the protections bestowed on civilians. This movement reached its high point with the publication of the 1977 Additional Protocols that expanded the category of civilian to include decolonized populations while also sanctioning anticolonial struggles carried out by irregulars. However, since the end of the Cold War and most prominently after the war on terror was launched, the value assigned to civilian lives has been diminishing.

One of the ways the status of the civilian has been eroded is by expanding the scale of human shielding. A notable example occurred in 2009 in the final days of the Sri Lankan civil war when government forces cast about three hundred thousand civilians trapped in the midst of the conflict as human shields, a move that rendered it difficult to accuse the military, which ended up killing thousands of civilians, of having carried out a war crime. Simultaneously, the human shielding accusation was used to manipulate the principle of proportionality, which obliges a warring party to balance anticipated civilian harm and military advantage. The objective was to justify the inhumane violence that the military deployed against noncombatants.

KILLING FIELDS

One of the confidential cables dispatched in mid-May 2009 from the United States embassy in Colombo to the State Department in Washington, DC— and intercepted by WikiLeaks—describes the plight of civilians in the civil war's final days. The cable recounts how the bishop of Mannar had called the embassy to ask it to intervene on behalf of seven Catholic priests caught in a so-called no-fire zone that had been set up by the Sri Lankan military as a space that was supposed to grant civilians protection from the fighting while providing them with humanitarian assistance. The bishop estimated that there were still 60,000 to 75,000 civilians confined within that particular zone located on a small sliver of coastal land about twice the size of Manhattan's Central Park. Following the bishop's phone call, the US ambassador spoke with Sri Lanka's foreign minister, asking him to alert the military that most of the people remaining in the no-fire zone were civilians stranded in what had become a death trap.[1]

Thousands of Sri Lankan civilians were killed in the weeks before and after the cable was sent as the twenty-six-year struggle waged by the Liberation Tigers of Tamil Eelam came to a horrific end. Having vied for a tiny sovereign state in parts of Sri Lanka, the Tigers had spent years enhancing their social, economic, and military capacities. They demanded independence from Sri Lanka's Sinhalese Buddhist government, which controlled the island's linguistically and religiously diverse population of over 21 million people. From the early 1980s, the government had become more and more authoritarian, stifling criticism and deploying violence against the country's religious and ethnic minority groups, not least its Tamil population. They experienced disappearances, unlawful killings, torture, rape, and sexual exploitation along with the ongoing clampdown on freedom of the press.[2]

The Tamil Tigers, who controlled the majority of the territory in the northern and eastern provinces of Sri Lanka at the peak of their strength, responded to state violence with ruthless techniques of warfare, weaponizing human bodies through the systematic deployment of suicide bombers. Frequently targeting civilians, over the years they managed to kill several politicians, including the prime minister of India in 1991 and the president of Sri Lanka in 1993. The Tigers also massacred Sinhalese and Muslims living in villages bordering the front lines of the areas they controlled, while forcefully recruiting child soldiers from the Tamil population.[3]

After four failed peace talks, an unsuccessful deployment of Indian peacekeeping forces, and a cease-fire agreement that lasted from 2002 until 2005, sporadic fighting resumed. By January 2008, the government declared a full military operation against the Tigers. Blasting its way through the northeast tip of the island, the Sri Lankan military slowly regained control of most of the regions previously held by the rebel group, while the civilian population that either sympathized with the Tigers or were afraid of the government forces moved deeper and deeper into the small swath of land still controlled by the Tamil guerrillas—an area characterized by the government as the "Tiger cage."[4]

At one point, the Sri Lankan military unilaterally declared the creation of three no-fire zones within the cage (including the one mentioned in the intercepted cable), urging the civilian population to gather in these zones by dropping leaflets from planes and notifying them through the wireless and loudspeakers.[5] As an estimated 330,000 internally displaced people assembled in these zones, the United Nations erected makeshift camps and, together with several humanitarian organizations, provided food and medical assistance to the desperate population—not unlike in the safe areas the United Nations had created in Bosnia in 1993.[6]

The Tamil Tigers also retreated to the no-fire zones on the coastal strip, where they had prepared a complex network of bunkers and fortifications and where they ultimately mounted their final battle. Not unlike other instances of guerrilla insurgency, they positioned their artillery batteries among the civilians and prevented many of them from leaving the area once the shelling began, in some cases shooting those who tried to exit the zone.[7]

While the Sri Lankan military claimed that it was engaged in "humanitarian operations" aimed at "liberating the civilians," it was in fact reclaiming the northeast tip of the island that was still in Tamil hands. An analysis of satellite images as well as numerous testimonies revealed that the military continuously pounded the enclosed land with mortar and artillery fire, transforming the designated no-fire zones into killing fields.[8] Between 10,000 to 40,000 caged-in civilians perished in the so-called safe zones, while thousands more were severely injured, often lying for hours or days on the ground without receiving medical attention because virtually every hospital—whether permanent or makeshift—had been hit by artillery.[9]

SHIELDING ZONES

The Sri Lankan civil war was subjected to international legal scrutiny. Following the government's defeat of the Tamil Tigers, a panel of experts appointed by the United Nations secretary-general published a damning report accusing both the Tamil Tigers and the Sri Lankan government of having carried out war crimes and crimes against humanity. In addition to charges of murder, mutilation, cruel treatment, and torture, the panel accused the Tamil Tigers of using civilians as a human buffer and killing civilians attempting to flee the no-fire zones. The Sri Lankan military was charged with intentional, indiscriminate, and disproportionate attacks on civilians, starvation and denial of humanitarian relief, and attacks on medical and humanitarian objects.[10]

In response, the Sri Lankan president established a governmental commission to examine the allegations and weigh in on the matter.[11] The government understood that it was not so much a question of who committed war crimes but rather whose war crimes would be recognized as such, and at whose political expense. To bolster its legal defense, the commission enlisted several leading experts in international humanitarian law from the United States, the United Kingdom, and Canada, asking them to provide legal opinions that would help exonerate the government and the military from the atrocities carried out during the war.

While the commission as well as the experts used international law's human-shields clauses to mount their defense of the Sri Lankan government, they interpreted the act of human shielding in a relatively novel way. One of the people hired by the commission was Michael Newton from Vanderbilt University's School of Law. Newton was not a neophyte when it came to investigating war crimes. He had served as a senior adviser to the United States ambassador-at-large for war crimes issues, had been the representative on the United States Planning Mission for the Sierra Leone Special Criminal Court, and had helped coordinate the government's support for the prosecution of Slobodan Milosevic, the president of Serbia during the humanitarian wars in the Balkans.

The kernel of Newton's legal defense was that the Tamil Tigers "refused to permit some 330,000 fellow Tamils to flee towards safer areas away from the zone of conflict, and in essence used them as human shields to deter offensive operations by the Sri Lanka Army," adding that the "Government of Sri Lanka [had] previously declared the entire area as a safe civilian or no fire zone in order to protect the innocent civilians."[12]

Newton's claim that *all* the civilians trapped within the no-fire zones were human shields stands in sharp contrast to the finding of the United Nations panel of experts, which stated that the Tamil Tigers' refusal to allow civilians to leave the combat zone "did not, in law, amount to the use of human shields."[13] Newton's analysis, however, actually reflects a shift in the way human shielding began to be conceptualized at the time.

Up to this point, the charge of involuntary human shielding had referred to individuals or small groups of civilians who were coerced into becoming a buffer in the midst of fighting. However, Newton, the other experts hired by the Sri Lankan commission, and even Human Rights Watch and the International Crisis Group significantly expanded the scale of what is considered shielding, rendering the act of shielding as partially determined by the proximity of civilians to the fighting. Even before Newton wrote his opinion, Human Rights Watch had spoken about "several hundred thousand people [used] as human shields," thus arguing that the no-fire zones had, in effect, become shielding zones.[14] The International Crisis Group adopted a similar interpretation of the use of human shields in Sri Lanka, as did other prominent human rights groups.[15]

To make this claim, the experts and organizations relied on the existing legal conception of a human shield as a passive civilian who can only become a shield if coerced to do so, but they articulated this conception within a specific spatial framework. In their various legal opinions and reports, human shielding is depicted as coextensive with the no-fire zones because these spaces were used by the insurgents to hide and launch rockets, while at least some of the civilians were prevented from leaving them.

The Tamil Tigers, so their argument goes, converted the humanitarian spaces into enclosed shielding zones by establishing bunkers and fortifications within them, thereby transforming the entire civilian population that had been urged by the government to assemble in these zones into human shields. In none of the cases that we have examined so far in this book had the legal figure of the human shield been mobilized to include such numbers. To be sure, the fact that the militants intermingled with the displaced people and built barricades in their midst is important for understanding why so many people were characterized as human shields, but it is also important to stress that the factor determining how a person is transformed into a shield had been radically modified.[16] If in the past specific individuals or a group were forced to become shields through coercive acts, such as tying people on trains (France, 1870–71) or forcing a group of civilians to march in front of soldiers (Belgium, 1914), in Sri Lanka civilians became shields due to the space they occupied and its proximity to the fighting.

It is useful to compare the way the government and numerous experts framed the civilians within the Sri Lankan no-fire zones as human shields with how Generals Jones and Foster understood human shielding during the siege on Charleston in the American Civil War. In Charleston, a city inhabited by thousands of civilians living alongside barricaded Confederate troops who were constantly shooting back at the Union forces, the civilians trapped in the city were not perceived by either side to be human shields. The only people who were considered to be human shields were the high-ranking Union officers who were prisoners of war and had been forcibly dispersed by Confederate troops in areas of the city that were being bombarded by General Foster. In Sri Lanka, by contrast, the thousands of civilians trapped in the no-fire zones alongside actively fighting Tamil insurgents were categorized as human shields by prominent legal experts.

In the hundred and fifty years separating the two civil wars, the person considered a shield had shifted partially due to changes in social hierarchies, which increased the number of people who could serve as human shields, and partially because the space civilians occupy and their proximity to enemy combatants had become factors in whether they could be considered human shields or not. This kind of legal thinking has become common in other conflict zones where civilians are caught in densely populated urban spaces and open-air prisons, such as the Gaza Strip, allowing the attacking armies to legitimize the use of lethal violence against otherwise legally protected people. New interpretations of international law and new calculations of what constitutes humane violence have been developed as a result of these transformations.

PROPORTIONALITY ALGORITHMS

Scale denotes not only the size of a unit but also the tool used to measure the weight of two things in order to determine whether they are balanced. The Sri Lankan commission and its hired hands used the term *scale* in both ways. They first expanded the meaning of human shielding so that it could encompass the entire civilian population within a given space. Then they argued that the military's offensive in the shielding zones did not breach international law's principle of proportionality because the civilian harm caused by the attacks weighed less than the military advantage that had been achieved as a result of the assaults on the no-fire zones.[17]

The principle of proportionality—which originally derived from just war theory, a doctrine that aims to establish the ethical criteria determining the justifiability of conducting a war and the ethical ways of fighting it—is designed to ensure that the ends of a battle justify the means of the battle by weighing the balance between the anticipated military advantage and civilian harm. Unlike human rights law, the law of war allows, or at least tolerates, the killing of civilians not directly participating in an armed conflict, but the killing must be proportional to the military advantage that the belligerent expects to gain from the attack.[18] The legal requirement to balance the military advantage against civilian losses was not an established practice before the adoption of the United Nations Charter in 1945 and was codified only in the 1977 Additional Protocols.[19] However, even after its codification, the way proportionality is assessed, measured, and calculated remains vague, and it is often subject to manipulation.

One way to justify civilian deaths is by inflating the weight of the expected military advantage. As one scholar expressed it: "The more the military task can be presented as crucial, the more civilian casualties the principle is willing to tolerate."[20] Another way is by downplaying the harm civilians have been subjected to in order to render the military attack more acceptable. In legal debates about proportionality, computations frequently determine the meaning, legitimacy, and ethics of violence, while the political circumstances in which the calculations are applied and the human face of those who have been killed or injured are elided. Proportionality can thus readily become a form of depoliticization and dehumanization.

Despite the clashing narratives about the unfolding of events during the civil war in Sri Lanka, two things became clear when the guns finally fell silent: the Tamil Tigers had been defeated and thousands of civilians had died. In the eyes of the Sri Lankan government, the military advantage of the offensive was clear: the end of a protracted civil war that had threatened Sri Lanka's stability and had cost thousands of lives. Accordingly, the ensuing legal debates focused on the degree of civilian harm in the war's final stages and whether it outweighed the military advantage.[21]

More specifically, one of the disputes revolved around the number of civilians who had died. The difference in the estimates provided by government proponents and government detractors was huge, with one side claiming that fewer than 10,000 civilians had died and the other side asserting that over 40,000 had perished. But even if the lower figure were accurate, the number of civilian deaths was still extremely high, compelling the government to find other ways to reduce the weight of civilian harm in the proportionality calculations. This is precisely why human shielding came to play a crucial role.

Sir Geoffrey Nice and Rodney Dixon, two lawyers from the United Kingdom who bear the esteemed title of Queen's Counsel, suggest at the outset of the opinion they submitted to the commission that the various reports blaming the government for unlawfully killing civilians did not properly consider the "complex legal standards applicable to [such] military operations." International humanitarian law, they claim, permits commanders to "adjust the ratio of civilian deaths" in human shielding situations.

The two lawyers go on to stress that because the Tamil Tigers used tens of thousands of civilians as shields in the final weeks of the fighting, "a marked adjustment" needs to be applied to the proportionality algorithm,[22] reducing the value ascribed to civilians so that in the final computations they have less weight. The bottom line is clear: because civilians were transformed into human shields by the Tigers, they could be killed on a wide scale without violating the principle of proportionality.

The idea of "adjusting" the proportionality calculation in favor of the attacking forces in human shielding situations is articulated in detail by Michael Newton (the expert who framed all the civilians in the Sri Lankan no-fire zones as human shields) and Larry May in their book *Proportionality in International Law,* published right before Newton delivered his opinion to the Sri Lankan commission. According to the authors, the presence of human shields produces a situation where a belligerent is "forced to choose" between refraining from attacking a legitimate target and targeting civilians. Human shields, they explain, are mobilized by one side or the other in order to manipulate proportionality calculations by increasing the number of civilians harmed. Accordingly, when civilians who have been transformed into shields are killed, they should not be classified as civilian deaths (which is a war crime), but rather as unintended collateral damage, even though their deaths were predictable.

The logic is that those who place civilians in front of legitimate military targets intentionally violate the principle of distinction and therefore bear full responsibility for the civilians' deaths.[23] This rationale shows how the interpretation of proportionality in human shielding situations can erode the principle of civilian immunity by condoning the targeting of noncombatants. When it comes to human shielding, proportionality can become what philosopher Achille Mbembe has called a "necropower," a form of power that facilitates the exercise of lethal violence.[24]

COMPUTATIONAL ACROBATICS

A third opinion supporting the Sri Lankan government's stance was written by David Crane from the College of Law at Syracuse University and Sir Desmond de Silva from the United Kingdom, both of whom had served as chief prosecutors in the international war crimes tribunal for Sierra Leone. These two experts take the calculations several steps further.

After claiming that the government forces never *intended* to strike civilian objects and were merely returning fire against enemy targets embedded amidst civilians and close to hospitals, Crane and de Silva accuse the Tamil Tigers of employing thousands of civilians as involuntary human shields. These civilians, they explain, cannot be considered as taking an active part in hostilities, and thus their presence would have to be weighed on the civilian side of the proportionality scale. However, they go on to claim, factoring involuntary human shields as civilians within the proportionality equation enables those who deploy the shields "to profit from a clear violation of the laws of war, and thus should not be allowed."[25] According to this rationale, belligerents would be incentivized to use civilians as human shields—an act that is prohibited by laws of war and considered an inhumane method of warfare—to deter their enemy from attacking.

Echoing Nice and Dixon, Crane and de Silva add that there appears to be consensus among international legal experts supporting the notion that casualties resulting from the use of involuntary human shields *"are at least somewhat diminished in the proportionality analysis,"* by which they mean that in the proportionality equation a dead involuntary shield is worth less than a dead civilian.[26] In this sense, their opinion anticipates the 2015 United States law of war manual which intimates that condoning the use of human shields would translate into a military disadvantage for the attacking forces and that human shielding alters the way proportionality is calculated.

Up to this point the different legal experts appear to concur, but then Crane and de Silva do the math, revealing, as it were, how the calculations enable them to adopt an even more extreme stance. They begin by assessing the weight of the military advantage:

> First, the humanitarian operation launched by the [government of Sri Lanka] was justified by a host of compelling military objectives, namely ending the nearly 30 year campaign of violence by the [Tamil Tigers] which included assassinations on duly elected officials and attacks on civilian objects. . . . It is clear the termination of such insidious and wholesale threats to civilian life represents a compelling military objective which already sets the bar fairly high relative to the acceptable level of civilian casualties in achieving that objective. This is a factor that could weigh heavily in favor of a finding of proportionality on behalf of [the government's] operations overall as this is a factor which must be put into the balance of the proportionality equation.

Next, they factor civilian deaths:

> Even taking the highest figures ascribed to the deaths of Vanni civilians [a primarily Tamil population living in the mainland area of the Northern Province of Sri Lanka], assuming that there were up to 330,000 civilians in the [no-fire zone] as the [UN] Report contends—7,000 of whom were killed—this presumes a loss of life of approximately 2% of that civilian population.... If there were as many as 40,000 killed, this would be a loss of approximately 12% of that population. Whatever the figure in terms of a hostage rescue operation where some 295,000 were saved—it is a successful operation.[27]

In fact, this proportionality analysis is legal maneuvering, and not only because the authors leave out of their legal arithmetic important forms of civilian harm, such as displacement, injury, and destruction. Crane and de Silva assume that incidents of involuntary human shielding are identical to hostage rescue operations by stating that the 295,000 civilians who survived "were saved." The computational ruse is clear: once one supposes that all civilians could have died and that only 12 percent were in fact killed, then the operation can be viewed as successful. Their argument follows the logic of the lesser evil, justifying the Sri Lankan attacks against civilians by claiming that a greater evil could have been carried out and was ultimately warded off.[28] This line of thinking transforms the proportionality computations into a tool for legitimizing the wide-scale killing of civilians, because one can always find a greater evil with which harm can be compared. Ultimately, in their eyes, it does not really matter what the military advantage was or how many civilians were killed, so long as some civilians were saved as a result of the operations.

Crane and de Silva's legal attempt to render the civilians in the no-fire zones killable becomes even clearer when they argue that not all the civilians in these spaces were involuntary human shields. "As a matter of logic," they maintain, "there is a powerful case for saying that it is extremely unlikely that some 20,000 cadres of [Tamil Tigers] could have taken up to 330,000 hostages against their will. The probability is that a large section of the civilians went voluntarily with the Tamil Tigers in order to play a part, albeit passive," in the war effort.[29] The two experts go on to suggest that these alleged voluntary human shields directly participated in hostilities and therefore should not be afforded the protections offered to civilians. Thus, when assessing the balance between military advantage and civilian harm, the deaths of these civilians should not be counted.

Crane and de Silva's effort to compute civilian deaths in relation to military advantage is not entirely exceptional and reveals how proportionality is operationalized by legal advisors in many theaters of violence across the globe. Moreover, the way all of the legal experts hired by the Sri Lankan commission made use of human shielding in their arguments highlights the central role human shields have come to play in these calculations.[30] The dual use of scale, first in order to dramatically increase the number of civilians who are considered human shields and second to decrease the legal value of the civilians who were killed as human shields, is a strategy that has become increasingly common in recent years.

Many legal experts maintain that proportionality is always an ambiguous concept because several significant variables cannot be quantified, yet when an incident is disproportionate, that imbalance cries out for all to see. However, large-scale violence never speaks for itself, and, as past conflicts have taught us, widespread killings always generate political debates about the use of lethal force and whether it was driven by an ethics of humane violence. In the case of Sri Lanka, we see how the work of prominent legal experts who mobilize the legal figure of the human shield on a large scale to manipulate the proportionality calculations can be decisive in legitimizing the killing of many thousands of civilians.

FIFTEEN

Hospitals

The Use of Medical Facilities as Shields

IN SRI LANKA, SPATIAL CLOSENESS OF CIVILIANS to the fighting was crucial to their being identified as human shields. However, the significance of proximity to the fighting did not originate in relation to shielding accusations in Sri Lanka—or even more generally in relation to humans being used as shields. Rather, it began a century before the Sri Lankan civil war with regard to hospitals being used as shields.

Not long after Louis Blériot became the first person to fly across the English Channel, European militaries woke up to the significance of airplanes for war. The Italians rushed to acquire a squadron of Caproni planes and, two years after Blériot's 1909 flight, introduced aerial bombings to armed conflict as they quelled a popular revolt in Libya, their North African colony. It was also then—more than two decades before the Italians began bombing Red Cross hospitals in Ethiopia—that medical units were first targeted from the air.[1]

The Italian pilots, who at the time could not fly much faster than 100 kilometers an hour, opened their cockpits over Libya and threw out five-kilogram bombs both at demonstrators and at medical units. In response, the local affiliate of the Red Cross, the Ottoman Red Crescent, sent a cable to the International Committee in Geneva, asking it to "protest indignantly against bombing by Italian airplanes of hospitals marked with Red Crescent flag in Tripolitania."[2] While the newly established air force continued bombing medical facilities in the colony, Geneva relayed the complaint to the Italian government, asking for a response.

In its reply, the Italian government contested the facts but also requested that protective markings "should be clearly visible on tents, detachments, convoys, etc., so as to make them recognizable even from afar and from the air."[3] It added that during the fighting, medical personnel should keep a fair distance away from the forces engaged in combat and that in military camps, separate and clearly visible areas should be allotted to hospitals and medical staff. A century before legal experts defended the Sri Lankan military's bombing of the no-fire zones, the Italians intimated that proximity to a military target rendered hospitals vulnerable to attack.

In conclusion, the Italian government declared that it would be unwilling to assume responsibility if such precautions were not observed at all times, for "it could not give up its capability of using all methods of attack authorized by international law, any more than the presence of *[medical] units could be allowed to serve as a safeguard for the enemy against its action.*"[4] Thus, from the very first instances in which medical units were bombed from the air, the charge that these units were being deployed to shield legitimate military targets was introduced to justify the attacks. Military necessity trumped the protection of medical structures and aid workers.[5]

The rules of the game were thus established in Libya. Over the years the claim that hospitals become legitimate targets when they are used to shield enemy combatants became part of accepted wisdom—so much so that belligerents would frequently assume responsibility for the attack, claiming that they had not violated international law because the hospital was deployed as a shield. Tracing the history of hospital bombings alongside the clauses dedicated to the protections of medical units in international law reveals not only that the shielding argument is part of black letter law but also that the notion of *proximate shields*—whereby humans become shields due to their proximity to belligerents (see chapter 16)—first appears in relation to hospitals and only later is applied to people. What also emerges with particular clarity from this history is the process through which international law has been developed as a tool not only for outlawing war crimes but also for humanizing them.[6]

DETERMINING CULPABILITY

World War I was the first war in which airplanes were systematically used as instruments of violence. The International Committee of the Red Cross collected eighty complaints relating to the bombardment of hospitals and medical installations by artillery or aircraft.[7] One case that received considerable media attention involved the German bombing of several hospital wards in

FIGURE 20. Bombed hospital in Étaples, 1918. Credit: United Kingdom Ministry of Information, First World War Official Collection.

Étaples on the northern coast of France in May 1918 (figure 20). The medical wards were hit repeatedly, with 182 patients and nurses killed and 643 injured.[8] In one of the raids, a German pilot was shot down, and while being cared for in the damaged hospital he had bombed, he was interrogated about the attack.

"He tried at first to excuse himself by saying that he saw no Red Cross," one newspaper reported, adding that "when challenged with the fact that he knew that he was attacking hospitals, he endeavored to plead that hospitals should not be placed near railways, or if they are, they must take the consequences."[9] The pilot's claim was straightforward: during war, those who help sustain life cannot expect to be protected if they are located in proximity to military targets.

In May 1939, while Britain was preparing for another world war, the attack on medical facilities at Étaples and the German pilot's claim about why the hospitals were bombed was raised in the House of Lords in London and reaffirmed by a much more prominent soldier. Hugh Trenchard, who had served as an infantry officer in the Second Anglo-Boer War and later helped found the Royal Air Force, which he headed from 1918 until 1930, actually supported the explanation provided by the pilot. He told his fellow parliamentarians that he was aware of the "popular idea" that "every hospital flying the Red Cross is purposely bombed." "One heard very much the same about the bombing of the hospitals and camps at Étaples during the War," he continued, "and it apparently did not occur to anybody that the real objectives there were the railway and the dumps."[10]

Trenchard referred his colleagues to the *History of the Great War Based on Official Documents*—a chronicle of Britain's military efforts during the First World War—and pointed out what the director of military operations at the

War Office said: "We have no right to have hospitals mixed up with rein-forcement camps, and close to main railways and important bombing objec-tives, and until we remove the hospitals from the vicinity of these objectives, and place them in a region where there are no important objectives, I do not think we can reasonably accuse the Germans."[11] In other words, the British War Office agreed with the Italian government and the German pilot that a hospital's proximity to a legitimate military target makes it susceptible to attacks, while also intimating that the culpability lies with those who place the hospital in such a location, not with those who bomb it.[12]

BLACK LETTERS

During the Second World War, the intensity of aerial bombings increased dramatically and whole cities were systematically being bombarded, some until they were completely flattened. Indeed, a mere thirty-four years after the first handheld explosives were thrown from a cockpit at Libyan protes-tors, the United States dropped atomic bombs on Hiroshima and Nagasaki, making the singling out of hospitals moot. In what some have called "total war," civilian life becomes expendable and bombing medical units is par for the course.[13]

As we have seen, following the Second World War the International Committee of the Red Cross drafted a new convention dedicated to the pro-tection of civilians and civilian infrastructures that included legal clauses aimed at protecting hospitals. Several provisions were adopted obliging war-ring parties to refrain from attacking medical facilities that display the Red Cross emblem. Civilian hospitals "may in no circumstances be the object of attack, but shall at all times be respected and protected by the Parties to the conflict," reads article 18 of the Fourth Geneva Convention. The following article, article 19, then prohibits shielding military activities behind Red Cross emblems, noting that the "protection to which civilian hospitals are entitled shall not cease *unless* they are used to commit, outside their humani-tarian duties, acts harmful to the enemy." The article also prohibits placing medical facilities in proximity to military targets. It reads: "In view of the dangers to which hospitals may be exposed by being close to military objec-tives, it is recommended that such hospitals be situated as far as possible from such objectives."[14] International law thus combined the protection of hospi-tals with the prohibition of using hospitals as shields.

The tenuous nature of these provisions became apparent during conflicts that took place in Southeast Asia immediately following the Second World War. In North Korea during the Korean War in the early 1950s, American and United Nations forces destroyed scores of medical facilities, forcing the Koreans to move their hospitals underground.[15] In Vietnam, the French air force was accused of bombing medical units and evacuation convoys with napalm during the 1954 defeat of the Viet Minh at Dien Bien Phu, to which the French government responded by accusing the Vietnamese resistance of violating the laws of war and "transporting munitions in medical aircraft marked with the Red Cross emblem."[16]

A decade and half later, the Americans were charged with deliberately bombing Vietnamese hospitals marked with the Red Cross emblem, to which the military commanders responded by blaming the Viet Cong of having used the hospitals to shield their forces.[17] Similarly, after the infamous bombardment of the 940-bed Bach Mai Hospital, the United States military maintained that Vietnamese militants had shielded themselves behind the Red Cross emblem, explaining that the hospital "frequently housed antiaircraft positions to defend the military complex," adding that it was located less than 500 meters from the Bach Mai airfield and military storage facility.[18] The deployment of hospitals to conceal legitimate military targets and their proximity to such targets were thus invoked together as justifications for the attack.

Due to these and other attacks on hospitals, medical units again received significant attention during the Diplomatic Conference on the Reaffirmation and Development of International Humanitarian Law Applicable in Armed Conflicts in the mid-1970s, which led to the formulation of the 1977 Additional Protocols to the Geneva Conventions. During the conference, the international delegates again outlined the two conditions in which protections offered to hospitals can be forfeited: "The Parties to the conflict shall ensure that medical units are situated as far as possible [from military targets] so that attacks against military objectives cannot imperil their safety. Under no circumstances shall they be used in an attempt to protect military objectives from attack."[19] In the final version of Additional Protocol I, these conditions were formulated as a form of shielding and incorporated into article 12, which states that "under no circumstances shall medical units be used in an attempt to *shield* military objectives from attack. Whenever possible, the Parties to the conflict shall ensure that medical units are so sited that attacks against military objectives do not imperil their safety."[20]

In the wording of the article we can see that proximity and hospital shielding have a parallel history in international law. The charge that a medical unit is located in proximity to a military target implies that it is shielding the target and can therefore lose its protection under law. It is as if the Italian government's arguments voiced after the bombing of medical facilities in Libya and Ethiopia became international norms.

IN THE MIDST OF TERROR

The claim that hospitals were being used as shields became pervasive with the subsequent war on terror. From the war in Afghanistan and the US-backed Saudi intervention in Yemen to the Israeli campaigns in Gaza and the Syrian civil war, in recent years hospitals have constantly been bombed by military forces under the guise of counterterrorism, while the shielding argument has been invoked time and again.[21] According to the World Health Organization, in 2016 a hospital was bombed on average every day and a half, and in 2017 and 2018 a hospital was bombed every two days.[22] Clearly, hospital bombings are neither sporadic nor a series of isolated events but rather a strategy of warfare aimed at weakening the enemy's infrastructure of existence. And while a few hospitals may have indeed been used as shields, the sheer number of bombings suggests that belligerents use the shielding accusation ex post facto in order to legitimize the strikes.

In Syria it has been primarily President Bashar al-Assad's regime and its ally Russia that have bombed hospitals in rebel-held territories, while in Yemen and Gaza it is Saudi Arabia and Israel whose planes have been destroying medical facilities held by nonstate actors. International and local human rights and humanitarian groups have consistently condemned these attacks, claiming that they are in flagrant violation of international law.

The states charged with bombing medical units are not disputing the claim that the facilities were used for medical purposes. They simply maintain that the hospitals were shielding insurgents, harboring weapons, or used as a cover for militants launching rockets. Consequently, the bombings do not violate international law, since the law allows militaries to bomb medical facilities that serve as shields, provided that the attackers give adequate warning to those on the ground and do not breach the principle of proportionality.

During the 2014 Gaza War, for example, Israeli strikes destroyed or damaged seventeen hospitals, fifty-six primary healthcare facilities, and forty-five ambulances.[23] To defend these attacks, Israel accused Hamas of using hospitals to store weapons and hide armed militants.[24] In a similar vein, after the bombardment of an underground medical facility in a rebel-controlled area, a Syrian regime official declared that militants would be targeted wherever they were found, "on the ground and underground," while his Russian patron explained that rebels were using "so-called hospitals as human shields."[25] Saudi officials attempting to justify the high number of air strikes targeting medical facilities in Yemen adopted the same catchphrases, accusing their adversaries, the Houthi militias, of using hospitals to hide their military forces.[26]

Such explanations can serve as a robust defense because medical personnel actually lose the protections allocated to them by international law if they "exceed the terms of their mission" or carry out "acts harmful to the enemy"[27] According to the International Committee of the Red Cross, "Such harmful acts would, for example, include the use of a hospital as a shelter for able-bodied combatants or fugitives, as an arms or ammunition dump, or as a military observation post; another instance would be the deliberate siting of a medical unit in a position where it would impede an enemy attack."[28]

In an effort to legitimize its bombing of Palestinian medical facilities following the 2014 war on Gaza, Israel invoked both exceptions in a legal report. It accused "Hamas and other terrorist organizations" of exploiting "hospitals and ambulances to conduct military operations, despite the special protection afforded these units and transports under customary international law." It claimed that hospitals were used both as "command and control centers, gunfire and missile launching sites, and covers for combat tunnels" and also as proximate shields for Hamas militants who fired "multiple rockets and mortars within 25 meters of hospitals and health clinics."[29] Sometimes Israel would call the hospital in advance, warning the staff that it was about to bomb their facility.[30] This allowed the Israeli government to claim that it had provided due warning and reasonable time to evacuate the buildings before it launched a strike, and therefore had not violated international humanitarian law articles requiring belligerents to warn medical units before bombing them.[31]

Following protests by Médecins Sans Frontières (Doctors Without Borders) against the 2016 bombardment of one of its medical units in Yemen, the Joint Incidents Assessment Team of Saudi Arabia's military coalition released a response similar to Israel's argument in its legal report on the attack on Gaza: "The [Assessment Team] found that the targeting was based on solid intelligence information. . . . After verification, it became clear that the building was a medical facility used by Houthi armed militia as a military shelter in violation of the rules of international humanitarian law." According to the self-exonerating report, one of the medical facilities targeted by the coalition "was not directly bombed, but was accidentally affected by the bombing due to its close location to the grouping which was targeted, without causing any human damage. It is necessary to keep the mobile clinic away from military targets so as not to be subjected to any incidental effects."[32] Even though hospitals had been bombed, the Assessment Team concluded that coalition forces had not violated the law.

HUMANIZING WAR CRIMES

Different actors with different political agendas have thus invoked the same legal vocabulary used to classify humans as shields for classifying hospitals as shields. What connects these two types of shielding accusations is the similar rhetoric and, even more important, the same underlying assumption: when a protected entity becomes a shield, it loses the protected status bestowed upon it by international law.[33]

Although the legal condemnation of those who use hospitals as shields is unconditional and that act is always considered a war crime, the protection offered to hospitals is conditional. All a warring party has to do in order to legally justify an attack is to claim that a medical unit was located near a target or was used to conceal it, assert that it warned the medical personnel before the attack, and argue that the assault followed the principle of proportionality. The history of bombing hospitals, the legal debates surrounding it, and the formulation of legal clauses pertaining to the protection of medical facilities reveal that international law privileges those who attack over those who shield and can serve as a tool for humanizing the use of lethal force against entities that the law itself purports to protect.

SIXTEEN

Proximity

Civilians Trapped in the Midst of the War on ISIS

DUBBED WE ARE COMING, NINEVEH (Qadimun Ya Nainawa), the campaign to retake the city of Mosul from ISIS's hands was announced on 16 October 2016.[1] Located some 390 kilometers north of Baghdad, Mosul stands on the bank of the Tigris River, opposite the ancient Assyrian city of Nineveh, and is one of the largest cities in Iraq.[2] Two years after ISIS militants captured the city, its population had shrunk from 2.5 million to an estimated 1.5 million because many residents had fled the Islamic extremists and their ruthless governing practices.[3]

Reports document that during this two-year period minorities in Mosul had been persecuted, and residents had been executed, tortured, or brutally punished for contravening the jihadists' interpretation of Islamic law, while the population in general experienced shortages in food and fuel.[4] Civilians who lived under ISIS's reign described the militants as an agile and mobile "ghost force," taking advantage of the architectural character of each neighborhood. Residents of Wadi Hajjar, for instance, recounted how ISIS fighters would move between houses through holes they had made in the walls. Residents of Mosul's Old City said that the militants primarily moved underground, as most of the houses in the neighborhood had cellars that ISIS fighters linked via tunnels in order to conceal their military activities and ambush the coalition forces.[5] Others testified that they were forced to keep their house doors open to allow the insurgents to move quickly from house to house without being detected from the air.[6]

In preparation for the pro-government operation to recapture Mosul from the hands of ISIS militants, Kurdish forces swept through villages northeast of the city, while the Iraqi army advanced from the southeast and US-led coalition fighter jets and drones prepared to strike. In the days leading up to the attack, accusations that ISIS was deploying human shields became increasingly prominent. Pope Francis expressed his concern about the use of over two hundred boys and men as human shields in the Iraqi city.[7] In a campaign rally the following day, Donald Trump decried the enemy's use of "human shields all over the place," and the *New York Times* reported that the Islamic State was driving hundreds of civilians into Mosul and using them as human shields.[8]

A few days later, the number of civilians employed as human shields in Mosul appeared to have soared. The United Nations, for instance, disseminated a series of press releases, the first of which warned that ISIS militants were using "tens of thousands" Iraqis as human shields, while a later release rounded the figure up to "one hundred thousand" (figure 21).[9] The fact that political leaders and global institutions depicted massive numbers of Iraqi civilians being used as weapons of war underscores just how prominent the figure of the human shield had become.[10]

After the fighting had subsided, Amnesty International also blamed ISIS militants for turning the legal imperative "to protect civilians on its head, ruthlessly and unlawfully exploiting civilian immunity from attack in an attempt to shield its own forces." According to the rights group, the militants prevented civilians from "evacuating to safety, trapping them in their homes by welding their doors shut, rigging booby traps at exits [from neighborhoods], or summarily killing those attempting to escape." One person described how he and his family had been moved from a small village into Mosul to serve as human shields and testified that ISIS fighters had transferred one hundred other families from his village into the city, at times using buses to transport them.[11]

Even though evidence of ISIS's use of human shields is overwhelming, the suggestion that tens of thousands of Iraqis were deployed as shields by a few hundred militants appears to be a blatant exaggeration. Most of those labeled as shields by the United Nations were categorized in this way due to their *proximity* to the fighting. Not unlike Sri Lankan civilians in the no-fire zones and Palestinians trapped in Gaza during Israel's military campaigns there, the fact that the city's inhabitants remained in Mosul when the fighting commenced was enough to brand them as potential weapons, thereby stripping them of some of the protections international humanitarian law bestows on civilians.[12]

Proximate human shields are in many respects different from their voluntary and involuntary counterparts.[13] Whereas involuntary shields are coerced by belligerents to protect military targets and voluntary shields choose that action, proximate human shields become shields simply because they are "too

ISIS HOLDS 100,000 'HUMAN SHIELDS' IN MOSUL'S OLD CITY, U.N. SAYS

BY JACK MOORE ON 6/16/17 AT 12:54 PM

Members of Iraqi forces stand guard in a house on the front line in Mosul's Old City on May 24, during an ongoing offensive to retake the area from Islamic State (ISIS) group fighters.

AHMAD AL-RUBAYE/AFP/GETTY

FIGURE 21. Iraqi soldiers guarding a house in Mosul's Old City. Credit: *Newsweek* website, June 2017.

close" to a legitimate target. Put differently, proximate shields become human shields without doing or being forced to do anything. This is in part what distinguishes them from other shields and helps explain why this kind of shield is increasingly invoked to legitimize inhumane violence.

99 PERCENT

The accusation by one warring party that the other party is using proximate shields undoubtedly has to do with the disappearance of the traditional battlefield. As uniforms, emblems, or the location of a person in relation to the fighting lose their usefulness in distinguishing between civilian and combatant, and as civilians and combatants become increasingly indistinguishable in numerous conflict zones,[14] experts have argued that the old notion of battlefield is becoming obsolete and should be replaced by the concept of battlespace.[15] *Battlespace* is used to describe situations where "regular armed forces seem to be a minority" and "there are many different actors" among whom it becomes extremely difficult to distinguish international law's axiomatic classes of civilian and combatant.[16] According to the International Committee of the Red Cross, this is due primarily to the exponential rise in urban warfare, which is characterized by the uncertainty, volatility, complexity, and risk produced by the unavoidable overlapping of military and civilian facilities and personnel.[17] As the political geographer Stephen Graham puts it, cities have become "the lightning conductors for our planet's political violence."[18]

Considering that civilians are inevitably caught in the midst of urban conflicts, practically all fighting within cities potentially involves the presence of proximate shields. It should not come as a great surprise, then, that in the past few years numerous states and international organizations have been warning the world that the use of human shielding is on the rise. From media reports about Syria, where ISIS militants in Raqqa used "an elaborate labyrinth of mines and civilians as human shields to stop coalition forces from advancing," through testimonies from Yemen, where Houthi fighters were blamed for using children as human shields, and back to Iraq, where government forces halted the "Fallujah advance amid fears for 50,000 human shields," the deployment of civilians as proximate shields is continuously reported on and criticized.[19]

Indeed, a search in major English newspapers for the phrase *human shields* from November 2015 through October 2016 corroborates that proximate shields have become by far the most prominent type of shield in contemporary discourse on war.[20] Of the 1,221 articles that mention human shields during this period, 65 describe voluntary shields, 272 depict involuntary shields, and 731 portray civilians who became shields because they lived in the midst of the fighting, while another 153 use the phrase as a metaphor. The actual number of people who are described as human shields in these articles is remarkable: there are references to 7 voluntary shields, 9,456 involuntary shields, and 3,354,800 proximate shields. The percentage of voluntary human shields is negligible, and involuntary shields account for only 0.2 percent, while proximate shields comprise over 99 percent of the civilians who are characterized as shields.

The massive percentage of proximate shields is worth dwelling on. Usually voluntary or involuntary shielding involve small numbers. A few hundred Western activists travelled to Iraq during the Gulf War to become voluntary shields, while dozens of activists joined the International Solidarity Movement in Gaza to stop bulldozers from destroying Palestinian homes. Involuntary shielding is similar. In Syria ISIS militants used scores of civilians as human shields to flee the town of Manbij after being defeated by US-backed fighters. By contrast, accusations of proximate shielding, because it routinely refers to the use of shields in cities, tend to involve thousands of people, at times hundreds of thousands.

This striking shift in the number of people who can become human shields, from individuals and small groups to masses of unidentified civilians, underscores an important historical transformation, whereby shielding is becoming more impersonal. And the dramatic expansion of the circle of humans who can indiscriminately become shields is, in turn, translating into a devaluation of humanity.

AGENCY

What makes this type of shield susceptible to political and legal manipulations? To address this question, it is important, first, to underscore that one of the features distinguishing voluntary and involuntary shields from proximate ones is human agency. In the struggles waged by Greenpeace, for example, civilian activists voluntarily chose to convert their bodies into shields in order to save the lives of beings endangered by nuclear testing or whales hunted in the Pacific Ocean. In the case of involuntary shields, agency is on the part of soldiers or militants—rather than civilians—who coercively convert presumably passive noncombatants into shields to deter their enemies from carrying out attacks.

In both voluntary and involuntary shielding, a person is defined as a shield because she or he either acts volitionally or is forced to act as a buffer between a belligerent and a target. Thus, agency is vital to these types of shields. Just as important, the voluntary or involuntary human shield occupies a specific space *in between* the two sides. By contrast, people become proximate shields due to their *nearness* to the fighting, without either volunteering or being coerced and without necessarily being positioned physically between the two sides. Proximity to a target seems to be the only factor that transforms them into shields.

Proximate shielding is also not necessarily an effect of an action, but rather it involves a peculiar relation to agency: *inaction* in urban warfare—remaining in cities that have become battle spaces—is sufficient to convert civilians into shields. In order *not* to become a shield, one has to take action, leaving the conflict zone and becoming a displaced person.[21] This difference helps explain the large number of people who are considered proximate shields as compared to voluntary and involuntary shields.

The passivity of proximate shielding also creates a legal conundrum. Precisely because international law considers the civilian to be passive, the agency involved in both voluntary and involuntary shielding helps justify stripping voluntary and involuntary shields of the protections bestowed on civilians. Insofar as passivity is the hallmark of civilianhood in international law, one might expect that proximate shields would retain the protections conferred on civilians that voluntary and involuntary shields stand to lose. Instead, some of the proximate shields' protections are also stripped away once they are labeled as shields.

The Mosul operation illuminates this point. Supporting Iraqi forces on the ground, the US-led coalition, which included a dozen countries, carried out more than 1,250 strikes in the city, hitting thousands of targets with over 29,000 munitions, according to official figures provided to *The Atlantic*.[22] Although the exact number of civilians killed in Mosul remains unknown, the Associated Press estimated that 3,200 were killed by the Iraqi government and the US-led coalition. The coalition acknowledged responsibility for only 10 percent of the deaths. Its spokesperson defined as "irresponsible" any accusations against the coalition for the "inadvertent casualties" of the remaining 90 percent of civilian casualties.[23] Once all civilians in Mosul had been framed as proximate shields, their lives mattered less.

Although it is true that in instances of voluntary and involuntary shielding, the framing of the event is crucial for determining what repertoires of violence can be employed and the ethical meaning of the fighting, with proximate shields the framing is everything.[24] Since practically any person trapped in a war zone can be cast as a proximate shield rather than as an innocent bystander without the accuser having to demonstrate anything about the action of that person or of the belligerents, it becomes relatively simple to frame hundreds of thousands of civilians as human shields. This act of framing converts entire urban populations trapped in a war zone into killable subjects.

Importantly, not every civilian who is ensnared in the midst of urban fighting is framed as a proximate shield. Whereas in Mosul in 2016 practically all the civilians who remained in the city were depicted by Western governments, media outlets, and even human rights organizations as shields even before the Iraqi army, assisted by a US-led coalition, invaded it, this was not the case two years earlier, when ISIS had captured the city.

At that time, hundreds of Iraqi troops were stationed inside the city in an effort to defend it from imminent attack. Neither the United Nations nor any government or media outlet cast the civilians among whom the Iraqi army was stationed as shields. Considering that hundreds of newspaper articles blamed ISIS for deploying tens of thousands of human shields in the days leading up to the 2016 Mosul campaign, it is remarkable that there was not a single mention of human shielding in the articles covering the 2014 ISIS offensive to conquer the same city.

The major difference between Mosul 2014 and Mosul 2016 lies in who the belligerents were and their relation to the state. During both military campaigns, the statist conception of international law, which we saw espoused by positivist jurisprudence in the aftermath of the 1871 Franco-German War, continued to reign. This means that the intervention of irregulars—today's insurgents, guerrillas, or terrorists but also at times protestors or rioters—is still decisive when interpreting international law and the ethics of violence.[25] By those terms, civilians trapped in areas where nonstate actors are fighting lose some of the protections bestowed upon them by international law, while those caught in similar circumstances but surrounded by a state's military do not lose these same protections. In this sense, proximate human shields are the weapon of the state par excellence.

Indeed, the statist approach informing international law helps to account not only for why Iraqi civilians in Mosul were framed as shields in 2016 but not in 2014, but also why civilians were framed as shields in Sri Lanka and again in the 2012 and 2014 wars on Gaza. Israeli citizens in Tel Aviv are not classified as shields when Hamas launches rockets towards the Israel Defense Forces military command headquarters located in the city center. By sharp contrast, Palestinian civilians are cast as human shields when Israel bombs Hamas command centers and military infrastructures in Gaza. In other words, if Hamas kills Israeli civilians, it is to blame, and if Israel kills Palestinian civilians, then Hamas is also to blame, since, at least ostensibly, it is Hamas that has deployed these civilians as shields.[26] This kind of comparison reveals how the irregular continues to pose a threat to the international legal order.

In the nineteenth century the intervention of irregulars legitimized the use of human shields as a form of reprisal by a military operating on behalf of a sovereign state, while in the twenty-first century it is the closeness of civilians to irregulars that legitimizes their transformation into proximate human shields. This difference reveals, as it were, the inner logic of the accusation of proximate shielding. According to the common use of the term, civilians become proximate shields due to their closeness to the fighting between warring parties. But the Mosul, Sri Lankan, and Gaza examples suggest that proximity refers not to the distance between civilians and the fighting but to the distance between civilians and nonstate militants who are waging a war with a state military. It is the nearness to irregulars in the midst of war that produces the proximate shield, and not merely the presence of civilians within a conflict zone. In this way, the specter of the irregular continues to haunt and inform international law.

ASSIGNING GUILT

While proximity to insurgent forces explains the absence of proximate shields in Mosul in 2014 and the framing of civilians as proximate shields in 2016, it does not explain why this form of shielding has suddenly become so prominent in battlespaces around the globe—from Africa through the Middle East and all the way to Southeast Asia. Part of the answer clearly has to do with the involvement of nonstate actors. Another factor is also at play here: specifically, the fact that proximate shielding introduces numerical, spatial, and temporal dimensions that do not exist with respect to the two other kinds of shielding.

Numerically, entire urban populations can be framed as proximate shields precisely because no agency—by either belligerents or civilians—is needed in order to render a person a proximate shield. With a single press release or a single pronouncement by a spokesperson (representing a state, military, or humanitarian organization), tens of thousands of civilians can be transformed into proximate shields—such as when the United Nations claimed that "ISIS is using one hundred thousand civilians as human shields."

Spatially, the portrayal of a city's whole civilian population as proximate shields allows the attacking forces to frame an entire city as a legitimate target. If voluntary and involuntary shields tend to be identified when they occupy a specific space in between a belligerent and its target, proximate shields can be anywhere, and are often everywhere, in a particular urban space.

Temporally, proximate shielding can endure far longer than either voluntary or involuntary shielding; the latter two are restricted to the time during which the civilian acts or is forced to act as a shield in the space between the warring party and its target. By contrast, civilians do not become proximate shields by their own actions or the actions of someone else. Therefore, they can be characterized as shields for days, weeks, and, at times, months on end. Indeed, since proximate shielding coincides with urban life in times of war, elements of everyday life such as going to fetch water or to shop for produce can potentially be framed as a form of shielding. Proximate shields can exist as long as the fighting persists.

Crucially, the numerical, spatial, and temporal features characterizing proximate shielding expand the ability of a warring party to claim that the civilians it killed were human shields and to assign the guilt to the enemy. In other words, if a warring party kills innocent bystanders in an urban setting, it can always exonerate itself because in its view there are no civilians in war-struck cities. There are only proximate shields, and their deaths lie on the shoulders of those who hid behind them.[27] Proximate shielding simultaneously allocates culpability and contributes to the erosion of the category of civilian in international law.

This certainly has to do with the fact that like other human shields, proximate shields can be mobilized to justify the use of lethal violence *after the fact.* But what makes the accusation of proximate shielding particularly insidious is that it frames vast populations as human shields even *before a conflict has taken place,* and this act of framing helps shape the repertoires of violence the attacking forces can use. In Mosul, the portrayal of the civilian population as proximate shields functioned as a "speech act" that allowed the Iraq- and US-led coalition to classify the whole urban space as a military target, and this legitimized the employment of munitions whose explosive reach impacts very large areas and whose use in spaces occupied by civilians is legally prohibited.[28] The act of framing Mosul as a city full of proximate human shields in the days leading up to the fighting helps explain why in its effort to recapture the city the coalition used weapons that razed large parts of the city to the ground.

In addition to revealing the large numbers of people who have been framed as proximate shields, our search for the phrase "human shield" in major newspapers also revealed that proximate shields appear *almost exclusively* in conflict zones taking place in decolonized parts of the world.[29] If one were to color a map of the world using darker shades for countries where accusations of human shielding have been most prevalent since the Second World War, then ex-colonies such as Afghanistan, Iraq, Lebanon, the Palestinian territories, Sri Lanka, Syria, Vietnam, and Yemen would certainly have the darkest contours.

One way many legal and military experts account for the concentration of shielding accusations in these countries is by pointing out that human shields are deployed at higher rates in asymmetric armed conflicts between powerful high-tech militaries and irregular fighters as the preferred weapon of the weak. According to the experts, rebels and terrorists in the Global South (where most ex-colonies are located) are increasingly using human shields to protect themselves from cutting-edge surveillance technologies and armed drones.[30]

However, our historical reconstruction of human shielding suggests that the story is more complex than that, not least because the darker shades on the proposed map correspond with darker-skinned populations. The fact that practically all invocations of proximate shielding are connected to nonwhite civilians in ex-colonies exposes how the figures of the colonial subject and the proximate shield are inextricably linked. Hence, another way to interpret the map is that shielding accusations by the strong function as a pushback against the integration of ex-colonized people into the international legal order, since such accusations have helped to justify the killing of large numbers of civilians in former colonies.

The political geography of the proximate shield not only reveals how this legal figure has, in many ways, come to stand for the colonial subject of old, but it also exposes how race reasserts itself within international law. As we have seen, human shielding was codified in international law during the period of decolonization, when the laws of war became applicable to conflicts taking place in the former colonies and civilianhood was extended to indigenous populations. This shift is often construed, in canonical interpretations of history, as a progressive move from a system informed by Western-white prerogatives to a system that promotes a universal sense of humanity.[31] Yet, ironically, it was soon thereafter that accusations of human shielding became pervasive specifically in the former colonies. Precisely when increasing numbers of nonwhites were finally recognized as fully human, they also become potential human shields, and when they are either used or framed as human shields, they lose some of the legal protections they gained following decolonization.

To be sure, international law does not make overt racial distinctions, but just as its logic once excluded the colonial subjects of old, its formulation today enables state actors to deploy the human shield clause to legitimize the killing of racialized civilians in wars waged against nonstate actors taking place in ex-colonies. More specifically, while the Additional Protocols to the Geneva Conventions prohibit the use of human shields, they also reiterate the legitimacy of militaries to bomb military targets protected by human shields, provided they abide by the principles of distinction and proportionality.[32]

Notwithstanding the common assumption that decolonization has led to the creation of a universal humanity in which all people are acknowledged as humans who are entitled to equal rights, proximate shielding reveals that assumptions about who is considered an equal human being retains traces of the colonial past. In the cases of the 2016 operation to recapture Mosul and Israel's wars in Gaza—in which the human shield argument was mobilized against entire populations—the figures of the colonized subject and of the civilian transformed into a proximate human shield coincide.[33] Whereas it would be difficult to imagine entire populations being transformed into proximate shields in Western cities—unless perhaps they are racialized minorities— from Mosul to Gaza, we see how the colonial subject is still very much alive.

SEVENTEEN

Info-War

The Gaza Wars and Social Media

IN JULY 2014, AROUND THE SAME TIME that ISIS first captured Mosul from the hands of the Iraqi army, Israel launched its third war on the Gaza Strip in six years, dubbing the campaign Operation Protective Edge.[1] Not unlike the previous campaigns, Protective Edge produced extensive damage to this densely populated swath of Palestinian land. Ten days before Israel withdrew its ground forces, the United Nations Human Rights Council adopted a resolution accusing Israel of collective punishment and urging all parties to respect the law. "The deliberate targeting of civilians and other protected persons and the perpetration of systematic, flagrant and widespread violations of applicable international humanitarian law and international human rights law in situations of armed conflict constitute grave breaches and a threat to international peace and security," the resolution declared.[2]

Correspondingly, accusations that Hamas and other Palestinian armed groups had used human shields served as one of Israel's key arguments for deflecting accusations of having committed war crimes. During an appearance at the United Nations General Assembly not long after Protective Edge, Israeli Prime Minister Benjamin Netanyahu exhibited a picture of children playing in the vicinity of a rocket launcher (figure 22). "Hamas," he averred, "deliberately placed its rockets where Palestinian children live and play."[3] Explaining that Israel was facing an enemy who constantly weaponizes vulnerable human bodies, Netanyahu concluded his address by claiming that the United Nations Human Rights Council was a "Terrorist Rights Council" that grants legitimacy to the mobilization and deployment of human shields.[4]

A few months later, Israel released a report providing legal defense of the 2014 Gaza invasion.[5] The report analyzes a variety of materials as it accuses

FIGURE 22. Israel's Prime Minister Benjamin Netanyahu at the UN General Assembly, 29 September 2014. Credit: Brendan McDermid, Reuters.

the different Palestinian resistance groups of having drawn "the fighting into the urban terrain," where they "unlawfully intertwined their military operations with the civilian environment."[6] Adopting language strikingly similar to the arguments used by the Italian government during the 1935–36 war in Ethiopia and by the American administration during the Vietnam War, the document blames Palestinians for using tactics that violate the customary prohibition against perfidy under international humanitarian law. The report concludes that Hamas deployed defenseless Palestinian civilians as human shields and resorted to other unlawful practices—such as the use of combatants disguised as civilians—with the hope of obfuscating the distinction between civilians and combatants and "deliberately distort[ing] assessments of the legality of Israel's Defense Forces (IDF) activity in the Gaza Strip."[7]

The narrative and key arguments for the governmental report were developed by the IDF on its social media sites during the fight itself. In fact, while it was attacking the Gaza Strip, the Israeli military waged another kind of war, this one on social media with the aim of defending the military campaign by legitimizing the killing of Palestinian civilians. It produced a series of sophisticated YouTube videos and infographics in which the legal figure of the human shield was mobilized to justify lethal force and disseminated them widely through its Twitter, Instagram, and Facebook accounts.[8]

By introducing human shielding to these social media platforms, the IDF helped popularize the figure of the human shield while transforming the cyberworld into a site of semiotic warfare.[9] The goal was to shape the visual perception of the battlespace by portraying the Palestinians as morally inferior and Israel as the humane actor.[10] Indeed, one should understand the dissemination of images of human shielding on social media as part of an info-war: a media campaign whose role is to provide ethical legitimacy to the deployment of lethal violence against civilians.

WHAT WOULD YOU DO?

According to data gathered by the United Nations, at least 2,251 Palestinians were killed during Operation Protective Edge. Of the verified cases, 1,462 were believed to be civilians. Many of these fatalities involved multiple family members, with at least 142 Palestinian families having three or more relatives killed in the same incident, for a total of 739 deaths. In addition, approximately 18,000 housing units were either destroyed or severely damaged, leaving approximately 108,000 people homeless. On the Israeli side, 73 people were killed during the war: 67 combatants and 6 civilians.[11] The discrepancy with respect to the number and proportion of civilian deaths—65 percent of all those killed by Israel were civilians compared to the 8 percent of civilians killed by Palestinians—created a legal problem, since according to these figures it appears that in its assault on Gaza, Israel did indeed commit egregious war crimes.

It is precisely in this context that one needs to understand Israel's extensive use of social media during and after the 2014 Gaza War to defend the level of violence it wielded against Palestinians. One of the first images the IDF circulated sets the stage for the Gaza War by portraying Israel's assault as an attempt to defend the very essence of liberalism. It shows rockets with bloody smoke heading towards the Statue of Liberty, one of liberal democracy's icons, and asks the Western public, "What would you do?" (figure 23). In this way, Israel both positioned itself as a liberal democracy and drew an analogy between the Gaza War and America's post-9/11 concerns about terrorist attacks against the United States. The war on Gaza was, according to the infographic, part of the war on terror.

FIGURE 23. Israel Defense Forces infographic justifying the assault on Gaza, 2014. Credit: IDF Blog.

Most of the infographics produced during Protective Edge were, however, dedicated to human shielding. One of the themes of Israel's claims about the Palestinians' use of human shields is the depiction of the asymmetric context in which the Gaza War took place as if it were symmetric. "Some bomb shelters shelter people. Some shelter bombs" (figure 24) is just one of numerous infographics where the radically disproportionate power differential and spatial disparity between a besieged population confined to an enclave (Palestinians) and its besiegers (Israelis) are depicted as if the two were equal. The assumption of equality not only elides the reality on the ground but is necessary for Israel to be able to justify—through the human shielding argument—its destruction of Gaza.

In this and several other infographics Israel accuses the Palestinians of illegally using civilian spaces for shielding purposes. By depicting Palestinians as hiding rockets in their homes, the IDF intimates that a single function (hiding weapons) overrides existing functions (home, shelter, intimacy, etc.) so that the meaning usually associated with homes, including their attribute as a space of protection, is compromised. Legally speaking,

FIGURE 24. Israel Defense Forces
infographic claiming Palestinians
hid rockets under their homes.
Credit: IDF Blog.

this is the "dual-use" doctrine, whereby an object serves both civilian and military purposes.

While dual use is not explicitly part of international humanitarian law,[12] Marco Sassòli from the Geneva Academy of International Humanitarian Law and Human Rights stresses that "an attack on a dual-use object is in any event unlawful if the effect on the civilian aspect is intended," but he adds that "respect of that particular rule is impossible to assess in the heat of the battle."[13] Therefore, in instances where a house that shelters civilians is simultaneously used as an arms depot or a militant hideout, which is illegal, belligerents can legitimately attack it and claim that its military function was a threat, and consequently the attack was necessary.[14] Accordingly, legal experts have noted that the dual-use doctrine ultimately enables "extraordinarily permissive" use of lethal force, allowing belligerents to sway the proportionality between civilian immunity and military necessity in their favor.[15]

In such circumstances, a house can no longer be a refuge, even when the majority of the people in the targeted area are, in fact, refugees, as in Gaza.[16] The space's resignification from a space of life to a space of death is crucial, since it allows the IDF to transform the meaning ascribed to the people within this space and to the violence that it deploys. Put differently, Israel's "moral cartography," to borrow political geographer Derek Gregory's phrase describing how morally acceptable violence relates to space, is acutely apparent here: the way a place is defined can facilitate the killing of civilians without it being a crime.[17] The inevitable overlapping of civilian and military functions in urban warfare creates new challenges for international law and the articulation of the ethics of violence. In its info-war, Israel tried to turn that challenge into a legal argument in its favor and portrayed Palestinian homes as well as the people inhabiting them as part of Hamas's military defense system.[18]

In the same infographic, Israel also accuses Palestinians of perfidy, which in customary international law is defined as "acts inviting the confidence of an adversary to lead him to believe that he is entitled to, or is obliged to accord, protection under the rules of international law."[19] The charge is that Palestinians are deceptive, using civilian spaces for military purposes, thereby legitimating attacks on those homes.

It is, nonetheless, highly unlikely that Palestinians were shielding weapons in all eighteen thousand homes that, according to the United Nations, were either destroyed or severely damaged during the war. Hence, one of the objectives of categorizing civilian homes as shields is to help conceal the fact that Israel's "pinpoint strikes" and "surgical capabilities" were often not precise and could neither predict nor guarantee discrimination between civilian sites and military targets. Another objective was to help Israel justify the high percentage of civilian deaths and the destruction of civilian spaces in Gaza.

WEAPONIZING CIVILIANS

This mobilization of dual use and perfidy in the Israeli info-war on Gaza is not an isolated case but reflects a major discussion in international humanitarian law on the principle of distinction between combatants and civilians. In addition to changing the traditional meaning of civilian spaces and criticizing Palestinians for not distinguishing between combatants and civilians, the Israeli infographics also accuse Hamas of transforming civilians into weapons, as shown in the IDF ad "Human Shields Are Hamas' Strategy" (figure 25). This infographic includes a photograph of Palestinians standing on top of a building, and underneath is a drawing of a home with warheads in it and people standing on the roof. The caption reads: "Hamas uses civilians to protect its weapons & its terrorists," while the image presents Hamas as transforming the civilian population into threshold beings—half human, half weapon.

The infographic portrays human shields as simultaneously both protected persons and nonprotected persons—a condition of in-betweenness that anthropologist Victor Turner defines as liminality.[20] For Turner the liminal

FIGURE 25. Israel Defense Forces infographic accusing Hamas of using civilians as human shields. Credit: IDF Blog.

figure occupies a temporal in-betweenness while transitioning from one social or political category to another; however, the human shield does not pass from the status of civilian to combatant but remains trapped in its liminal status. Precisely because the human shield is neither combatant nor noncombatant, he or she loses the traditional protections offered to civilians. Hence, Israel's mobilization of the figure of the human shield on social media is manipulative, since it avows the civilian status of these civilians while using the legal figure of the shield to justify why so many Palestinian civilians were killed.

THE ETHICAL FRAME

The IDF's info-war suggests that the struggle over the interpretation of violence can be as important as the violence itself. States and militaries invest considerable resources in framing acts of war for public consumption in order to demonstrate that violence was deployed in accordance with the law; in the wake of the new millennium, many of these resources focus on social media. States and militaries know that the morality of the event is determined in the public arena often through the circulation of images and that most people access images through their cell phones, tablets, and computers.

The info-war ultimately aims to frame the enemy as the guilty actor,[21] as in a video clip released by the IDF during the 2012 Operation Pillar of Cloud that depicts an incident when the Israeli military "tapped" on the roof of a Palestinian apartment building. Tapping is used by the IDF to alert civilian populations that it has marked a building as a target and intends to destroy it within minutes. In the clip, one sees an aerial image of an apartment building in Gaza. The moment the roof is "tapped" by a small bomb—a warning technology that does not kill—civilians are shown running outside the building. Suddenly some civilians change course and run back inside, climbing onto the roof. By so doing they blur the threshold between civilian and combatant and position themselves as human shields. The clip's message is straightforward: while the IDF wants to observe the principle of distinction by allowing time for civilians to leave a designated military target, Palestinians violate that distinction by refusing to leave the building.

The clip underscores that the principle of distinction is not merely a descriptive force differentiating among numerous actors who are already in the field; it also has a capacity to produce different legal figures.[22] It is the tapping that turns these Palestinians into figures who occupy the threshold between civilian and combatant, while it is the law that gives them the status of human shields; the naming—"they are human shields"—confers on these civilians a new legal and political reality.[23] The irony of this clip is that while the tapping is meant to ensure the distinction between civilian and combatant, it is at least partially responsible for producing a legal figure that represents the blurring of that distinction.

In fact, the clip can also lend itself to a very different interpretation than the one intended by the Israeli military. After all, when the camera first focuses on the apartment building, there are no human shields inside. Only when the apartment building is designated as a target through the act of tapping do the civilians who remain within the building, climbing up to its roof, become human shields. The tapping dictates a course of action, and those who refuse to follow its fiat—namely, flee the building—become human shields and thus abdicate their status as civilians. Distinction, as the tapping example reveals, can at times be a force used to undermine distinction itself.

In the clip, which was disseminated widely by the Israeli military as a visual weapon, the pilot decides to abort the attack—a decision that assumes a humanitarian motive precisely because the Palestinians who were spared have been framed as human shields rather than civilians. According to this legal-military frame, the Palestinians intentionally blurred the distinction between combatants and civilians, while the Israeli military reveals its ethical superiority by upholding the distinction. Even though human shields are legally killable, the pilot decided to show mercy, reiterating yet again the ethical incommensurability between Israel and the colonized Palestinians.

EIGHTEEN

Posthuman Shielding

Drone Warfare and New Surveillance Technologies

FLYING OVER A RUGGED MOUNTAINOUS REGION of South Yemen, helicopter gunships and armed Reaper drones provided cover as a Navy SEAL team advanced toward an al-Qaeda compound. The operation's objective was to seize a number of computers containing "clues about future terrorist plots."[1] When the commandos attempted to enter the compound, those inside returned fire, killing one officer before succumbing to American air power. Initially, the military reported that fourteen al-Qaeda militants had been killed during the operation, but medics at the scene said that actually thirty people had died, including ten women and children.[2] The Pentagon later confirmed that civilians were among the dead, though some of the women appeared to have been "combatants," and analysts were "busy determining whether the terrorists used women and children as human shields."[3]

Descriptions of US operations in the Middle East like this one, which occurred in 2017, are not uncommon. When the violence that was deployed in a military operation becomes the object of public and legal scrutiny, we often witness an ethical debate about how lethal force has been deployed and to what degree the principle of distinction was observed by the actors in the battlefield. Politicians as well as military and legal experts describe situations where it is difficult to draw distinctions between enemy combatants and civilians in what Prussian military theorist Carl von Clausewitz termed the "fog of war."[4] The claim that forces could see through the fog serves to convince the public that they abided by the principle of distinction and deployed humane forms of violence. However, in the Yemini compound, where women and children were killed, it appears that the "fog" was too thick for distinctions to be made, and the human shielding accusation was invoked to cover up the failure of the advanced surveillance technologies deployed by the US military.

NEW SURVEILLANCE TECHNOLOGIES

Military tools of observation have changed dramatically over the years.[5] During the nineteenth and early twentieth centuries, military targets were identified primarily from hilltops and watchtowers through optical magnification with binoculars. Later in the twentieth century, airplanes equipped with radar and soldiers with night-vision equipment extended the possibilities for detecting enemies and distinguishing them from noncombatants. Today, satellites and drones not only provide live video streams and GPS locations but are also able to gather a massive amount of electronic signals used to identify and locate military targets and distinguish them from innocent bystanders. These technologies have fundamentally expanded the visibility of different actors in the field in terms of both their geographical reach and their ability to render observable people and interactions previously impossible to detect.[6] Former US president Barack Obama's drone wars were a pronounced manifestation of these developments. Using new surveillance technologies, pilots sitting thousands of miles away could identify and follow targets for extended periods of time.[7]

The developments in military perception and associated weaponry have altered not only the ways high-tech states wage wars but also the ways guerrillas fight back. As highlighted by political scientist Antoine Bousquet, both militaries and militants have always adapted their tactics according to how they are observed, and in this new round of the war of perception, nonstate forces have increasingly adopted new practices of concealment and dispersal that often involve blending into the "community of noncombatants."[8] This has changed both how combatants fight and the nature of warfare itself. Partially in response to the development of technologies that increase their visibility and detectability, insurgents have moved from mountainous deserts and jungles to densely populated urban settings, blending with civilians and multiplying the situations in which noncombatants can be used as human shields. In turn, high-tech militaries are now spending much of their resources hunting militants in city spaces.[9]

Crucially, these transformations in military perception and warfare strategies have also had a major impact on how international law is being mobilized: the fact that the historically unstable boundary between civilians and combatants has been blurred even further has led some experts to develop new proportionality calculations (as we saw in chapter 14 on the Sri Lankan civil war) and expand the range of people who can be killed legally in the battlespace. For these experts, assassinations and killing people who are deployed as human shields are now a legitimate part of warfare.[10]

A POSTHUMAN TURN

Because in contemporary battlespaces a person's garb and location often do not signal whether he or she is an armed militant, the only way to distinguish between combatants and civilians is by assessing whether a person is actually "participating in hostilities."[11] Michael Schmitt, an expert in international law, explains how during the US invasion of Afghanistan guerrilla groups were scattered and "wore no uniforms or other distinctive clothing that allowed immediate visual identification," and "the mere position of a group, vehicle or other mobile target seldom served as a reliable indicator of its enemy character."[12] Accordingly, new technologies have been developed that aim to analyze human activity within theaters of violence. Determining what a person *does* is now considered vital for understanding what a person *is*.

This new way of identifying combatants translates into a shift in the military gaze. Complex surveillance and identification technologies have increasingly been adopted for gathering data from mobile phones, emails, and social media, while also using satellite images, heat-seeking sensors, electronic signal detectors, thermal imaging, GPS, GIS, aerial photos and videos, and acoustic vector systems. Their function is to alter ways of "seeing" so as to expand what militaries can observe.[13]

For instance, according to the Drone Papers—a series of secret documents published by *The Intercept* on the US drone wars in Afghanistan, Pakistan, Somalia, and Yemen—a device attached to drones collects electronic signals, which are analyzed and used to produce the military's Geolocation Watchlist of targets.[14] This vast amount of data is assembled by an array of agencies and other actors, including some civilian institutions, and it is then subjected to algorithms that aim to draw distinctions among people by detecting anomalies in the relationships among multiple data points.[15] These relationships are then translated into various "patterns of life," some of which are believed to coincide with the "life of a terrorist."[16]

As former National Security Agency (NSA) employee and whistleblower Edward Snowden revealed, the use of electronic signals as standard procedure for identifying combatants in the battlefield has dramatically broadened the pool of potential legitimate targets. In Pakistan, for instance, the NSA used metadata gathered from mobile phones to generate algorithms that aimed to identify couriers who shuttle between targets. Working like an email spam filter, the algorithm then produces a kill list.[17] But just like email spam filters, the lethal algorithms can make mistakes, adding innocent people to the list of those who the US Administration thinks should be killed. Moreover, if a phone is handed from one person to another, the person who ends up being targeted is not necessarily the person who has been tracked but the one who has the SIM card. Drone attacks targeting patterns of life rather than a specific person are called "signature strikes," because their objective is to kill "men who bear certain signatures, or defining characteristics associated with terrorist activity, but whose identities aren't known."[18] In such attacks, drones target data but kill people.

The fact that targets are identified electronically underscores the posthuman turn in how distinctions are made between combatants and civilians, or, in post-9/11 language, between terrorists and innocent bystanders. In environmental activism the term *posthuman* refers to the decentering of humanity by attributing equal value to other forms of biological life, but, in this context, *posthuman* signifies both the move in surveillance away from the human senses to computerized analysis of big data and the reconceptualization of the human body as a repository of digital signals for military purposes.

We witness, then, how the original conception of surveillance, which artificially replicated the human senses, such as with binoculars, is "increasingly being demoted or even altogether displaced" by other systems of surveillance that are based on different forms of mathematical computing.[19] Concurrently, contemporary technologies of distinction conceptualize the human body in ways that are similar to the scientific reconceptualization of the body as a molecular entity or a genomic figure.[20] The human target now appears as a digitized pattern of life.

The crucial point here is that the posthuman military surveillance apparatus does not merely reflect interactions in the world; it constitutes a *productive force* that shapes how battlespaces are perceived legally and ethically. It informs the invention of a new arsenal of weapons that can be used from greater distance and are more precise, radically modifying the way wars are fought. It has also propelled combatants, who are hiding from the surveillance technologies and new weapon systems, to change their positions in space—particularly moving into urban settings—and to change the ways they fight, using tunnels, for example, to advance in the terrain. Finally, the novel forms of seeing have also transformed how militaries interpret the lethal violence they use.

But at times the reduction of targets to an amalgamation of electronic data does not provide enough clarity to develop an unequivocal ethical interpretation of an attack. This is where human shields enter the picture, and their appearance—whether real or fabricated—within conflict zones is invoked to justify the failures of the posthuman apparatus.

COVER-UP

The posthuman surveillance technologies have three functions. First, they are used to gather intelligence through reconnaissance aimed at distinguishing between the guilty and innocent in an effort to identify "terrorists." Second, they are used to guide the attacking forces as they attempt to kill the target, and in this function, they should be considered an integral part of the military's arsenal of weapons. Third, they are used to interpret the meaning of violence before, during, and after the fighting to assess whether the acts of war conform with the law, usually in order to claim that the forces were acting ethically.[21] Thus, investigators, warriors, and judges are all dependent on the apparatus.

The problem is that the surveillance apparatus often fails to draw accurate distinctions, and the fog of war can be too foggy even for the new technologies. Indeed, increased visibility and tracking have not necessarily translated into more clarity when applying international law to battlespaces. In the words of international relations scholar Thomas Gregory, "the ability to zoom in on potential targets with high-definition cameras and track them for weeks on end has drawn attention to the difficulties we face when it comes to categorizing combatants and noncombatants, as well as the way in which belligerents have sought to justify their violence and legitimize their targets."[22] Paradoxically, then, the new technologies, which aim to produce more clarity, often expose the fuzziness of the processes through which legal categories are mobilized.

These technologies' shortcomings are especially apparent in the drone wars, where the high-tech wizardry often fails in its most elemental purpose:

"to tell the difference between friend and foe."[23] Even though the exact number of civilian deaths as a result of drone strikes remains unclear, the Drone Papers suggest that US targeting is accompanied by significant civilian casualties referred to as "collateral damage."[24] Considering that the surveillance apparatus is meant to improve the ability to distinguish between combatant and civilian and thus reduce the level of suffering inflicted on innocent people and that the missiles carried by most drones are considered extremely precise, the relatively poor level of discrimination in drone wars is disturbing. The high civilian casualty rates have led the UN and various international human rights organizations to call for an investigation into US drone targeting.[25]

The US military's legal department has addressed this line of criticism in part by redefining its collateral damage protocol, introducing new legal categories and invoking old ones to classify those who die. In certain instances, new categories—like "enemy killed in action"—have been coined to reframe civilians killed in the battlefield and to justify collateral damage. In other instances, existing legal figures like that of human shield are deployed to cover up the failures of posthuman surveillance technologies and to secure impunity from any wrongdoing. In a certain sense, we have entered the era of *posthuman shielding,* where a person is categorized as a human shield following the analysis of posthuman surveillance technologies in order to cover up the failure of these technologies, like the "women and children" in the al-Qaeda compound attacked by US special forces in Yemen.

NINETEEN

———

Women and Children

Gender, Passivity, and Human Shields

THE FRAMING OF WOMEN AND CHILDREN as human shields by state militaries is carried out not only to cover up the killing of innocent civilians in the era of drone warfare. It also points to a more radical transformation in the history of human shielding, particularly regarding who can be classified as a human shield. In general, over the past 150 years there has been a pronounced change in the gender associated with human shielding. In the American Civil War, the Franco-German War, and the Second Boer War, only men served as involuntary shields. Starting from World War I both men and women were deployed as shields. But in our contemporary moment, women and children have become the major protagonists in shielding accusations.[1]

Although it is unclear if women and children are actually used more often than men as human shields, political scientist Helen Kinsella notes that the concept of shielding has congealed to denote "mostly women and children"— and mostly among populations that are nonwhite.[2] One explanation for this change is that with the expansion of notions of civilianhood and universal humanity, people who in the past were not deployable as shields because they were considered socially marginal, like women and children, are now deemed more valuable, making them usable as shields. Yet, this does not explain why such shielding accusations refer almost solely to nonwhite women and children rather than to woman and children in general. To grasp the reasons why women and children have become the central characters in shielding accusations and why the accusations are directed towards people of color, we need to understand what kind of political work these accusations attempt to carry out in the defense of humane violence.

Even though women and children have been used as human shields since World War I, it is only with the war on terror that they have become the main characters in shielding accusations. These accusations frequently appear in media portrayals of war zones, where the media typically reproduces the information it receives from military spokespeople—who are speaking on behalf of states that have a vested interest in obfuscating the number of civilians killed by their own forces.[3] To this end, and as we have seen in previous chapters, militaries the world over have begun to reclassify civilians according to an array of categories that render their deaths defendable in a court of law as well as more palatable for public consumption.

With the war on terror, the US military resurrected the use of a legal category it coined during the Vietnam War and began referring to all men who are killed during strikes as "military-aged males"—or MAMs. In this way, it classifies practically all men whose age is estimated to be between 16 and 65 as potential terrorists or combatants, and thus as people whom it is "acceptable to put to death."[4] A report published by the International Human Rights Clinics at New York and Stanford Universities explains that, absent exonerating evidence, "the US government counts all adult males killed by strikes as 'militants.'"[5] These men are not included in the civilian death count, so they are not part of the collateral damage calculations. And because they are considered combatants, they are also not characterized as human shields.

Once the category of combatants is expanded so dramatically to include all men and teenage boys within war zones, then women and children become the only possible recipients of the human shielding charge. This is one explanation why women and children, rather than men, have become the protagonists of shielding accusations. It also reveals why it is often assumed that Western militaries very rarely kill civilians: when nearly all the men are characterized as killable MAMs and the women and children as human shields, then very few people are left in the category of "civilian." This gives credence to Derek Gregory's claim that, according to those waging the war on terror, their enemies "don't have any" civilians.[6]

GENDER AND PASSIVITY

There are several other reasons why women and children have become the protagonists of the shielding accusation. One has to do with the category of "women" in international law and the persistence of gendered frameworks in interpreting the legitimacy of violence. While technically all individuals are guaranteed equal protection under the laws of war, as Kinsella points out, women are granted special protections as a consequence of their biological sex, or as the Fourth Geneva Convention states: "Women are to be treated with all the respect due to their sex." Kinsella goes on to point out that the "respect" due to women is rooted in normative assumptions about "the suffering, distress, or weakness women, literally and figuratively, embody at all times, owing to their sexual and reproductive characteristics."[7]

The naturalization of sex, bolstered by a certain conception of gender that presents women as passive subjects, has informed the way the category of civilian has been construed in international law. The civilian has long been feminized as a quintessentially defenseless subject with no agency, while the combatant has been portrayed as active—thus replicating gendered social norms.[8] According to this rationale, women—and children, who are also feminized—are assumed to be innocents, people who must be protected, and consequently their deaths always require explanation and justification. By claiming that they were killed because they were forced to become human shields, Western militaries uphold the naturalization of women and children as passive in international law, while simultaneously shifting the blame for their deaths onto their enemies.

THE RETURN OF THE BARBARIANS

The reason why the shielding accusation is directed primarily against the use of *nonwhite* women and children is less about the actual use of women and children as shields and more about the effort to depict men of darker skin color as inhumane. In 2019, during the final stages of the war against ISIS in Baghouz, an eastern Syrian village considered to be the last bastion of the jihadist organization, news outlets reported that "ISIS fighters who stayed in the terror group's last piece of territory before it succumbed to US-backed forces used their wives and children as human shields."[9] "ISIS," one news report explained, "has a long history of putting women and children on front lines to slow or stop offensive advances against it." But then, a few lines later, the report adds: "Over the past few weeks, ISIS told fighters and their families that they could leave Baghouz if they want. Since SDF [the Syrian Democratic Front] launched an offensive on Baghouz in February some

60,000 people—mostly women and children—left the village for the nearby al-Hawl refugee camp, according to Reuters."[10]

The extremist organization is portrayed, on the one hand, as using the wives and children of its own fighters as human shields, a practice depicted as common, and, on the other hand, as allowing most of the population to flee, such that only an estimated "1,500 civilians and 500 fighters" remained in Baghouz by the time the offensive began.[11] Whether some of these 1,500 civilians were indeed used as human shields is a matter of speculation. What became apparent after we began to write this book is that in literally thousands of news articles ISIS is accused of using women and children as human shields. While some of these claims are probably accurate, this refrain about the way Islamist extremist use women and children as shields requires further explanation.

As we have seen, since decolonization, ex-colonized men have often been framed as using women and children as shields, and this accusation becomes a sign of their barbarity. In saying this, we are not denying the existence of patriarchy, misogyny, and child abuse in ex-colonized societies. However, the continuous reiteration of the mistreatment of women and children by ex-colonized men (people of color who are often Muslims) has the effect of framing these men as uncivilized even though they have been welcomed into the family of nations and given full political and legal status as human.[12]

It is not mere coincidence that the moment ex-colonized men gain full political status as human, they are accused of deploying women and children as human shields and are thus reconstructed as uncivilized.[13] The ex-colonized should not, of course, be exempt from being held to account for using brutal means of warfare, and as groups like ISIS have proven time and again, some have no qualms about carrying out extensive and cruel violations against civilian populations, not least of which is wide-scale rape. Still, invoking the trope of defenseless women and children to justify the use of lethal violence against civilians in neo-imperial wars highlights a crucial element of the political and legal history of human shielding. Through this narrative, the principle of distinction is racialized: nonwhites fight by intentionally undermining the distinction between combatants and innocent women and children. The ability to make distinctions and the insistence on their significance continue to be presented as part of the West's cultural, technological, and ethical superiority, especially in relation to the war on terror—a war waged in the name of humanity even though it regularly fails to distinguish between civilians and combatants.

FIGURE 26. Mother and child "human shields" at a US-Mexico border crossing, 2018. Credit: Ueslei Marcelino, Reuters.

XENOPHOBIA

The specter of women and children as shields also haunts nonwhites when they migrate from war zones and areas afflicted by economic and environmental disaster in an effort to attain political asylum in countries located in the Global North. In the United States, a 2014 report published by the right-wing Tea Party organization portrays the movement of migrants from the Global South as an "invasion, not led by troops, but by divisions of mothers and children and young adults marching north from Central America and Mexico." The Tea Party report goes on to claim that "civilian women and children are directly marched into the target nation so that permanent settlement locations may be secured for more advancing insurgents. In effect, the civilians become political human shields for the insurgents coming in behind them, which are part of a much larger (and more dangerous) offensive."[14]

Four years later, in the weeks leading to the 2018 midterm elections, a "migrant caravan" of several thousand people, mainly from Guatemala, Honduras, and El Salvador, marched northward for hundreds of kilometers. They were fleeing abject poverty and violence, some of which had been spurred by US economic and military intervention over the past several decades.[15] These migrants intentionally formed a large group because in the past many people travelling as individuals or in small groups had been kidnapped by traffickers and drug gangs. Travelling en masse offered them a degree of protection, or so they thought (figure 26).

President Donald Trump, however, had no sympathy for the migrants. He rebuked the Mexican government and accused it of being complicit with the migrants by using "trucks and buses to bring them up to our country in areas where there is little border protection."[16] Building on deep-rooted anti-Latino racism, he also characterized the asylum seekers as "invaders" who sheltered among their ranks "unknown Middle Easterners"—a fabricated accusation, as he was later forced to admit—and then threatened to send thousands of soldiers to meet them.[17] Secretary of State Michael Pompeo and the head of the Department of Homeland Security parroted their boss and also warned the American people that the migrants were "putting women and children in front of this caravan to use as shields as they make their way through."[18]

The portrayal of women and children as human shields is a way of framing the migrants' attempt to enter the United States as an act of war waged by an inhumane nonwhite enemy. Here, too, the trope of the uncivilized brown man using women and children to advance his goals was mobilized, this time as a rallying cry aimed at uniting the American people behind the policies of a xenophobic presidency.

TWENTY

Spectacle

Viral Images That Dehumanize or Humanize Shields

VIDEO CLIPS AND PHOTOGRAPHS POSTED ON social media in early November 2015, using the hashtag ‎#أقفاص_الحماية‎ (Cages of Protection), showed dozens of civilians locked in metal cages as they were paraded through the rubble-laden streets of the Syrian town Douma located in the Eastern Ghouta region.[1] A spokesperson for the rebel group Jaysh al-Islam is seen explaining to the person shooting the clip that the caged people are human shields and are part of a new strategy for stopping the Syrian regime's aerial bombings. A short press release accompanying the footage states: "Rebels in Ghouta have distributed 100 cages, with each cage containing approximately seven people and the plan is afoot to produce 1,000 cages to distribute . . . in public places and markets that have been attacked in the past by the regime and Russian air-force."[2]

Two years earlier, the rebels had abducted hundreds of Alawite civilians in Eastern Ghouta, scattering them in unidentified locations, and it is very likely that those held in cages on top of pickup trucks were taken from among their ranks (figure 27). During those two years, Syrian government forces had imposed a siege on the region, limiting access to food, clean water, and medical care, while repeatedly bombing residential areas and markets. Just two days before the human shields were paraded in the street, President Bashar al-Assad's regime's airplanes had attacked a popular marketplace in Douma, killing at least 70 people and wounding 550 more.[3]

The Syrian regime's attacks and the rebels' response have many similarities with the first instance of human shielding examined in this book: the siege on Charleston and the use of human shields by the rebels there. Standing near one of the cages on a street in Douma, a teenage boy is filmed saying, "If you want to kill my mother, you will kill them too," echoing the logic adopted by

191

FIGURE 27. Jaysh al-Islam parading captured civilians and fighters in a town on the outskirts of Damascus, 2015. Credit: Twitter.

Confederate General Samuel Jones when he deployed human shields in the southern city. Yet, in the hundred and fifty years separating these two wars, technology and the media have dramatically developed, providing numerous platforms for the Syrian rebel group to stage an unnerving performance of cruelty and to circulate the macabre images of caged prisoners through YouTube, Facebook, Instagram, and Twitter. Knowing well that mainstream media outlets like to broadcast sensational images in order to attract large audiences—which, in turn, fuels their advertising revenue—those who choreographed the event were probably not surprised when Reuters, BBC, CNN, and scores of other news agencies aired the shocking violence and made the human shielding performance into a global spectacle.

GLOBAL SPECTATORSHIP

The Syrian rebels thus converted the human shields into a commodity for mass consumption, projecting the deployment of human shields from the battlefield into the domain of global spectatorship, where the circulation of those images became part of the semiotic struggle over the ethics of violence.[4] This spectacle, like other spectacles emerging from the front lines, is not really separate from war but constitutes one of its essential components.[5] War and the spectacle of war—in this case *human shielding and the viral image of shielding*—can hardly be disjoined. The act of war produces the spectacle, and the spectacle, in turn, becomes a weapon of war.

The images of civilians in cages are seductive because they are so disturbing; like other spectacles, they are open to various interpretations and are directed towards multiple audiences. In one sense, the video is straightforward and follows a common human shielding script: to urge the enemy to hold its fire or else risk killing its own civilians and imprisoned soldiers. It was addressed to the Syrian regime and, just as important, to the people supporting Assad by producing, to borrow political geographer Yi-Fu Tuan's expression, a "landscape of fear."[6]

Simultaneously, the grisly performance was also directed inward—namely, to the rebels' constituency. In this second sense, the imprisoned Alawites represented the Syrian regime. The prisoners were degraded in order to convey the message that despite Assad's overwhelming airpower and the utter desolation his military had wrought on Eastern Ghouta, the regime could still be defeated. The spectacle was thus also produced to boost morale among the besieged insurgents and their social milieu.

The third and probably most pronounced impression this spectacle creates, at least among certain audiences, is that the rebels deploying the shields are barbaric. One commentator with over forty thousand followers immediately tweeted: "Footage of the barbaric 'rebel' fighters transporting Alawite civilians in cages around Douma/E. Ghouta, #Syria."[7] Another observer added: "Barbarian traitors attempt to save their lives, they use #HumanShields in #Syria #Douma!!"[8] Not unlike the snuff clips showing ISIS militants beheading prisoners, audiences around the world were captivated by the pictures of people confined in cages and paraded like animals in a zoo. The charged frames may have stirred compassion toward those who were forced to become shields, but they also presented the rebels as savages.

BARBARISM, LAW, AND IMAGES

International law and barbarity are intricately tied. The law, according to the canonical perspective, developed as a set of norms introducing and regulating humane ways of waging warfare, while barbarism designates the violation of these norms. To substantiate the accusations of violations, images are often circulated and then interpreted as depicting instances of barbarity—as we saw, for example, in the Italian media campaign against Ethiopia (chapter 6).

This is even more pronounced today, in an age where brutal images of war can circulate and become viral through various media platforms.

By the time the rebels displayed the caged human shields, Assad's regime had killed many hundreds of civilians in Douma, and, as the images in the video suggest, most buildings in the town had been damaged by air strikes. Just two months earlier, a series of Syrian aerial attacks had killed 112 civilians in one of the town's markets.[9] Immediately after the bombings, several international actors accused the regime of indiscriminate bombings that breached the laws of war.

In response, Damascus insisted that like the United States it was waging a war against "terrorists," while its foreign minister Walid Muallem asserted that "many of the terrorists use civilians as human shields, so what is claimed about massacres in Douma or elsewhere is fabricated news."[10] Those who died, the regime declared, were not civilians but human shields deployed by the rebels. Echoing liberal militaries engaged in the war on terror, the Assad regime asserted that the rebels were the ones responsible for the deaths.

There was, however, no evidence of rebels using human shields in or around the market during that period, so the regime presumably made up the charge in order to frame the rebels as the ones violating international law. The rebels' decision to place Alawite civilians in cages a few weeks later can thus be understood as a reaction that made the charge real. Their message was straightforward: since you do not abide by international law when you bomb civilians, we will not abide by the law either; we will actually deploy Alawite prisoners as human shields.

Both the Syrian regime and the rebels carried out egregious violations, yet only the rebels were tagged as barbarians. This suggests that while appalling violations of international law may be a necessary condition for being branded barbarian, they are insufficient. Barbarity is not only about the disruption of dominant norms and the breakdown of the systems of rules by which societies regulate the relations among their members.[11] Rather, contemporary conceptions of barbarity during war are dependent on the production and circulation of images and on the sensibilities of the targeted audiences. The circulation of images thus becomes a necessary tool for mobilizing a range of emotions around trauma and suffering and for framing certain acts as barbarous and others as legal and legitimate.[12]

This had definitely been the case in Ethiopia when the Italian government labeled the Ethiopian forces as savages in its propaganda campaign, even though the Italians had perpetrated the most egregious war crimes in the

African country, including the use of nerve gas and widespread aerial bombings. In the reports it sent to the League of Nations, the fascist government included numerous images of dead Italian soldiers who had been mutilated by the Ethiopians and of injured combatants who had been shot by prohibited weapons such as dumdum bullets.[13] Mussolini understood that circulating images of barbarity can shape the interpretation of international law.

Although there are many reasons why certain images manage to frame belligerents as barbarian and others do not, when it comes to human shields, the perception of militants as savages is informed by the suffering they inflict to the human body. The shock produced by the images of caged humans appears to emanate from the conversion of the human into both an animal and a weapon. And the transformation of the human body into a weapon, as Banu Bargu has shown in her accounts of both human shields and political prisoners on hunger strike, is an outrage against liberal morality, rendering those who weaponize the body as uncivilized.[14]

In Syria, however, the rebels were not fighting an anticolonial war, and, more crucially, they produced and circulated their own homemade spectacle of barbarity. It seems that they generated this image in order to assert their existence and legitimacy in the global political sphere while simultaneously rejecting the order—in this case, the law of armed conflict—that distinguishes between civilized and barbarian. After four years of fighting, the rebels knew all too well that armed opposition groups do not have formal legal status unless they are recognized as a national liberation movement, a rare occurrence given that such recognition amounts to a state confessing to being a colonial power, alien occupier, or racist regime.[15] They understood that the distinction between state and nonstate actors is at the root of the opposition between civilized and uncivilized.[16] Since these rebels were not recognized by the international legal order, including being denied participation in the development and ratification of the laws of war that bind them, it appears as if they chose to reject the system altogether and play the role of the barbarians.

COLONIAL PRESENT

A year and a half after images of caged shields in Douma began circulating on social media, a clip showing a twenty-six-year-old Kashmiri civilian tied to the front of an army jeep transformed another act of coercive human shielding into a global spectacle. The incident occurred on the day

FIGURE 28. Farooq Dar tied to a jeep and used as a human shield in Kashmir, 2017. Credit: Twitter.

parliamentary by-elections were held in Kashmir, a predominantly Muslim region that for decades has been at the center of a dispute between India and Pakistan. Police reports suggest that the man, Farooq Dar, a local shawl weaver, had cast his vote at a polling booth and was then picked up by an army patrol and strapped to the spare tire lodged at the front of a jeep with a sign saying "This is the fate that will befall stone throwers" pinned to his chest.[17] For an excruciating five hours he was held in this position, paraded at the head of an army convoy that traveled through several villages (figure 28).[18]

Unlike in Douma, where the rebels staged the deployment of human shields and distributed the grotesque images on social media, in this case the act of forced shielding was carried out by the state's army. A bystander captured a short clip on his cellphone of Dar strapped to the jeep and posted it on Twitter, thus turning the Orwellian nightmare where civilians are being incessantly watched by an omnipresent state apparatus on its head. In the era of digital citizenship, a civilian armed with a phone can expose the practices of state militaries and transform them into a global spectacle broadcast by major news agencies.

This incident was also different from the one in Douma in that the clip exposed the state's criminal activity, rather than wrongdoing by rebels or insurgents. Yet despite widespread international condemnation, neither the Indian government nor its military apologized. The officer responsible said Dar had been seized because he had led a stone-throwing mob that was

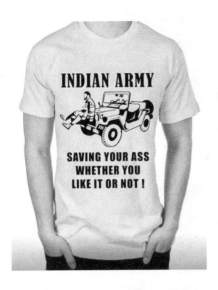

FIGURE 29. T-shirt with an image of Dar strapped to the jeep. Credit: India Today.

besieging a polling station—an accusation denied by both Dar and witnesses. The same officer also claimed that the decision had been spontaneous and justified tying Dar to the jeep by asserting that doing so "had saved 12 lives."[19]

Instead of trying to suppress the spectacle, which depicts an act that the International Committee of the Red Cross called "cruel and barbaric," the ruling Bharatiya Janata Party (Indian People's Party) celebrated it. A party spokesperson who owns an online fashion company, began selling T-shirts with an image of Dar strapped to the jeep; its caption read: "Indian army . . . saving your ass whether you like it or not"[20] (figure 29). Within a few days the shirts were sold out. Through the spectacle, human shielding had become a political commodity.

At one point the Indian government did announce that there would be an inquiry into the incident, but on 22 May 2017, before the inquiry had been completed, the army awarded the officer a commendation medal for his "sustained efforts during counter-insurgency operations."[21] General Bipin Rawat, commander of the Indian army, explained that the medal was given as a way of boosting the morale among young officers. He described the deployment of a human shield as an "innovation" and went on to note that the armed forces have the right to self-defense, and by using Dar as a shield, the army avoided the need to fire on the crowd. Human shielding was portrayed as a humane act of violence. "People are throwing stones at us, people are throwing petrol bombs at us. If my men ask me what do we do, should I say, just

FIGURE 30. Two Palestinians used as human shields on a train's pony truck extension, 1930s. Credit: Haganah Museum.

wait and die? I will come with a nice coffin with a national flag and I will send your bodies home with honor. Is it what I am supposed to tell them as chief? I have to maintain the morale of my troops who are operating there."[22]

Actually, strapping Dar to the jeep was by no means innovative, not even in the Indian landscape. The British had often deployed human shields in their colonies, indicating that the decision to decorate the officer reflects how colonial strategies of domination and oppression bleed into the present.[23] Indeed, in a 1920 British governmental report about how colonial forces dealt with disturbances in Punjab, the investigating committee found that "in some places [British forces] took certain people from villages as hostages. It appears to have been done on a fairly large scale. These people were not themselves guilty of having done anything but they were taken in order to ensure the good behavior of their respective villages, and for the purpose of creating a general impression and also to put pressure on the villagers to give information about offences that had been committed."[24]

The idea of using hostages for ensuring the "good behavior" of the population was also put to use in other British colonies. Major A. F. Perrott of Peshawar suggested in a 1938 letter to the British Mandatory police in Palestine that it "might be worthwhile forming a 'hostage corps' composed of the sons of hostiles. A couple of these in the front car of a convoy would discourage the use of land mines. On the Frontiers we often push the relatives of an outlaw in front of a police party when entering a house where an outlaw is suspected of hiding."[25] At the time, Palestinians had carried out frequent acts of anticolonial sabotage against British installations, including railway lines and trains. In response, the British equipped the train with a "pony truck" on which "hostages could be made to sit" (figure 30). These Palestinians served both as human shields against ambush and as "human mine sweepers" against any land mines placed on the tracks.[26]

The similarity between these colonial practices and the way the Indian army dealt with civil protests in Kashmir suggests that although the context has changed, the specter of colonial rule lingers in India.[27]

RESISTANCE SPECTACLE

Spectacles of human shielding do not always depict the shield as vulnerable, particularly if they are voluntary shields who resist the powers that be. A good example of this is the image of Ieshia Evans, an African American woman who had traveled from her home in New York City to Louisiana to protest the killing of Alton Sterling, an unarmed black man shot to death by Baton Rouge police officers. As thousands gathered for the July 2016 demonstration, Evans walked into the middle of the street to oppose an advancing row of officers dressed like Robocops in military garb. She confronted them, the lone woman against the armed men whose faces are covered.

The image represents the unequal power differential between the police and the African American community, while her gender fits perfectly with the stereotypical assumptions about contemporary human shields. Yet her stoic gaze, planted feet, and perfect posture undermine this stereotype since the image presents a woman who is willing to put her life on the line to defend all those standing behind her, people who are located outside the photograph's frame.

Captured by a Reuters photographer, the image immediately went viral on social media, because it highlighted the way the militarized police confront demonstrations organized by the Black Lives Matter movement, while simultaneously underscoring a single woman's unfaltering courage as she confronts a platoon of men armed to their teeth. Evans appears by no means weak or helpless, and therefore her image became a symbol for civil resistance (figure 31).[28]

After being arrested and then released from custody, she explained: "I have a six-year-old son, Justin, and I fear more for his life than I do for my own."[29]

FIGURE 31. Ieshia Evans in front of an advancing line of police officers in Baton Rouge after the police killing of an unarmed black man, 2016. Credit: Jonathan Bachman, Reuters.

She was alluding to the precarity of black boys and men in the United States, who have been systematically targeted by police forces.[30] The power of her image emerges not only from her willingness to shield the protestors standing behind her but also because her body functions as a screen that renders visible racism against blacks and the oppression that accompanies it. Evans is, in other words, shielding the whole black community in the United States, whose lives, she asserts, matter.[31]

The image of Ieshia Evans standing opposite the police thus works in a very different way than the two other spectacles of human shielding. If the images of Syrians held in cages and of Farooq Dar tied to a jeep became iconic because they highlighted how human beings can be debased, the image from Baton Rouge presents the figure of the human shield as upright in both the literal and ethical sense of the word. It becomes an icon of power that highlights the "contributions of black people to humanity," while underscoring "their resilience in the face of deadly oppression."[32] In this case, then, the spectacle of human shielding stands in stark contrast with Syria and Kashmir and highlights a form of human liberation rather than dehumanization.

TWENTY-ONE

Computer Games

Human Shields in Virtual Wars

OVER THE YEARS HUMAN SHIELDING has also made its way into computer games. One of the early hints of the power and influence of virtual games is in Orson Scott Card's 1985 science fiction novel *Ender's Game,* about an alien race that intends to colonize Earth and obliterate the human race. In preparation against the attack, Earth's international fleet creates a program for gifted children, training them to command military spacecrafts through simulation games. Ender Wiggin is recruited by one of the colonels when he is about six years old, and after four years of training, he is asked to command a fleet in a series of simulated battles against the aliens, who are disparagingly called buggers. In the final test, Ender's fleet is outnumbered by the buggers, but he manages to fire a molecular detachment device that destroys the bugger fleet and their whole planet. Afterward, Ender is informed that the battle was not a simulation game and that he had actually won the war by killing millions of buggers.[1]

With the gradual "gamification of combat,"[2] aspects of *Ender's Game* have migrated from fiction into reality. Although flight simulations have been employed by militaries since the mid-twentieth century, it was in 1980, five years before the publication of *Ender's Game,* that Atari marketed for military use a first-person shooter game, *Army Battlezone,* in which the player occupies the character of a virtual protagonist and experiences weapon-based combat through the character's eyes.[3] In 1997, a US Marine general recognized that virtual games operate both on the body and mind and improve a soldier's preparedness for combat. Consequently, he sent out a directive allowing the use of computer-based war games when training infantry troops for warfare.[4]

Since then, virtual games have had a dramatic effect on the military's education and training programs, with the US Department of Defense spending

$4 billion annually to develop and integrate computerized war games into the curriculum of every war college in the United States.[5] These games prepare cadets for battle by simulating the use of automated weapons, such as drones and killer robots currently being developed for the military.[6] Most of these games are designed in countries whose militaries and governments claim the moral high ground in their deployment of lethal violence during war. But paradoxically, several computer games include functions that enable the player not only to deploy ruthless violence, but also to weaponize innocent civilians—a practice that these countries condemn as inhumane human shielding.

HOME SCHOOLING

Orson Scott Card certainly forecast that computers would play a central role in training combatants, that future wars would be fought from a distance using computers, and even that computer games might be used as an interactive recruitment device. Yet he envisioned combat training as remaining a military enterprise operated by a centralized authority.[7] Today, however, war simulations have also become permanent fixtures in the private sphere, allowing millions of civilians across the globe to participate in virtual wars from the comfort of their homes.

About 2.2 billion gamers regularly sit at home on their computers around the world, many of them playing action-packed war games that fuse virtual boot camps with special operations aimed at eliminating enemies. They can learn about warfare through games like *Call of Duty* and *America's Army*. A 2015 report suggests that in the United States alone, 80 percent of households have a gaming device and over 155 million citizens play games, many of which are extremely violent.[8]

Unlike the passive consumption of other forms of military-themed entertainment, such as television or movies, in virtual war games participants are not merely active spectators who either support or oppose war, but they are transformed into virtual combatants, engendering fantasies of military participation among civilians. In fact, a recent recruitment drive by the British Army targeted gamers with one of their posters reading, "Are you a binge gamer? The Army needs you and your drive."[9] In many ways, war games have managed to merge the battlefield with the private home, creating a culture that in its own unique way undermines the distinction between civilians and combatants.[10]

FIGURE 32. A drone pilot with his joystick. Credit: Carsten Rehder, Alamy.

The invasion of computer war games into leisure activities is part of what communication studies scholar Roger Stahl has called "militainment": state violence translated into an object of pleasurable consumption.[11] The interactive mode of computer games, which invites citizens to step through the screen and become virtual protagonists in the action, serves as a primary interface governing the civic experience of war.[12] The war games, many of which receive development funding from both the military and the military industry, are, however, not merely entertaining but also assume an important educative role.[13]

One commander explained that the use of computer simulations in the military "proved to be a smooth transition for younger generations of soldiers, who, after all, were spoon fed on Nintendo and computer games."[14] This suggests that high-tech militaries the world over are now enjoying the fruits of home schooling.[15] In the words of two experts, "Young military personnel raised on a diet of video games now kill real people remotely using joysticks" (figure 32).[16] In a culture dominated by simulations, where automated weapons are rapidly becoming an instrument of choice among high-tech militaries, it is not an exaggeration to say that today civilians can train themselves to become killers.[17]

Considering that millions of the civilians playing virtual war games every day are children, then these games not only help to undermine the principle of distinction between civilian and combatant but can also be said to educate children to become soldiers.[18] They are not only trained to "rapidly react to fast moving visual and auditory stimuli, and to switch back and forth between different subtasks," but they also gain "cognitive flexibility" as they are taught what constitutes "correct comportment."[19] Operating on both the body and the mind, these games circulate different messages about good and bad, humane and inhumane, and the meaning of heroism and manliness, which engender and help normalize certain habits and dispositions toward violence and war. Some of these learned habits involve the use of human shields.

THE HUMAN SHIELD FUNCTION

In several first-person shooter games, players can deploy human shields. How the human-shield function operates in these games reveals not only how shields are imagined and deployed in this interactive world of militainment. It also lays bare a series of ethical messages about human shields and those who use them.[20] In *The Last of Us, Army of Two,* and many other games, the protagonist occupied by the player is the one deploying human shields. When the gamer presses a button, the character he or she incarnates randomly grabs a nearby figure—frequently an enemy combatant but at times a civilian— and uses this figure as a shield against enemy fire (figures 33 and 34). As the game continues, the shield is often killed in the fray, frequently by enemies who shoot at the gamer's character but strike the shield instead. In other instances, the shield is killed by the gamer's character, who, after using the hostage as a shield, executes him or her.

The gamer's successful deployment of human shields attests to his or her swift reactions, flexibility, and adaptability and is part of mastering the game's increasing levels of difficulty. Significantly, the use of shields is cast as the product of the virtual combatant's spontaneous decision rather than a specific order coming from above. The act of deploying human shields is part of a broader inculcation process, whereby the gamer qua combatant is incited not only to exploit anything that may advance the mission but also to assume responsibility for the situation. Instead of receiving specific instructions, the gamer is encouraged to be creative and imagine what needs to be accomplished in each level in order to carry out the mission. Through trial and error, he or she is trained to imagine in the "correct" way. The gamer is thus

FIGURE 33. Scene from *The Last of Us*.

FIGURE 34. A human shield in *Army of Two*.

shaped as an individualized, self-reliant, and self-sufficient combatant who is responsible for the mission's success.

The act of shielding in the games is always one on one, where the gamer grabs a character and uses him or her as a shield. This stands in sharp contrast to the real-life accusations of shielding that have become common in the past decade—for instance, in Sri Lanka and Mosul—where militants were blamed for transforming thousands of civilians populating safe zones, neighborhoods, and even whole cities into human shields. In the games, the shield is always a single character, the space in which shielding occurs is circumscribed, and the interaction between the gamer's character and the human shield reproduces and reinforces well-established norms of manliness and heroism.

Actually, the format of virtual human shielding in computer games is reminiscent of real shielding practices used in war. During the Second Intifada (2000–2005), for instance, while invading the main Palestinian population centers, the Israeli military routinely coerced Palestinians to act as shields. Soldiers would "pick a civilian at random and force him to protect them by doing dangerous tasks that put his life at risk." These tasks included entering buildings to check if they were booby-trapped, removing suspicious objects from roads used by the army, standing inside houses where soldiers had set up military positions so that armed resistance groups would not fire at the soldiers, and walking in front of soldiers to shield them from gunfire while the soldiers held a gun to their back and sometimes fired over their shoulder.[21]

Similar forms of involuntary human shielding were practiced during the two world wars, in the former Yugoslavia, and in other conflicts, and presumably these serve as the model for the human shielding function in virtual games. In this way, games and reality are mutually constitutive. Yet, in games involuntary shielding becomes even more cruel.

VIRTUAL BARBARITY

In first-person shooter games, human shields are more like props than humans. The value ascribed to human beings is completely deflated. Unlike real human shields, they lack any legal and political value and therefore are incapable of producing deterrence. Instead, they are objectified to such an extent that they come to represent sponge-like beings that have the capacity to absorb enemy bullets. Like other figures who appear on the screen, there is nothing really human about them; they lack any depth and are portrayed as exploitable instruments to be disposed of if doing so advances the protagonist's goals.

Significantly, the human shielding function is featured in the games' marketing appeals. In the description on Amazon.com of the action-shooter game *Dead to Rights: Retribution,* shoppers are told that players get to personify Jack Slate and take part in "extensive hand-to-hand fighting functionality, including numerous branching combos, blocks, counters and even the ability to toss enemies aside or into each other and use them as human shields." The blurb goes on to encourage gamers to deploy human shields "for dynamic cover."[22] Among the challenges advertised on Tom Clancy's *Splinter Cells* is a task called "Human Kevlar" that prompts gamers to "mark & execute 3 enemies while holding a human shield"; in another task, called "Collateral Damage," gamers are incited to "grab an enemy into [*sic*] human shield, then use him to bash down a door."[23] The online write-up for *Turning Point: Fall of Liberty* says that players get to adopt "guerrilla tactics to outflank superior enemy forces," including the use of human shields.[24]

Strikingly, in this virtual orbit, the illegal deployment of involuntary human shields is not only presented as legitimate but, at times, is even romanticized as a means for advancing liberation. This stands in stark contrast to the widespread moral aversion against the coercive use of human bodies as military buffers and its depiction in the media as a barbaric act. Obviously, much can be said about the moral registers advanced by first-person shooter games and how they shape the conduct of players. Certainly, in encouraging gamers to use human shields, the games invert the racist analogy between civilized and barbaric and between Western and non-Western warfare that has been central to the ethical condemnation of human shielding practices. From the comforts of their homes, gamers prepare for battles where the "civilized soldier" is urged to become a barbarian.

TWENTY-TWO

Protest

Civil Disobedience as an Act of War

IN NOVEMBER 2016, HEADLINES ACROSS the United States, ranging from the *New York Times* to Fox News, announced that two thousand veterans were heading to Standing Rock Sioux Reservation to serve as human shields. The veterans had decided to defend the indigenous "water protectors" from fellow uniformed officers after seeing footage of how the peaceful protestors were "brutally attacked by security dogs, blasted with water cannons in subzero temperatures, and fired on with rubber bullets, pepper spray, and bean-bag rounds" while demonstrating against the construction of the Dakota pipeline on their native land. Many veterans felt it was high time to stand up to the government that had once sent them to war (figure 35).[1]

A few months earlier, former Army officer Wes Clark Jr. began following the debate over the controversial 1,170-mile pipeline that would risk contaminating water reservoirs as it shuttled an estimated 470,000 barrels of crude oil every day from North Dakota to Illinois. Watching the standoff, he was appalled by the harsh measures adopted by the law enforcement–backed security contractors against Native Americans. He was appalled by the conclusions of a United Nations investigation that brought testimonies of protestors characterizing the security contractors' conduct as "acts of war."[2] In solidarity with the water protectors, he spent a few weeks trying to assemble a legal team but gradually came to realize that, given the gravity of the situation, legal action would not be sufficient and only peaceful direct action could propel change. Together with a few friends, he began organizing a peaceful army of fellow veterans ready to put their lives on the line.[3]

For some veterans who heeded the call, the mission to shield the water protectors was a way of reconnecting politically to their ancestry. Loreal Black Shawl, who travelled to the reservation from New Mexico, is a

FIGURE 35. Veterans serving as human shields for indigenous water protectors at Standing Rock Sioux Reservation. Credit: Stephen Young, Reuters.

descendant of two Native American tribes, the Oglala Lakota and Northern Arapaho. She had served in the Army for nearly eight years, ending her tenure as a sergeant. When questioned by one news agency about why she had travelled to Standing Rock, she rhetorically asked: "O.K., are you going to treat us veterans who have served our country in the same way as you have those water protectors? We're not [here] to create chaos. We are [here] because we are tired of seeing the water protectors being treated as non-humans."[4] Black Shawl understood that her military fatigues bestowed upon her privileges that her brethren Native Americans did not enjoy; she believed that the police officers would think twice before blasting veterans with water cannons or squirting them with pepper spray.

MILITARIZED POLICE

The veterans were, in a sense, adopting strategies developed by transnational activists, like those involved in the Human Shield Action who had volunteered to shield civilian targets in Iraq. Yet at Standing Rock, the veterans carried out an act that symbolically inverted the legal definition of human shielding. If, according to international law, human shields tend to be civilians who protect military targets, in North Dakota the shields came dressed in military fatigue to protect civilian targets. They hoped that the security forces would identify with them and that this identification, alongside the privilege they wield as a result of having put their life at risk for their country, would generate deterrence. Whereas in Iraq the shields' privilege emanated from being white Western civilians within a space where nonwhite civilians were attacked by a Western military, at Standing Rock the shields' privilege derived mainly from having served in the military.

The veterans' actions exposed in two ways how the border between war and civil protest is increasingly being blurred. First, they highlighted how, in the United States, some citizen-protestors, especially those who are not white, can become legitimate targets, people who can routinely be attacked through quasi-military violence. Second, they underscored how police forces and private security contractors have become highly militarized. The introduction of warfare strategies into the civil sphere, including the use of flash grenades, rubber bullets, and riot teams in full military gear, have propelled citizens to adopt new forms of protest and defense.[5]

The militarization of the police is not a new phenomenon. In the United States it is often traced back to the social upheaval, civil unrest, and culture wars of the 1960s—followed, as writer and educator Anna Feigenbaum notes, by "Nixon's rhetorical wars on crime and drugs in the 1970s, Reagan's all-too-literal drug war of the 1980s, and the massive expansion of SWAT [Special Weapons and Tactics] teams in the 1990s." Over time, military experts, "who saw all protesters as rioters and all rioters as enemies," acquired the status of celebrities in the policing sector.[6] As one investigative reporter points out, in many cities, police departments have given up the traditional blue garb for "battle dress uniforms" modeled after soldier attire, and have acquired armored personnel carriers designed for use in battlespaces, with some departments even boasting of the purchase of Humvees, helicopters, and tanks. Numerous police officers now carry military-grade weapons and are trained by former Special Forces soldiers, Navy SEALs, or Army Rangers.[7] The change has been so dramatic that some legal experts are currently asking whether the protections normally bestowed on civilians in international armed conflict should not be applied to situations of domestic protests and unrest.[8]

The introduction of warfare techniques to deal with civil protests extends beyond the United States and characterizes numerous liberal democracies as well as authoritarian regimes. This helps explain why human shielding, which used to be restricted to civil and interstate wars, is becoming more common in domestic protests. From Venezuela, where priests shield anti-Maduro activists attacked by riot police, to Catalonia, where firefighters shield their fellow citizens from state violence, privileged civilians engage in acts of shielding because unarmed protestors are routinely subjected to fierce violence not unlike the violence used in conflict zones.[9] And like civilians who are targeted in conflict zones, these citizens often come from marginalized backgrounds that can be traced back to colonialism and slavery.

Yet, even as privileged individuals and groups across the globe put themselves on the line as they defend marginalized citizens in acts of solidarity, privilege is not always an effective form of protection. During the American civil rights movement, for example, when African American protestors were subjected to brutal violence by white supremacists and police forces, progressive white activists often joined the demonstrations. Despite their privilege, these whites could not serve as shields because they were considered race traitors and were hated by white supremacists with as much fervor as the black protestors they had joined; accordingly, they had also lost their political value in the eyes of the aggressors.[10] By contrast, in present-day South Africa, where the apartheid color lines still play a role in the public sphere, white students have successfully used their privilege to shield black students as they rallied against unaffordable tuition fees.[11] The ability of privilege to serve as a deterrent is thus contingent on history and geography. For it to be effectively mobilized, the attacking forces must not only acknowledge the shield's privilege—as well as vulnerability—but also identify with it.

HUMAN BARRICADES

Shielding in civil protests is not only about the mobilization of privilege, however. It is also often about engaging the power of a group of people acting collectively.[12] Shielding informed by these two strategies simultaneously tends to be the most effective. A single person acting as a shield, regardless of his or her privilege, can only rarely evoke sufficient deterrence to protect those who he or she wants to shield. The veterans' ability to influence the situation at Standing Rock, even if only for a few days, was due not only to the place veterans occupy in the US public's imagination, but also because two thousand of them created a human barricade between the water protectors and the security forces.[13] More often, it is the collective action rather than the use of privilege that does the job. Indeed, in numerous countries across the globe, acts of human shielding have been successful when masses of people joined together to protect a target. One of the best-known instances took place in the Philippines during the final days of Ferdinand Marcos's military regime.[14]

Political anthropologist Kurt Schock chronicles how, after two years of sustained unrest marked by campaigns of nonviolent action, Philippine dictator Ferdinand Marcos called early elections in an attempt to shore up his rule. Following the February 1986 vote, Marcos immediately declared himself the winner, but his opponent, Corazon Aquino, organized a rally of approximately two million people where she proclaimed victory for herself and "the people." Simultaneously, the minister of defense and a group of officers decided to force Marcos out of office, gathering their soldiers in two military bases just outside of Manila, while announcing their allegiance to Aquino.[15]

Marcos was furious and ordered the military to crush the resistance, but that evening, Archbishop Sin urged people to support the mutiny, and, in response, tens of thousands of pro-democracy sympathizers assembled around the military bases where the rebels had retreated.[16] As the tanks approached the bases, unarmed civilians led by nuns and priests formed a human barricade between the tanks and the rebels. The human barricade effectively immobilized Marcos's troops, and they subsequently retreated. These dramatic events sparked a nationwide defection of soldiers and officers who were unwilling to fire at the thousands of civilians gathered outside the military bases. This allowed Cory Aquino to form a parallel government on February 25, and, as she took the presidential oath, four United States military helicopters transported Marcos and his entourage to an air base north of Manila and, the following day, to Hawaii.[17] Collective human shielding carried out by the people had won the day.

From 1968, when students across Europe routinely created human chains to protect fellow protestors who were targeted by police, to Tahrir Square in Egypt in 2013, when hundreds of men formed a shield to protect female protestors from attacks by supporters of former President Morsi, citizens have formed human barricades as a form of shielding.[18] Again, these barricades achieve deterrence not so much due to the privileged status of those who stand together, but because the forces they challenge were unwilling to exert violence against the masses.

While the purpose of such collective shielding is usually to protect targeted people from violence, it also protects the public sphere—the space where people can assemble and act in concert. Indeed, the formation of human barricades to protect fellow citizens is not only a political act par excellence, it is an act that shields the sphere of protest, deliberation, and persuasion from violence that aims to destroy it.[19]

THE PARADOX OF SHIELDING

As government forces try to restrict and condense spheres of protest and resistance, activists across the globe are drawing connections between different struggles and producing forms of transnational solidarity. In August 2014, after police officer Darren Wilson shot and killed Michael Brown, an eighteen-year-old African American, in Ferguson, Missouri, SWAT teams were sent in to quell the protest of hundreds of African Americans who filled the streets. And as images emerged of armed police in riot gear and armored vehicles tear-gassing the demonstrators, Palestinians who had experienced similar violence expressed their solidarity from thousands of miles away.[20] Mariam Barghouti, a Palestinian American writer and at that time a student at Birzeit University in the West Bank, sent off a supportive tweet: "Always make sure to run against the wind / to keep calm when you're teargassed, the pain will pass, don't rub your eyes! #Ferguson Solidarity."[21] Standing opposite a row of police officers, protestors in Missouri reciprocated the gesture, chanting, "Gaza Strip! Gaza Strip!"[22]

As tactics of oppression travel across the globe, so do the tactics of resistance; yet the forms of struggle adopted in each new setting are often reshaped in order to fit the specific political, cultural, and legal context.[23] When citizens in Toronto, Canada, took to the streets to express their anger at the grand jury's decision to exonerate Darren Wilson for the killing of Michael Brown, the organizers asked white protestors to stay away from the center of the action and instead to serve as human shields between black protestors and the police. They posted the following statement on their Facebook page: "While we appreciate the solidarity shown by White and Non-Black POC, [we] want to remind folks of some things: Please refrain from taking up space in all ways possible. Remember that you are there in support of black folks, so should never be at the center of anything. Refrain from speaking to the media. Black voices are crucial to this. Stand behind black folks or between us and the police. If you see a cop harassing a black person, come in and engage (chances are they are least likely to arrest you)."[24]

In a blog published on *Huffington Post,* Eternity Martis, one of the black activists in Toronto, noted that some white protestors "decided to rage and whine on the Black Lives Matter protest Facebook group about how this was segregation, and how your life matters too, and how we should screw ourselves if we don't want to include you."[25] She described how towards the end of the protest white activists were politely asked to move: "A small act of kindness to let your fellow black protesters get a glance at the center." After thanking those who did move, she criticized those who didn't, or who moved but didn't want to: "If you're having trouble with that, you either disliked having a black person tell you what to do, or you are so full of your white privilege that you didn't feel you needed to move."[26]

Martis was underscoring the fact that strategies of resistance—in this case, human shielding—can, at times, replicate and reinforce the structures they are fighting to dismantle. The concerns she expressed were similar to those voiced by political theorist Banu Bargu, who was among the first to analyze the paradoxical effect of voluntary human shielding in war zones. Bargu claims that insofar as the global public responds favorably to voluntary human shielding, this form of shielding actually risks lending recognition and legitimacy to Western privilege, reinstalling "a colonial hierarchy of lives in the very process of challenging that hierarchy. It devalues the work, suffering, and death of local, non-Western activists and at times even deflects attention away from the deaths of the populations that human shields ultimately seek to protect."[27]

At the same time, Bargu recognizes that voluntary shields are carrying out courageous nonviolent acts, at times risking their own lives to protect the lives of others.[28] Human shielding thus operates simultaneously on two levels: the civilian's *body* and the social *perception* of the civilian by the global public. The shield's body—frequently that of a privileged citizen—is subjected to risk as part of a strategy of protection and resistance, yet the perception of the privileged shield, who is ostensibly worth more than those he or she is shielding, can reinforce existing structures of domination.

Many progressive organizers around the world are acutely familiar with this paradox. The Palestinian popular committees that for over a decade organized weekly protests in West Bank villages such as Bil'in and Nabi Saleh invited both international and Israeli activists to join them, recognizing that the presence of white Westerners might lower the levels of violence exerted by the Israeli military forces confronting them. The non-Palestinians were asked to join the protests and, if need be, serve as shields, on the condition that they follow their hosts' instructions. Frequently, whole villages would take part in the protests, with Israeli and foreign activists serving as human shields.

WHERE ARE THE CHILDREN?

Unlike the Native Americans in Standing Rock and Palestinians in the West Bank, Palestinians in the Gaza Strip cannot invite foreign citizens to join their weekly demonstrations because Israel keeps the Strip under a state of siege that restricts the entry of non-Gazans into the area. Moreover, in Gaza, no one has enough privilege to serve as a shield. Even so, the figure of the human shield is often invoked by the Israeli military to frame demonstrators taking part in civil protests.

In March 2018, thousands of Palestinian civilians began marching every Friday towards the militarized fence surrounding the Gaza Strip. They called the protests the Great March of Return, alluding to their right to return to the lands from which their families were expelled in 1948; simultaneously, they were protesting their incarceration in the world's largest open-air prison.[29] Week in and week out, they marched towards the fence in the hope that people around the world would heed their call and exhibit solidarity.

As thousands strode towards the fence in what became a weekly ritual, Israeli snipers ended up killing hundreds and wounding thousands of unarmed protestors. On numerous occasions, not long after the week's protest, the military spokesperson unit disseminated images and videos depicting young children intermingling with the demonstrators through its Facebook, Twitter, and YouTube accounts. Similar to the info-war waged during its 2014 war on Gaza, this time the Israeli military also blamed the Palestinians for deploying human shields, even though the accusation came in a context of civil protest. The goal was to stir moral indignation against Palestinians while also providing a legal defense for the snipers lined up at the border.

One short video clip plays a lullaby interspersed with the sound of gunfire and rhetorically asks, "Where are the children of Gaza today?" After showing children amid the protestors, it then displays the word "HERE" in large letters across the screen (figure 36). Such montages are used as proof that

Israel Defense Forces @IDF

Do you know where your children are?

HERE

43.9K views   0:16 / 0:18

4:36 PM · May 14, 2018 · Twitter for iPhone

615 Retweets   1K Likes

FIGURE 36. Israel Defense Forces video clip asserting that Palestinians use their children as human shields, 2018. Credit: IDF Twitter.

Palestinians are using children as human shields.[30] Morally, the charge intimates that the Palestinians are savages, that they have no problem sending their young sons and daughters to the front lines. As with the infographics that were disseminated during the Gaza War, the subtext is that civilized people protect their children whereas Palestinians sacrifice them.

This is precisely the message Danny Danon, Israel's ambassador to the United Nations, conveyed in a letter he sent to the Security Council. "Hamas is committing grave violations of international law" during the weekly protests, he declared, adding that "their terrorists continue to hide behind innocent children to ensure their own survival."[31] By portraying the protestors as Hamas terrorists hiding behind shields, Danon, in effect, categorizes any Palestinian from Gaza who participates in civil protests as a terrorist who is consequently killable.

The fact that Israel has employed the same accusation of human shielding in order to justify its indiscriminate killing of civilians both in situations of war, such as the 2014 aggression, and in civil protests, such as the Great March of Return, suggests that in Israel's eyes, the notion of civilianhood for Palestinians has disappeared.[32]

PROPHECY

The framing of the Palestinian civilians taking part in the protests as human shields intimates that all of the protestors are legitimate targets; therefore, the Israeli military cannot be accused of perpetrating crimes against civilians for the simple reason that there are no civilians among the protestors in Gaza.[33] This is the argument Israel has constructed to justify the deployment of lethal violence against Gaza's civilian population. Like in many colonies of old, in which colonial armies disregarded the distinction between combatants and noncombatants, Israel refuses to differentiate between the military and civil spheres in the Gaza Strip.

However, in this case the way Israel invokes the figure of the human shield also exposes an inherent relationship between civilianhood and citizenship. For the stateless Palestinians trapped in Gaza, the right to enjoy the protections offered to civilians by international law is intertwined with the right to liberate themselves from colonial occupation and achieve the status of citizens within a state of their own. In Gaza, the protections offered by international law and the right to self-determination and citizenship are simultaneously denied.

Arguably, in many ways the situation in Palestine may also very well be predicting our future. Israel's treatment of Gaza's civilian population is undoubtedly extreme, but the logic driving Israel's security forces is not that different from the logic informing security forces in other areas of the world that cast their own citizenry, especially marginalized groups, as security threats, as the protests from Standing Rock to Kashmir and back to Ferguson reveal. The threat of using lethal violence against demonstrators is dangerous not only because of the harm it inflicts, but also because it frames civil protestors as enemies who can be confronted with military force.[34] It is precisely in this sense that Gaza becomes a terrifying prophecy, exposing how the denial of civilian protections in war zones is informing attacks on citizens participating in protests from the Americas to Europe and the Middle East and all the way to Asia and Australia. The almost complete erosion of the civilian in Gaza is an omen, a sign of the increasing precarity of citizenship and the protections that it promises.

ACKNOWLEDGMENTS

This book, like our previous one, *The Human Right to Dominate,* is the result of friendship and an ongoing fertile scholarly exchange. We consequently share equal responsibility for both the contributions and the mistakes it might contain. We would like to thank Niels Hooper from the University of California Press for believing in the book and for pushing us to make it accessible to a wide audience. The manuscript has benefited a great deal from Carolyn Bond's meticulous editing, brilliant suggestions, and insistence that the narrative and arguments should be as clear and tight as possible. Barbara Armentrout intervened at a later stage, and her eye for the details did wonders to the manuscript.

We wish to thank Benedikt Buechel, Jacob Burns, Samantha Freeze, and Sophie Knowles-Mofford for providing vital research assistance, Ari Rottenberg for suggesting that we look at the use of human shields in computer games, and Aviv Rottenberg for helping to prepare the images. As we wrote the book, Catherine Rottenberg read each chapter, often several times, offering invaluable advice while urging us to sharpen our arguments. Elliott Colla, Laleh Khalili, Frédéric Mégret, and Jessica Whyte read the whole manuscript and provided extremely helpful suggestions on how to improve it.

Like most books, this one also took several years to write. During this process, different people read drafts of chapters, commented on presentations, or offered insightful suggestions in the course of casual conversations. In an early discussion, Kate Wahl provided an incredibly helpful recommendation that helped us structure the book. For their helpful suggestions along the way, we are also extremely grateful to Lori Allen, Lorenzo Alunni, Merav Amir, Sarah Banet-Weiser, Lisa Baraitser, Banu Bargu, Simon Bayly, Nitza Berkovitch, Jack Bratich, John Chalcraft, Tanzil Chowdhury, Yinon Cohen, Ayça Çubukçu, Beshara Doumani, David Eng, Noura Erakat, Sara Farris, Dani Filc, Maayan Geva, Penny Green, Michal Givoni, Susan Gzesh, Markus Gunneflo, Lisa Hajjar, Samir Harb, Iain Hardie, Omar Jabary Salamanca, Craig Jones, Ratna Kapur, Tobias Kelly, Nadim Houry, Nadim Khoury,

Becky Kook, Hagar Kotef, Karin Loevy, Mark Levine, Thomas MacManus, Eva Nanopoulos, Vasuki Nesiah, Mihaela Mihai, Samuel Moyn, Donna Mulhearn, Kieran Oberman, Sharon Pardo, Renee Poznanski, John Reynolds, Massimo Riva, Teemu Ruskola, Farah Saleh, Adham Saouli, Yezid Sayigh, Tommaso Sbriccoli, Beth Van Schaack, Joan W. Scott, Lynne Segal, Hugo Slim, Thomas Spijkerboer, Rebecca Sutton, Andrea Teti, Mathias Thaler, Peter Thomas, Mandy Turner, Barbara Van Dyck, Christiane Wilke, Al Withrow, Jonathan Whittall, Niza Yanay, Oren Yiftachel, and Francesco Zucconi.

Neve wishes to thank Penny Green for her support, friendship and for being a wonderful interlocutor. His research was made possible by generous fellowships from the American Council of Learned Societies, the Leverhulme Trust, and European Union's Horizon 2020 Research and Innovation Programme MSCA-IF-2015–701891. Nicola's research and writing were made possible by a generous fellowship from the Mellon Foundation at Brown University and the European Union's Horizon 2020 Research and Innovation Programme MSCA-IF-2015–703225.

Finally, we wish to thank our families for their incredible support throughout the research and writing process: Rachel Gordon and Amnon Agami, Haim and Rivka Gordon, Nitsan Joy Gordon and Mordechai Gordon, Elizabeth Rottenberg, David and Shelly Rottenberg, Fulvio Perugini, Paola Sinibaldi, Enrica Perugini, Sala Ra'fat, and Sawsan Saleh. Most important, this book could not have been written without the love, care and encouragement of Ari, Aviv, Catherine, Emil, and Farah. This book is dedicated to them.

NOTES

INTRODUCTION

1. Gordon, 2012. Italics added.
2. Skaff, 2012.
3. Mégret, 2010: 23–38.
4. Lee, 2010.
5. National Defense Authorization Act for Fiscal Year 2018.
6. AFP, 10 October 2017, "Trapped in Syria's Raqa, Civilians Become Human Shields for IS," *Borneo Bulletin,* https://borneobulletin.com.bn/trapped-in-syrias-raqa-civilians-become-human-shields-for-is/.
7. AFP, 2017.
8. Gordon and Perugini, 2016b.
9. Bargu, 2013.
10. Throughout the book we use the terms *laws of war, laws of armed conflict, international humanitarian law,* and *international law* interchangeably. On law as power, see Foucault and Ewald, 2003.
11. Starobin, 2017.
12. Sheehan-Dean, 2019: 6–7.
13. Benvenisti and Lustig, 2017.
14. On legal uncertainty and ambiguity in shielding situations see, for instance, Crawford, 2015: 90–91.
15. Kinsella, 2016b.
16. Gregory, 2011a.
17. Chamayou, 2015.
18. Graham, 2009.
19. Bousquet, 2018.
20. Perugini and Gordon, 2017.
21. Cohen, 2013. On the relationship between naming violence and allocating the blame for violence, see Thaler, 2018.

22. Balko, 2013.

23. For a critique of the relationship between law, humanity, and violence, see Asad, 2015. See also Moses, 2020.

24. For a philological investigation of the Roman notion of *humanitas,* see Nybakken, 1939. On the multiple political meanings of the notion of humanity, see Feldman and Ticktin, 2010.

1. CIVIL WAR

1. Starobin, 2017.

2. Reprinted in Scott, 1891b: 145.

3. This correspondence appears in the official war records. Scott, 1891b: 132.

4. Jones, 1911.

5. This is not precise, since Union forces also used prisoners of war as human shields, not only in retaliation to the deployment of human shields by Confederate forces, as in the case described, but also in other instances. General William T. Sherman describes an incident where a young Union officer stepped on a land mine, called torpedo at the time. Consequently, the general "immediately ordered a lot of rebel prisoners to be brought from the provost-guard, armed with picks and spades, and made them march in close order along the road, so as to explode their own torpedoes, or to discover and dig them up. They begged hard, but I reiterated the order, and could hardly help laughing at their stepping so gingerly along the road, where it was supposed sunken torpedoes might explode at each step, but they found no other torpedoes till near Fort McAllister." Sherman, 1875: 194.

6. Jones, 1911.

7. Roman, 1884.

8. Cited in Witt, 2012: 99. For how the 1846–1848 Mexican-American War shaped American legal conceptions, see Grandin, 2019.

9. Cited in Grandin, 2019: 32.

10. Starobin, 2017.

11. Scott, 1891b: 134–135. Italics added.

12. Baxter, 1963.

13. Witt, 2012

14. Lieber, 1863: article 15.

15. Meron, 2000.

16. Lieber, 1863: article 29.

17. Lieber, 1863. See also Kennedy, 2009; Orford, 2003.

18. Scott, 1891b: 135.

19. Scott, 1891b: 143.

20. Dunlap, 2016b; Rubinstein and Roznai, 2011; Schmitt, 2008.

21. Winthrop, 1920: 797n61.

22. The notion that civilians could not be used as human shields was not universal even during the Civil War. On June 23, 1864, just a few days after General Samuel

Jones notified General Foster that he was using prisoners of war as human shields, General William T. Sherman wrote Maj. Gen. J. B. Steedman, "The use of torpedoes in blowing up our cars and the road after they are in our possession, is simply malicious. It cannot alter the great problem, but simply makes trouble. Now, if torpedoes are found in the possession of an enemy to our rear, you may cause them to be put on the ground and tested by wagon-loads of prisoners, or, if need be, citizens implicated in their use. In like manner, if a torpedo is suspected on any part of the road, order the point to be tested by a car-load of prisoners, or citizens implicated, drawn by a long rope." Scott, 1891b: 579. For an analysis of the gendered dimension of human shielding, see Kinsella, 2016b.

23. Cited in Starobin, 2017: 26.

24. Hartman, 1997.

25. Weheliye, 2014.

26. Phillipson, 1911; Hammer, 1944.

27. Kosto, 2012: 1.

28. "British Relations with the Neighbouring Tribes," 1898: 1–380.

29. Vattel, 2008: book 2, clause 245, 400; Oppenheim, 1912: 542.

30. Francis Lieber mentions the use of hostages in the Code's section dealing with prisoners of war, explaining that a "hostage is a person accepted as a pledge for the fulfillment of an agreement concluded between belligerents during the war, or in consequence." He immediately adds that "hostages are rare in the present age." Lieber, 1863: article 54.

31. Lieber, 1863: articles 55 and 56.

32. The Confederate Army also used human shields/hostages following General Lee's seized "unoffending citizens" from his successful attack on Pennsylvania and subjected "them to maltreatment in various ways, in order to effect a particular object, which became apparent when a demand was made for their release. For this purpose quite a number of citizens of Pennsylvania were carried into captivity." Draper, 1870: 500–501.

33. Scott, 1891b: 163.

34. Scott, 1891b: 164.

35. Bargu, 2016.

36. Gordon and Perugini, 2016b.

37. An analysis of this paradox appears in Bargu, 2013.

38. Chambers, 1999: 559.

39. For a detailed account of a confederate prisoner who was used as a human shield on Morris Island and who describes the inhumane conditions of the prisoners, consult Murray, 1911.

2. IRREGULARS

1. Howard, 2005.

2. Badsey, 2014: 58.

3. Förster, 1987.

4. Förster, 1987.

5. Wawro, 2005: 237.

6. Badsey, 2014.

7. For an interesting discussion of the "tellurian" character of partisans, see Schmitt, 2007.

8. Wawro, 2005: 288.

9. Meron, 1998.

10. Badsey, 2014: 58–59.

11. Howard, 2005: 299.

12. Cited in Howard, 2005: 299. See also Wawro, 2005: 279.

13. Wawro, 2005: 238, 265.

14. Hozier and Adams, 1872, vol. 2: 90.

15. Hozier and Adams, 1872, vol. 2: 90.

16. Nabulsi, 1999: 36–38.

17. Hall, 1890: 475.

18. Moltke and Hughes, 1995: 32. For an overview of the German response to the francs-tireurs, see Hull, 2006: 32.

19. Badsey, 2014: 59.

20. Imperial Cabinet of Russia, 1868.

21. These jurists were aware of the 1874 Brussels Declaration—the first attempt to establish international law for the conduct of occupying armies—which was initiated by the Russian Czar Alexander II and may have been the most progressive legal document ever introduced by a major power. The declaration, for instance, recognized the legitimacy of irregulars taking part in war. While it did not mention human shields, it did note that "the population of occupied territory cannot be forced to take part in military operations against its own country." It also insisted that "prisoners of war cannot be compelled in any way to take any part whatever in carrying on the operations of the war." However, due to the state-centric approach that was coalescing among the legal experts of the time, which denied the legitimacy of irregulars, the Brussels Declaration was not universally accepted among the prospective European signatories and was never ratified, and its basic tenets continued to be rejected long after they were formulated. Three decades after the war, the 1902 official German manual on the laws of land war, published by the General Staff in Berlin, discarded the declaration's legal reasoning, especially the sections concerning the prohibition against forcing civilians and prisoners of war to take part in conflict. The manual admits that the use of human shields to stop the destruction of trains was cruel but justifies it on the ground that it had proved completely successful in achieving its objectives. No damage occurred to the trains that carried notables, whereas all previous attempts to prevent "the undoubtedly irregular, even criminal, conduct of a fanatical population" had ended in failure. See Project of an International Declaration concerning the Laws and Customs of War, 1874: article 36. The German manual is cited in Spaight, 1911: 468. Another key

document that circulated at the time was Laws of War on Land, known as the Oxford Manual, 1880.

22. Bonfils, 1898; Hall, 1890; Pillet, 1901.

23. Pillet, 1901: 213.

24. Anghie, 2007: 33.

25. Kennedy, 2009.

26. Anghie, 2007: 43; Bantekas and Oette, 2013: 43.

27. Oppenheim, 1912: 272.

28. Aldrich, 1991.

29. Kalshoven and Zegveld, 2011.

30. Darcy, 2003: 184.

31. Meron, 2000.

32. Scheipers, 2015.

33. Spaight, 1911: 469, 123.

34. Spaight, 1911: 469. See also Sassòli, 2010; Whyte, 2018.

35. Oppenheim, 1912: 273. Italics added.

36. Hall et al., 2013.

37. In this sense they are the direct descendants of political thinkers such as Bodin, 1992, and Hobbes, 1991.

38. Scheipers, 2015: 28.

39. Hobbes, 1991; see also Williams, 1996.

40. Scheipers, 2015.

41. This threat is at the center of Carl Schmitt's reflections in his *Theory of the Partisan*. Referring to the Franco-German War, Schmitt claims that civilians who transform themselves into resistance fighters while hiding among other civilians naturally make state armies anxious. He notes that "the more strictly an army is disciplined—the more decisively it distinguishes between military and civilian, considering only the uniformed opponent as the enemy—the more sensitive and nervous it becomes when an un-uniformed civilian populace joins the battle on the other side." This situation of indistinction in which irregulars use "malicious ruses and treachery" propels militaries to adopt inhumane strategies that violate civilian immunity and may include human shielding. Schmitt, 2007: 17, 24. See also Schmitt, 2006; and Odysseos and Petito, 2007.

3. SETTLERS

1. Mégret, 2006.

2. Read, 2015: 139–144; see also Gallay, 2002.

3. Pakenham, 1979: 3–4.

4. Churchill, 1897.

5. "Boers Wreck a Train. Churchill Is Missing," 17 November 1899, *The Guardian*, https://www.theguardian.com/news/1899/nov/17/mainsection.fromthearchive.

6. Churchill, 2013: 39.

7. Bell, 2016.

8. Hague Convention No. II, 1899.

9. Erakat, 2019: 7.

10. Callwell, 1906. His counterinsurgency treatise was adopted as an army textbook by the British and was later used by the United States Marine Corps in its *Small Wars Manual,* a 1940 handbook that is still considered an essential resource by militaries involved in the war on terror. United States Marine Corps, 1940.

11. Callwell, 1906: 31.

12. Pakenham, 1979: 420–22.

13. Pakenham, 1979: 434–36.

14. Cited in Spies, 1977: 102

15. Spies, 1977: 103.

16. Doyle, 1901.

17. Doyle, 1902: 118.

18. Captain J. Feld, 1901, "Guerillas and Derailing: A Protest," *The Times,* 6 September 1901, 9.

19. Downes, 2008: 156–77.

20. Hobhouse, 1901.

21. Concentration Camps Commission, 1902.

22. Stead, 1901.

23. Frederic Mackarness, 1901, "Train Wrecking," *The Times,* 13 September 1901, 6.

24. Frederic Mackarness, 1902, "Methods of 'Humanity' Sanctioned by the Government," *The Speaker* 5, no. 127: 643–44.

25. "Columns 509–31," 1901.

26. "Columns 509–31," 1901.

27. Cited in Spies, 1977: 240.

28. Spies, 1977: 241–42.

29. One Labor MP asked the secretary of state for war whether noncombatant Boers were being compelled to travel on trains, if they were entitled the status of prisoners of war, and whether "such compulsion is in accordance with the rules laid down in the War Office Manual for the treatment of noncombatants." The MP went on to demand that the practice be stopped. The secretary of state for war, however, was unmoved, replying that the measures were legitimate, in line with the British customs of war contained in the manual and "in no way contrary to the practice of civilised warfare." Column 513," 1902.

30. On the imperialist character of pro-Boer activism in Great Britain, see Khalili, 2013: 220–21; Krebs, 1999; and Nash, 1999.

31. "Columns 707–708," 1902.

32. "Column 1025," 1902.

33. Mackarness, 1902: 644.

4. REPORTS

1. Cited in Lipkes, 2007: 39.
2. Hull, 2006: 120.
3. On *jus ad bellum* and *jus in bello,* see Kolb, 1997.
4. Horne and Krame, 2001: 10–20. See also Lipkes, 2007.
5. Geinitz, 2000: 216–17.
6. Hull, 2014: 17.
7. Hull, 2014: 16–20.
8. Pratt, 1915.
9. For a genealogy of the use of eyewitnesses to denounce mass atrocities, see Wieviorka, 2006; and Givoni, 2016. Wieviorka makes the era of the witness start from World War II and the Eichmann trial. Givoni's genealogy starts earlier, during the Great War, mainly focusing on the witnessing of veterans and survivors in their diaries. The occupation of Belgium with the international denunciations of German atrocities seems to be one of the first instances of massive evidence gathering and eyewitness testimonies in order to accuse an enemy of war crimes in an international conflict.
10. *Correspondence and Report from His Majesty's Consul at Boma,* 1904: 21–80.
11. Official Commission of the Belgian Government, 1915.
12. Hull, 2006: 119.
13. Official Commission of the Belgian Government, 1915: v.
14. Official Commission of the Belgian Government, 1915: xviii.
15. Enloe, 1990.
16. Official Commission of the Belgian Government, 1915: xviii.
17. Official Commission of the Belgian Government, 1915: xviii.
18. Official Commission of the Belgian Government, 1915: xviii.
19. Official Commission of the Belgian Government, 1915: xxxii.
20. Hague Convention No. IV, 1907: article 2.
21. German Imperial Foreign Office, [1915] 1921: viii-xv.
22. German Imperial Foreign Office, [1915] 1921: xv.
23. German Imperial Foreign Office, [1915] 1921: xviii.
24. German Imperial Foreign Office, [1915] 1921: xvi-xvii. On legitimate reprisals, see Oppenheim, 1912.
25. Kingdom of Belgium, 1918: 38.
26. Government of France, 1915: 189–190.
27. Great Britain, Committee on Alleged German Outrages, 1915.
28. Great Britain, Committee on Alleged German Outrages: 53, 61.
29. Wilson, 1979.
30. German Imperial Foreign Office, [1915] 1921: v.
31. Schabas, 2019: 139–49.
32. Pillet, 1916.

33. Risse, Ropp, and Sikkink, 1999. Samuel Moyn provides a much more nuanced genealogy, whereby the agenda of President Carter and non-governmental human rights organizations converged around the 1970s. Moyn, 2010.

5. PEACE ARMY

1. In the wake of World War II, Royden renounced pacifism, claiming that "Nazism is worse than war" and that one must fight against it. See Royden, 1941.
2. Falby, 2004.
3. Fletcher, 1989.
4. Royden, 1915: 6–7.
5. Royden, 1915: 8.
6. Royden, 1915: 12.
7. The idea of a peace army made of civilians who form a buffer between the fighting parties has many antecedents—for instance, the Quaker pacifist sects that used intervene in the American colonies to protect the Indian populations. But only in the political context of the twentieth century did this idea of peaceful interposition started to take shape. See Weber, 1996: 13.
8. Royden, 1949: 135.
9. Gandhi, 1939.
10. Gandhi, [1942] 1962: 117.
11. After Gandhi's death, the idea was adopted by his disciple Bhave Vinoba, who established the Indian peace army also known as the Shanti Sena. Weber, 1996.
12. Royden, 1941. On pacifist antiwar declarations, see also Hathaway and Shapiro, 2017.
13. Royden, Gray, and Sheppard, 1932.
14. Royden, 1932: 1–2.
15. Royden, 1941.
16. Bargu, 2016.
17. Royden, 1932: 5.
18. On the threats to the League of Nations, see Hathaway and Shapiro, 2017.
19. Royden, 1933: 1–2.
20. Letter from Sir Eric Drummond, March 1, 1932, Maude Royden Files, Women's Library Archive, London School of Economics.

6. EMBLEM

1. Mussolini, 1937: 9.
2. Labanca, 2015.

3. Du Bois, 1935.

4. Prominent historians of Italian colonialism such as Angelo Del Boca, Richard Pankhurst, and Giorgio Rochat have documented the ground invasion and aerial bombardments in detail, exposing the perpetration of a series of war crimes. See Del Boca, 1996; Pankhurst, 1999; and Rochat, 1988.

5. The historian Richard Pankhurst has identified at least twenty-two cases of Italian aerial bombing of Red Cross units throughout the war. Pankhurst, 1997; See also Baudendistel, 2006.

6. Hague Convention No. IV, 1907: article 27.

7. Perugini and Gordon, 2019.

8. Baer, 1976.

9. At the beginning of the 1930s, Liberia's membership was subjected to a pressure similar to those faced by Ethiopia. The Liberian government was asked to implement administrative and financial reforms and to abolish slavery as a condition to remain a League member. See Mackenzie, 1934.

10. The arms embargo had major repercussions on Ethiopia's capacity to defend itself against Italy's aggression.

11. Bhabha, 1994: 89.

12. In the Ethiopian context, the expression "white negroes" was utilized by the traveler Alejandro Liano, who defined the Ethiopians as "the most intelligent Negroes on earth, because they easily assimilate Western education, and if it wasn't for their superstition . . . they could . . . be at the same level of the men of white race." See Liano, 1929: 198. Rose Parfitt has highlighted how this racist cultural prism then influenced the Western construction of the Ethiopian international legal personality as hybrid, where whiteness denoted their sovereignty and acceptance into the League of Nations, while "negro" denoted their incomplete humanness and their contingent inclusion in the family of nations. See Parfitt, 2011. The racist notion of "white negro" had been used also in other contexts—for instance, to classify racially mixed people within the antebellum period in the United States. See, for instance, Bynum, 1998. In the colonies, the corresponding term "black albinos" was used to define the attitudes of colonized subjects who "want[ed] to be White" as a result of acculturation, according to Frantz Fanon's famous formulation. On black albinos, see Little, 1995; and on acculturation, see Fanon, 1952.

13. Friedrich Biever cited in Parfitt, 2011: 855.

14. Cited in Rochat, 1971: 26.

15. Carlo Cereti cited in Bartolini, 2012: 254.

16. Mussolini, 1937: 83–87.

17. Mussolini, 1937: 85–87.

18. Waugh cited in Zappa, "Quello che si nasconde in Etiopia sotto l'inviolabile 'Croce Rossa,'" *La Stampa,* 25 November 1935.

19. "Virgin ammette," *La Stampa,* 7 January 1936.

20. Baudendistel, 2006: 102–3.

21. League of Nations, 1936b; and League of Nations, 1936a.

22. League of Nations, 1936b: 408.

23. League of Nations, 1936b: 433–36.

24. Durand and Boissier, 1984: 303.

25. Julliot, 1936: 433–464; L.D., 1936.

26. Alter, 1936: 257.

27. Junod, 1951: 49.

28. Junod, 1951: 29

29. Baudendistel, 2006: 126.

30. On the racial bias of the Red Cross, see Moorehead, 1999: 122-131. On the historical tension between humanity and race in colonial situations, see Esmeir, 2012; and Çubukçu, 2017.

31. Owens, 2015.

7. NUREMBERG

1. Carlton, 2010.

2. Beevor, 2011: 122.

3. Beevor, 2011: 122

4. Beevor, 2011: 123.

5. Beevor, 2011: 123

6. United Nations War Crimes Commission, 1948a: 120.

7. United Nations War Crimes Commission, 1948a: 119.

8. United Nations War Crimes Commission, 1948b: 588.

9. One other Nuremberg case mentioned human shields. Gottlob Berger, a lieutenant general in the SS claimed in his testimony that Hitler had asked him to move prisoners of war to areas that were being bombed by the allies but he had suggested that it contravened the 1929 Geneva Convention. There is, however, no corroboration of this incident. Exhibit Number USA-529, Nuremberg Trials, United Nations War Crimes Commission, 1949.

10. Koskodan, 2011; Zander, 2017: 148.

11. Sayer and Dronfield, 2019.

12. Ramet, 2011: 79.

13. Two hundred years before the codification process began, Grotius (1583–1645) provided an eloquent argument why noncombatants should be regarded as excludable from the operations of war. Grotius, 2005. See particularly the chapters relating to noncombatants in Book 3. In a similar vein, Vattel's 1758 *The Law of Nations* is emphatic about noncombatant immunity, rendering him an extremely attractive thinker for many humanitarians. See Vattel, 2008. For a discussion about the penetration of legal discourse among European elites, see Best, 1994.

14. Lieber, 1863: article 19.

15. The 1868 St. Petersburg Declaration was the first legal document banning the use of certain lethal weapons, and although it is often cited as a foundational text for those advocating civilian immunity, it does not explicitly mention noncombatants. Imperial Cabinet of Russia, 1868.

16. Meron, 1998.

17. Hurd, 2017.

18. Meron, 2000.

19. Geneva Convention Relative to the Treatment of the Prisoners of War, 1949: article 9.

20. In 1921, the Geneva-based organization began to put forward a preliminary draft of a legal convention dealing specifically with civilian protections. However, members within the organization second-guessed how governments might react to this proposal, and in its 1923 conference the Red Cross rejected its own draft text, confining itself to voicing what amounted to a pious hope that civilians would not be targeted during wars. This episode highlights the difference between the Red Cross and the liberal internationalists who thought that war could be eradicated through enlightened diplomacy and collective action. See Bugnion, 2003; Hathaway and Shapiro, 2017.

21. The Armenian genocide (1915–23) alongside the Greco-Turkish War (1919–23), the occupation of the Ruhr (1923–25), the Chaco War (1932–35), the Italo-Ethiopian War (1935–36), the Spanish Civil War (1936–39), and the Sino-Japanese conflict (1937–39) all drew attention to the brutalities civilians were subjected to. For an overview of ICRC codification efforts between the two wars, see Bugnion, 2003: 118–27.

22. International Committee of the Red Cross, 1947a: 40; See also International Committee of the Red Cross, 1947b: 269–332.

23. International Committee of the Red Cross, 1947a: 55.

24. The final draft was, however, embryonic but, more importantly, failed to garner the necessary governmental approval. Concurrently, the Red Cross circulated the idea of creating safety zones immune from attacks during war, but again the drafted convention aiming to create "cities of refuge" as well as "hospital towns" did not receive the necessary support. International Committee of the Red Cross, 1934; International Red Cross Conference, 1938.

25. Bugnion, 2003: 127.

26. Bellamy, 2012.

8. CODIFICATION

1. Meron, 1989.

2. Seybolt, Aronson, and Fischhoff, 2013. On civilian protection, see also Slim, 2007, 2015. On the drafting of the conventions and the increase of the moral-legal focus on civilians after the Second World War, see Van Dijk, 2018.

3. International Committee of the Red Cross, 1946.

4. International Committee of the Red Cross, 1947b: 1.

5. International Committee of the Red Cross, 1947a: 3.

6. Crawford, 2013.

7. Geneva Convention IV, 1949: articles 3 and 20.

8. Meron, 2000.

9. Geneva Convention IV, 1949: article 28.

10. International Committee of the Red Cross, 1934: 1–6. See also Alexander, 2007.

11. Enemy civilians were defined as (a) not belonging to the land, maritime, or air armed forces of the belligerents, as defined by international law, and in particular by articles 1, 2, and 3 of the Regulations attached to the Fourth Hague Convention, of October 18, 1907; and (b) being the national of an enemy country in the territory of a belligerent, or in a territory occupied by the latter. See International Committee of the Red Cross, 1947b: 2.

12. For a more extended critique of the nonneutral character of international law, see Chimni, 2006.

13. International Committee of the Red Cross, 1947b: 2, 7. The governmental working group decided to expand the notion of civilianhood at the same time as another group of experts was drafting the United Nations Universal Declaration of Human Rights. For a discussion of the relation between human rights, international law, and humanitarian intervention, see Orford, 2010: 335–56.

14. For the way race pervades international law, see Grovogui, 1996. For international law and the use of emergency regulations as mode of governance in the colonies, see Reynolds, 2017; Arendt, 1973; Kakel, 2013; Césaire, 1972; and Mamdani, 2001.

15. For a discussion of the persistence of state-centric paradigm following the Second World War, see Jochnick, 1999; and Perugini and Gordon, 2015.

16. International Committee of the Red Cross, 1949b: 848.

17. International Committee of the Red Cross, 1949c: 381.

18. International Committee of the Red Cross, 1949c: 381.

19. Nabulsi, 1999: 45.

20. International Committee of the Red Cross, 1949c: 384. Article 3A as a whole was adopted 29 to 8 with 4 abstentions.

21. International Committee of the Red Cross, 1949c: 41.

22. International Committee of the Red Cross, 1949b: 581.

23. The exact wording of article 24 is "No protected person may at any time be sent to, or detained in areas which are particularly exposed, nor may his or her presence be used to render certain points or areas immune from military operations." International Committee of the Red Cross, Vol. I, 1949a: 118.

24. International Committee of the Red Cross, 1949b: 639–40.

25. International Committee of the Red Cross, 1949b: 712.

9. PEOPLE'S WAR

1. Zedong, 1968: 78.

2. Tse-tung, 1917.

3. For a genealogy of the notion of people's war, see Scheipers, 2018.

4. Zedong, 1968: 78.

5. Zedong, 1968: 172–73.

6. Tse-tung, 1989: 12–18.

7. Tse-tung, 1989: 92.

8. Nguyên Giáp, [1961] 2014: 62.

9. Cited in Catton, 1999: 928.

10. "Guerrilla Warfare," 1962, *Newsweek* 59, no. 7: 32.

11. Gilman, 2003; Khalili, 2012.

12. Vietnam Task Force, 2011: 2.

13. Boot, 2013: 413.

14. Vietnam Task Force, 2011: 14.

15. For an overview on modernization theory debates, see Gilman, 2003.

16. Huntington, 1968. See also Gusterson, 2004: 24–25.

17. Attewell, 2015.

18. Cushman, 1966: 24.

19. On indistinction and the absence of legal experts in US targeting decisions during the Vietnam War, see Dill, 2014: 147.

20. Douglas, 2014. On the notion of "Viet Cong infrastructure" according to the Phoenix program, see chapter 1.

21. Lawrence, 2008: 102.

22. Lawrence, 2008: 102. For an updated calculation of civilian casualties, see Turse, 2013.

23. Johnson, 1967.

24. On the body count paradigm in Vietnam, see Tyner, 2009.

25. Schmitt, 2004: 15.

26. Veuthey, 1983: 40.

27. "Protected by Human Shields, Viet Cong Kill 33 Americans," *Morning Record,* 7 September 1968: 1; and "Viet Cong Use Human Shields, 10 Die, 16 Hurt," *Gadsden Times,* 9 January 1967: 1. Other articles on the use of human shields were "Civilians Used As Shields," *New York Times,* 7 September 1968: 8; and "Vietcong Ambush U.S. Patrol, Kill or Wound Every Man in It: Children Used as Shields, One Believed Dead," *Washington Post, Times Herald,* 6 October 1965: 10.

28. "Human Shields in Vietnam," *Lewiston Daily Sun,* 6 November 1967: 4.

29. Text of the leaflet reproduced in Lewy, 1978: 69.

30. International Committee of the Red Cross, 1965: 1173.

31. Official statement of the U.S. Department of Defense, reproduced in Whiteman, 1968: 427.

32. For a comprehensive account of the history of the program, see Young, 2009.

33. Young, 2009: 3. On the relationship between visibility and imperial wars, in particular the Vietnamese postwar claim that lack of visibility was used as an excuse for reprisals against entire colonized populations, see Kinsella, 2011: 144–46.

34. Bui Thi Phuong-Lan defined the Vietnamese farmers as "eco-refugees." Phuong-Lan, 2003.

35. Swiss Federal Council, 1978b: 141–43.

36. Protocol Additional to the Geneva Conventions, 1977.

1. Weyler, 2004: 50–66.
2. Zelko, 2013.
3. Mitchell and Stallings, 1970.
4. Weyler, 2004: 65.
5. Tracy, 1996: 99–105.
6. Bigelow, 1959.
7. Treaty Banning Nuclear Weapon Tests in the Atmosphere, 1963.
8. Day, 1987.
9. Gottlieb, 2003.
10. Jain, 2016: 57.
11. Jain, 2016: 51. See also Gottlieb, 2003.
12. Shiva, 2016: 69.
13. Bargu, 2016; Gordon and Perugini, 2016b.
14. Braidotti, 2013.
15. Carter, 1977.
16. Carter, 1977.
17. For a history of nuclear testing with an emphasis on the French role, see MacKay, 1995.
18. Hunter and Naidoo, 2012: 58.
19. Hunter and Naidoo, 2012; see also Zelko, 2013.
20. McTaggart and Hunter, 1979: 88.
21. The fact that the crew was comprised solely of men reflected Greenpeace's gender politics, where male activists were not only calling the shots but had also barred women who were unmarried or did not have male partners from joining the crews and using their bodies as shields. Wittingly or unwittingly, this both reflected and helped reinforce a dominant military and legal perspective that posits men as active actors, and women and children as passive actors. A decade later, some thirty thousand women would challenge the gender restrictions of Western green politics, acting as human shields on British territory along the nine-mile perimeter of the US cruise missile base at Greenham Common, in the largest shielding protest in history. "Men were excluded from the demonstration" by the women shields "and told to run the creche, prepare food, and keep out of the way." "Peace campaigners want US missiles removed from British soil," 1982, *The Guardian*, 13 December 1982. For a more general analysis of gender and human shielding, see Kinsella, 2016a.
22. McTaggart and Hunter, 1979: 90.
23. MacKay, 1995.
24. Wittner, 1970.
25. Caprari, 2009.
26. "Gregory Peck Attacks on Japan's Whale Killing," 1981, *Vegetarian Times*, no. 50 (October): 15.
27. Day, 1987: 12.

28. Erwood, 2011: 28.

29. Mulvaney, 2003: 13.

30. Weyler, 2004: 316–19.

31. Nordquist and Nandan, 2011.

32. Raffi Khatchadourian, 2007, "Neptune's Navy," *New Yorker,* November 5, 2007.

33. Hobbes, 1991. See also in this respect Fitzmaurice, 2015.

34. Plant, 1983; Plant, 2002.

35. McTaggart and Hunter, 1979: 81.

36. This, to be sure, engendered considerable resistance from states, and in 1982 they managed to change the Convention on the Law of the Sea, reformulating articles and adding new ones to render the law more state-centric than it had been in the past. Boats continued to enjoy the same freedom in international waters, but, according to the 1982 convention, from then on only state actors would have the authority to enforce the law. The practical effect has, however, been minimal. Human shielding in the high seas is still legal, and the deployment of shielding boats has an enforcement effect even if, formally, they can no longer claim that they are applying the law. United Nations Convention on the Law of the Sea, 1982.

11. RESISTANCE

1. United Nations Security Council, 1990.

2. Burrowes, 1991.

3. Julie Bindel, 2008, "No Time for Battle Fatigue," *The Guardian,* 30 April 2008.

4. Arrowsmith, 1972.

5. For a history of unarmed peacekeeping led by civilians, see Weber, 1996.

6. Burrowes, 1991.

7. "Flashback: 1991 Gulf War," 2003, BBC World News: Middle East, 20 March 2003.

8. Habibzadeh, 2018.

9. Della Porta, Diani, and Mastellotto, 2003.

10. See Mulhearn, 2010; Temuge, 2005.

11. US Central Intelligence Agency, 2003.

12. US Central Intelligence Agency, 2003: 1.

13. Scott Peterson, 2003, "'Human Shields' in Tug-of-War," *Christian Science Monitor,* 17 March 2003.

14. Some of the shields were even expelled by the Iraqi government because of their unwillingness to make compromises. Mulhearn, 2010: 109.

15. Email communication with Donna Mulhearn, January 18, 2019.

16. Rajiv Chandrasekaran, 2003, "'Human Shields' Take Stand in Baghdad; Peace Activists Hope Presence Will Prevent U.S Attacks on Civilian Facilities," *Washington Post,* 25 February 2003.

17. Fassin, 2007.

18. Human Shield Action to Iraq, n.d., "Truth Justice Peace Human Shield Action to Iraq," https://humanshields.org.

19. Knights, 2003.

20. United States Court of Appeals, Seventh Circuit, 2009, Ryan Clancy, Plaintiff-Appellant, v. Office of Foreign Assets Control of the United States Department of the Treasury, No. 07–2254, FindLaw, decided 11 March 2009.

21. Julie Hilden, 2003, "Do Americans Have a Legal Right to Become 'Human Shields'?" CNN Law Center, 14 August 2003, http://edition.cnn.com/2003/LAW/08/14/findlaw.analysis.hilden.human.shield/.

22. On the intricacies of framing voluntary shielding, see Dill, 2016; Haque, 2017.

23. Unpublished ICRC report on file with Michael Schmitt, who published an excerpt in Schmitt, 2012.

24. Robert Fisk, 2012, "In the Line of Fire: Tom Hurndall," *The Independent,* 21 January 2012.

25. An initial military inquiry concluded that Hurdnall had been killed accidentally, but after British diplomatic pressure the investigation was reopened. The sniper was eventually convicted of manslaughter and sentenced to eleven and half years in prison. Sean O'Hagan, 2012, "Tom Hurndall: A Remarkable Man's Photographs of the Middle East," *The Guardian,* 1 March 2012; International Solidarity Movement, "In Memory of Tom Hurndall," 2017, *Gaza Reports,* 13 January 2017.

26. Donald Macintyre, 2010, "Bulldozer Driver Insists He Did Not See Rachel Corrie," *The Independent,* 22 October 2010.

27. Corrie Family, 2009: 247.

28. On white privilege, direct action, and shielding, see Mahrouse, 2014.

29. Haifa District Court, 2012, The Estate of the Late Rachel Aliene Corrie et al. v. State of Israel, Ministry of Defense, File 371/05, article 167, International Crimes Database, 28 August 2012.

30. Haifa District Court, 2012: articles 32, 397.

31. Israel Supreme Court, 2014, Rachel Aliene Corrie Foundation et al. v. State of Israel, Ministry of Defense, File 6982/12, Rachel Corrie Foundation, 21 May 2014.

12. HUMANITARIAN CRIMES

1. Elliott, 1995.

2. *National Security Strategy of the United States,* 1991: v.

3. Douzinas, 2007: 139. Douzinas uses the notion of "benign imperialism" to describe Michael Ignatieff's invocation of the creation of an "empire lite"—an empire without colonies—as a new post-Cold War global order based on the protection of human rights. See Ignatieff, 2003. For more recent cases of mobilization of humanitarian protection, see Mamdani, 2009.

4. United Nations General Assembly Resolution A/RES/60/1, 15 September 2005, section "Responsibility to protect populations from genocide, war crimes, ethnic cleansing and crimes against humanity," https://www.refworld.org/docid /44168a910.html.

5. Van Shaack, 2019: 464–514

6. United Nations Security Council, 1992.

7. United Nations Security Council, 1993a.

8. Carpenter, 2006: 151.

9. Smith, 2006: 333–36.

10. Prosecutor v. Radovan Karadžić, 2016: 2454.

11. Prosecutor v. Radovan Karadžić, 2016: 2459–60.

12. Chuck Sudetic, 1994, "Bosnian Serbs Set Free 43 U.N. Troops Held Hostage," *New York Times,* December 1, 1994; Roger Cohen, 1995, "After 2nd Strike From NATO, Serbs Detain U.N. Troops," *New York Times,* May 27, 1995; Joel Br, 1995, "Bosnian Serbs Seize More U.N. Troops," *Washington Post,* May 29, 1995. On the kidnapping of UN soldiers by Bosnian Serbs, see Tony Barber, 1995, "UN Troops Snatched as Human Shield," *The Independent,* July 19, 1995.

13. MacQueen, 2011: 154.

14. Smith, 2006: 344.

15. Cited in Wheeler, 2002: 259.

16. Wheeler, 2002: 243.

17. US Department of State, 1999.

18. Greg Steinmetz and Steve Stecklow, 1999, "Crisis in Yugoslavia: NATO Fears Threat of Refugee Shield," *Wall Street Journal,* April 9, 1999: 5.

19. Lieber, 1863: article 29.

20. Richard Norton-Taylor, 1999, "Air Strikes Hampered by Human Shields," *The Guardian,* 18 May 1999.

21. Jamie Shea and Ambassador David Scheffer, NATO briefing, May 18, 1999, https://www.nato.int/kosovo/press/b990518a.htm.

22. CNN, 1999, "NATO Says 'Human Shields' Account for Bombing Deaths," May 18, 1999.

23. United Nations Security Council, 1993b.

24. Dunlap, 2001; and Dunlap, 2008. For a critique of the concept of lawfare, see Gordon, 2014.

25. Gordon and Perugini, 2016a.

26. Gordon, 2014.

27. In 1999, the International Criminal Tribunal for the former Yugoslavia also extended its mandate to the conflict in Kosovo.

28. NATO, 1999, "Press Conference given by NATO Spokesman, Jamie Shea and SHAPE Spokesman Major General Walter Jertz," *NATO's Role in Kosovo,* 16 May 1999, https://www.nato.int/kosovo/press/p990516b.htm.

29. Prosecutor v. Radovan Karadžić, 2016: 198–99.

30. Prosecutor v. Ratko Mladić, 2017: 1178.

31. Scheffer, 2012.

32. Amnesty International, 2000; Human Rights Watch, 2000; Human Rights Watch, 2001.

33. Human Rights Watch, 2000: 2.

34. International Tribunal, 2000.

35. Amnesty International, 1999.

36. International Tribunal, 2000.

13. MANUALS

1. Kennedy, 2009: 7.

2. The United States issued several military manuals during the last century and half, but not all of them deal with the laws of war.

3. On the international lawmaking function of military manuals, see Reisman and Leitzau, 1991.

4. David Kennedy from Harvard University's law school says something similar when he notes that norms assume their force not through their pedigree but through persuasiveness. Manuals are a crucial instrument through which militaries produce, promulgate, and render norms persuasive. Indeed, manuals are texts that lay out the official military norms. The norms that are most persuasive have more of an effect, and, as Kennedy notes, those norms that have an effect should rightly be considered "legal." In this sense too, military manuals lay down the law. Kennedy, 2009: 93.

5. Yotam Feldman and Uri Blau, 2009, "Consent and Advise," *Ha'aretz*, 5 February 2009.

6. Kennedy, 2008.

7. Lieber, 1863.

8. For the impact of the Lieber Code on international law, see Meron, 1998.

9. Lieber, 1863. In a similar vein, the 1914 *Rules of Land Warfare* manual incorporated the rules of international law accepted by and for the "civilized powers of the world." US War Department, 1914: 13.

10. US War Department, 1914: 13. Ever since the Lieber Code, the idea that manuals are lawmaking instruments that could be deployed as part of a civilizing mission has been widespread not only for those published by the United States, but also for the ones issued by European countries until the 1960s and beyond. See, for instance, UK War Office, 1958.

11. US Department of the Army, 1956.

12. US Department of Defense, 2015.

13. Carvin, 2010: 361–62.

14. See article 1, paragraph 4 of Protocol Additional to the Geneva Conventions, 1977. On the expansion of the United Nations and its effects on international law, see Burke, 2010.

15. Lieber, 1863.

16. US War Department, 1914: 62.

17. UK War Office, 1914. See also Elliott, 1995.

18. US Department of the Army, 1956: 2.

19. Since the war on terror was launched, other states have issued new or updated versions of their law of war manuals in which they introduced a human shielding clause. The 2004 manual *The Law of Armed Conflict* put out by Britain frames human shielding as a violation of international law, requires its army to apply the principle of proportionality when attacking human shielding areas, and, similar to its 2015 US counterpart, concludes that "however, if the defenders put civilians or civilian objects at risk by placing military objectives in their midst or by placing civilians in or near military objectives, this is a factor to be taken into account in favour of the attackers in considering the legality of attacks on those objectives." The 2012 French *Manuel du droit des conflits armés* (Law of Armed Conflict Manual) prohibits the use of human shields and defines voluntary human shields as people who "directly participate in the hostilities." Ministère de la Défense, 2012: 27–28. No mention of involuntary or proximate shielding is made in the French handbook, leaving the question open to interpretation. The 2013 German *Law of Armed Conflict Manual* states that voluntary human shields lose their civilian protections, and targets protected by shields can be attacked provided the principle of proportionality is respected. Federal Ministry of Defense, 2013. As in the French case, involuntary or proximate shields are not made part of the manual's human shielding clause. Recently, Denmark, Canada, Australia, and Israel have also introduced provisions that explicitly outlaw the use of human shields in their legal-military doctrine.

20. Luard, 1989.

21. On wars of national liberation and the Additional Protocols to the Geneva Conventions, see Whyte, 2018; and Kinsella, 2011.

22. Charney, 1993; Gray, 2018.

23. Whyte, 2018.

24. Luis Eslava, Michael Fakhri, and Vasuki Nesiah define the political struggle triggered in Bandung as one "to both conform and to resignify the language and categories of the international legal order." Eslava, Fakhri, and Nesiah, 2017: 5–6. A vast number of works have problematized the colonial processes of formation and the decolonial processes of transformation of international law in the last two decades. See, for example, Anghie, 2007; Chimni, 1993; Eslava and Pahuja, 2011; Koskenniemi, 2001; Obregón, 2007; Pahuja, 2011; and Parfitt, 2019.

25. Bedjaoui, 1961: 10. On Mohammed Bedjaoui and international legal universality, see Özsu, 2015, 2019.

26. Protocol Additional to the Geneva Conventions, 1977: article 1, paragraph 4. On the expansion of the United Nations and its effects on international law, see Burke, 2010.

27. For a history of international law as international space of political contestation, see Pitts, 2018. Pitts focuses her analysis on the eighteenth and nineteenth centuries, but the theoretical framework she advances is still pertinent to our times.

28. Mantilla, 2019.

29. Britain and France were afraid that applying international law to national liberation struggles would legitimize "acts of terrorism, whether concerted or in

isolation." See Gaudreau, 2003. On the role of the Additional Protocols and their interpretation in delaying the publication of the 2004 UK *Manual of the Law of Armed Conflict,* see Rogers, 2010: 89–96.

30. Reagan, 1987.

31. Reagan, 1987.

32. Hays Parks, a senior legal consultant for different US administrations, recounts that in the 1980s and 1990s military and legal experts of the "Empire Club"—Australia, Canada, New Zealand, the United Kingdom, and the United States—held various informal meetings to define the concept of proportionality and other crucial legal issues. Their discussions did not translate into the publication of a new manual, both because the principle of proportionality does not have a clear universal definition on which the drafters could agree and because the United States got involved in a series of conflicts, including the first Iraq war and the wars in the former Yugoslavia and Kosovo. See Carvin, 2010: 361–62; and Parks, 2010: 3–4.

33. Cordesman, 2004; Schoenekase, 2004.

34. Dunlap, 2016a.

35. Parks, 2010.

36. Hays Parks interview in Dunlap, 2016a.

37. Dunlap, 2016b. See also Rosen, 2009.

38. "Full Text: George Bush's Address on the Start of War," 2003, *The Guardian,* 20 March 2003; and Barack Obama's press conference after meeting with national security officials, White House, 2006.

39. Dunlap, 2015; Schmitt, 2008.

40. Schmitt, 2008; Skerker, 2004.

41. US Department of Defense, 2015: 198.

42. US Department of Defense, 2015: 244.

43. A similar argument has been made by Michael Walzer, 2014, "Israel Must Defeat Hamas, but Also Must Do More to Limit Civilian Deaths," *New Republic,* 30 July 2014.

44. Butler, 2015: 233.

45. Haque, 2015.

46. Dunlap, 2015.

47. US Department of Defense, 2016: 201–2.

48. US Department of Defense, 2016: 269–70.

49. Aldrich, 1991.

50. Meron, 2000.

51. Rosen, 2009.

52. See the section on reprisals in chapter 2.

14. SCALE

1. United States Embassy Sri Lanka, Colombo, 2009, "Northern Sri Lanka Sitrep 74," May 17, 2009, https://wikileaks.org/plusd/cables/09COLOMBO535_a.html.

2. Weiss, 2011. United Nations Commission on Human Rights, 2006; United Nations Commission on Human Rights, 1999.

3. United Nations Secretary-General, 2011: 8–9.

4. Weiss, 2011: 96.

5. Holmes, 2015: 210–45.

6. Holmes, 2015: 230; United Nations Secretary-General, 2011: 19.

7. United Nations Secretary-General, 2011: 27–28.

8. Van Schaack, 2016; Ministry of Defense, Sri Lanka, 2011.

9. Human Rights Watch, 2009; United Nations Secretary-General, 2011: 27–34; United Nations Human Rights Council, 2015b.

10. United Nations Secretary-General, 2011: 67.

11. Paranagama, Ramanathan, and Vidyaratne, 2015.

12. Newton, 2015, "A Legal Opinion for the Commission Inquiring into Disappearances," 28 April 2015, http://www.lankaweb.com/news/items/2015/04/28/a-legal-opinion-for-the-commission-inquiring-into-disappearances/.

13. United Nations Secretary-General, 2011: 65.

14. Human Rights Watch, 2010.

15. International Crisis Group, 2009.

16. To justify this modification, the commission cites the International Criminal Court's *Elements of Crimes,* a document intended to assist the International Criminal Court in the interpretation and application of the legal articles defining the crimes under its jurisdiction. The relevant article defines human shielding as a situation where a perpetrator "moved or otherwise took advantage of the location of one or more civilians or other persons protected under the international law of armed conflict." See Dörmann, 2003: 344. Italics added.

17. The principle holds that it is illegal to launch an attack against lawful military targets if the attack "may be expected" to result in excessive civilian harm (deaths, injuries, or damage to civilian objects, or a combination thereof) compared to the "concrete and direct military advantage anticipated." A disproportionate attack may constitute a war crime if carried out intentionally. See International Committee of the Red Cross, n.d., "Rule 14: Proportionality in Attack."

18. Meron, 2000.

19. Gardam, 2004.

20. Weizman, 2017: 178.

21. In addition to the reports already cited, see Amnesty International, 2009; Norwegian Refugee Council/Internal Displacement Monitoring Centre, 2009; International Crisis Group, 2010.

22. Geoffrey Nice and Rodney Dixon, 2015, "Legal Opinion concerning the Law Applicable to Military Operations in the Final Stages of the Armed Conflict between the Government of Sri Lanka and the LTTE That Ended on 19 May 2009 following Intense Combat in the Vanni Area of Northern Sri Lanka," 20 March 2015, http://www.island.lk/index.php?page_cat=article-details&page=article-details&code_title=121064.

23. Newton and May, 2014.

24. Mbembe, 2003: 39.

25. Crane and de Silva, 2015, "Opinion to the Commission from Professor DM Crane and Sir Desmond de Silva, QC re.," 20 March 2015, http://www.lankaweb.com/news/items/2015/03/20/what-the-international-experts-say-3-war-crimes-in-sri-lanka/.

26. Crane and de Silva, 2015. Italics added.

27. Crane and de Silva, 2015.

28. Weizman, 2012.

29. Crane and de Silva, 2015.

30. Kasher and Yadlin, 2005b.

15. HOSPITALS

1. Lindqvist, 2001: 4, 75–78.

2. Durand and Boissier, 1984: 17.

3. Durand and Boissier, 1984: 17.

4. Durand and Boissier, 1984: 17. Italics added.

5. For attacks on aid workers, see Fast, 2014.

6. For a lengthier analysis of hospital shields, see Gordon and Perugini, 2019.

7. Durand and Boissier, 1984: 52.

8. Wynne, Miles, and Falls, 1927: 162.

9. Derek Gregory, 2016, "The Hospital Raids," *Geographical Imaginations: Wars, Spaces and Bodies,* September 25, 2016, https://geographicalimaginations.com/2016/09/25/the-hospital-raids/.

10. Lords Sitting of Wednesday, 15th March 1939: 214–88.

11. Lords Sitting of Wednesday, 15th March 1939.

12. Wynne, Miles, and Falls, 1927: 162–63.

13. Aron, 1965.

14. Geneva Convention Relative to the Protection of Civilian Persons in Time of War, 1949: Articles 18 and 19. Italics added.

15. Armstrong, 2010: 2.

16. Truninger and Bugnion, 1994.

17. Rey-Schyrr, 2007: 395. Perret and Bugnion, 2009: 392.

18. Parks, 1983: 12.

19. Swiss Federal Council, 1978a: 63–65.

20. Protocol 1 Additional to the Geneva Conventions, 1977: article 12. Italics added.

21. In 2016 alone, attacks on health care facilities occurred in twenty-three countries across the globe. In Syria, hospitals were attacked 108 times—one every three and a half days. In Afghanistan, the number of strikes targeting health facilities and personnel rose from 63 in 2015 to 119 in 2016, while in Yemen hospitals were attacked 93 times during a similar period. As the numbers clearly suggest, medical facilities have

become not only a legitimate target but also part of a recurrent strategy of war aimed at weakening the enemy. See Safeguarding Health in Conflict, 2017; Dewachi, 2017.

22. World Health Organization, "Attacks on Health Care Dashboard," for 2016, 2017, and 2018, https://www.who.int/emergencies/attacks-on-health-care/en/.

23. Helena Kennedy, 2015, "The 2014 Conflict Left Gaza's Healthcare Shattered. When Will Justice Be Done?" *The Guardian,* 29 June 2015.

24. IDF Blog, 2014, "Hamas Terrorists Confess to Using Human Shields," August 27, 2014.

25. Ellen Francis, 2016, "Even in a Bunker under a Mountain, Syrian Hospital Knocked Out by Strikes," *Reuters,* October 3, 2016.

26. Himmiche et al., 2014. The same claim was also reiterated in a more recent United Nations report. See Michelle Nichols, 2016, "U.N. Report on Yemen Says Houthis Used Human Shields, Islamic State Got Cash," *Reuters,* August 4, 2016.

27. Article 19 adds that "the fact that sick or wounded members of the armed forces are nursed in these hospitals, or the presence of small arms and ammunition taken from such combatants and not yet been handed to the proper service, shall not be considered to be acts harmful to the enemy." Geneva Convention Relative to the Protection of Civilian Persons in Time of War, 1949.

28. Pictet et al., 1987: article 21.

29. Ministry of Foreign Affairs, State of Israel, 2015: 76, 79.

30. Charlotte Alfred, 2014, "Hospitals Are Supposed To Be for Healing. In Gaza, They're Part of the War Zone," *Huffington Post,* July 30, 2014; Nora Barrows-Friedman, 2014, "Israel Used Fabricated Images to Justify Bombing Al-Wafa Hospital," 2014, *Electronic Intifada,* July 24, 2014.

31. Geneva Convention for the Amelioration of the Condition of the Wounded and Sick in Armed Forces in the Field, 1949: article 21; Geneva Convention Relative to the Protection of Civilian Persons in Time of War, 1949: article 19; Protocol 1 Additional to the Geneva Conventions, 1977, article 13; Protocol 2 Additional to the Geneva Conventions, 1977: article 11.

32. Government of Saudi Arabia, 2016.

33. Gordon and Perugini, 2016a.

16. PROXIMITY

1. Amnesty International, 2017.

2. Michael Georgy, 2016, "Factbox: Once-Tolerant Mosul Site of Iraq Push against Islamic State," *Reuters,* 17 October 2016.

3. Lizzie Dearden, 2017, "Life after Isis: People of Mosul tell of Horrors under the Rule of 'the Devil's Murderers,'" *Independent,* 6 May 2017.

4. BBC News, 2015, "Inside Mosul: What's Life like under Islamic State?," 9 June 2015.

5. Amnesty International, 2017; William Booth and Aaso A. Shwan, 2016, "Islamic State Tunnels below Mosul Are a Hidden and Deadly Danger," *Washington Post,* 5 November 2016.

6. Florian Neuhof, 2017, "'It Was Like the Apocalypse': Mosul Residents Caught between Coalition Strikes and ISIL Violence," *The National,* 26 March 2017.

7. Rome Reports, 2016, "Pope Francis Distressed at Use of Boys as Human Shields in Mosul, Iraq," *Rome Reports,* 24 October 2016.

8. Tim Hains, 2016, "Trump: Now We're Bogged Down in Mosul Because Obama Gave Away the Element of Surprise," *RealClearPolitics,*24 October 2016; Tim Arango, 2016, "Mosul Fight Unleashes New Horrors on Civilians," *New York Times,* 25 October 2016.

9. CBS News, 2016, "U.N.: ISIS using 'tens of thousands' as human shields in Mosul," 28 October 2016; Jack Moore, 2017, "ISIS Holds 100,000 'Human Shields' in Mosul's Old City, U.N. Says," *Newsweek,* 16 June 2017.

10. Kennedy, 2009.

11. Amnesty International, 2017: 15–16.

12. Protocol I Additional to the Geneva Conventions, 1977: article 51(7).

13. Ezzo and Guiora, 2009: 91–116.

14. Garraway, 2011; Sassòli, 2003.

15. "The spatial logic of violence, long dominated by the inside/outside dichotomization of the Cold War, has," Caroline Croser reminds us, "been expanded to include the more fluid, eventful, and relational logic of contingency, particularly as expressed in the figure of the network." Croser, 2007.

16. Garraway, 2011: 178; see also Graham, 2009; Gregory, 2011b.

17. On urban warfare, see Kilcullen, 2010; on the civilianization of conflict, see Wenger and Mason, 2008.

18. Graham, 2011: 16; Gregory, 2011a.

19. Waffa Munayyer and Kara Fox, 2017, "Raqqa in Ruins: Drone Footage Reveals Devastation in ISIS' Stronghold in Syria," *CNN,* 29 August 2017; Kuwait News Agency (KUNA), 2018, "Yemeni Report: 2,250 Violations against Journalists since Houthis' Coup," 12 January 2018; Martin Smith, 2016, "Iraqi Forces Halt Fallujah Advance amid Fears for 50,000 Human Shields," *United Press International,* 3 June 2016.

20. The search identified 1,903 articles that used the phrase *human shields,* but 682 of these were duplicates. When counting the number of people used as shields, we counted each incident only once but used the largest figure provided in the articles describing the incident.

21. We realize that often remaining in one's home during war can be an active act that not only points to agency but also to courage.

22. Samuel Oakford, 2018, "Counting the Dead in Mosul," *The Atlantic,* 5 April 2018.

23. Susannah George, 2017, "Mosul Is a Graveyard: Final IS Battle Kills 9,000 Civilians," AP News, 21 December 2017.

24. Butler, 2009.

25. Schmitt, 2007: 15.

26. Perugini and Gordon, 2015.

27. Rosén, 2016: 5.

28. Philosopher of language John Austin explained that perlocutionary speech acts "produce certain consequential effects upon the feelings, thoughts, or actions of the audience, or of the speaker, or of other persons: and it may be done with the design, intention, or purpose of producing them." Austin, 1975: 101. On how the preliminary framing of civilians as human shields functions as a speech act and enhances violence against them, see Butler, 2015.

29. A LexisNexis search in "major publications" for the phrase *human shields* over the one-year period between 1 November 2015 and 31 October 2016 found 1,221 articles where the vast majority refer to human shielding in Yemen, Iraq, and Syria. Another search we conducted, one that includes a five-year period ending in 31 October 2016 reveals that while a handful mention Ukraine, the phrase *human shield* is primarily and most often used in reference to Gaza, Nigeria, Iraq, Syria, and other ex-colonized spaces. See Gordon and Perugini, 2016a.

30. Dunlap, 2016b; Gross, 2015; Schmitt, 2008; Walzer, 2016.

31. Slim, 2015.

32. Protocol II Additional to the Geneva Conventions 1977.

33. Gordon and Perugini, 2016b.

17. INFO-WAR

1. The two campaigns that preceded it were the 2008–2009 Operation Cast Lead and the 2012 Operation Pillar of Cloud. For a meticulous account of all three attacks, see Finkelstein, 2018.

2. United Nations Human Rights Council, 2014.

3. Bob Frederick, 2014, "Netanyahu Reveals Photo of Children Playing near Hamas Rocket Launcher," *New York Post,* 30 September 2014.

4. "Full Text of Prime Minister Netanyahu's UN Speech," 2014, *Jerusalem Post,* 29 September 2014.

5. Ministry of Foreign Affairs, State of Israel, 2015.

6. Ministry of Foreign Affairs, State of Israel, 2015.

7. Ministry of Foreign Affairs, State of Israel, 2015.

8. To be sure, the deployment of images and slogans to justify political violence was by no means new. In *War and Cinema,* the French cultural theorist Paul Virilio (1989) shows how the development of contemporary military strategies have increasingly overlapped with cinematographic techniques and are used to justify certain instances of violence. Political theorist Judith Butler (2009) makes a similar claim in *Frames of War,* where she shows how war is often framed in texts and images to legitimize violence against vulnerable people. On the moral claims and human shields in the wars on Gaza, see also Butler, 2015.

9. By *semiotic warfare* we mean, following Edward Said, the array of discursive operations deployed in order to delegitimize an enemy and give meaning to the use of violence against it. Said, 1980: xi. See also Kuntsman and Stein, 2015.

10. On this point, see Butler, 2015: 226.

11. United Nations Human Rights Council, 2015a.

12. Dinstein, 2002: 252.

13. Sassòli, Bouvier, and Quintin, 2011; Henckaerts and Doswald-Beck, 2005.

14. On the notion of dual use in international law and its permissive use, see Shue and Wippman, 2001.

15. Shue and Wippman, 2001.

16. For the breakdown of Gaza's population, see Gordon, 2008.

17. Gregory, 2006a; Jones, 2016: 207–40.

18. For an analysis of the relation between space and human rights, see Blomley and Pratt, 2001.

19. Henckaerts and Doswald-Beck, 2005: 223.

20. Turner, 1969: 95.

21. Butler, 2009: 10.

22. Perugini and Gordon, 2017.

23. Bourdieu, 1986: 805.

18. POSTHUMAN SHIELDING

1. Eric Schmitt, 2017, "U.S. Commando Killed in Yemen in Trump's First Counterterrorism Operation," *New York Times,* 29 January 2017.

2. Glenn Greenwald, 2017, "Obama Killed a 16-Year-Old American in Yemen. Trump Just Killed His 8-Year-Old Sister," *The Intercept,* 30 January 2017.

3. Russ Read, 2017, "Civilians Killed in US Raid on Al-Qaida May Have Been Used as Human Shields," *Daily Caller,* 1 February 2017.

4. Clausewitz, 2007: 88–89.

5. For a history of the transformation of military perception, see Bousquet, 2018.

6. Halpern, 2015; Amoore, 2016.

7. Incidentally, one of the children killed during the assault on the compound was eight-year-old Nawar Awlaki, whose father, Anwar, and sixteen-year-old brother, Abdulrahman, had been tracked and hunted down in two separate drone strikes back in 2011. Greenwald, 2017.

8. Bousquet, 2018: 5–6.

9. Shaw, 2005; Chamayou, 2015.

10. Kasher and Yadlin, 2005a; Fields and Odeen, 2004.

11. Melzer, 2009; Schmitt, 2005.

12. Schmitt, 2009: 313.

13. Amoore, 2016.

14. Jeremy Scahill, Cora Currier, and Ryan Devereaux, 2015, "The Drone Papers" *The Intercept,* https://theintercept.com/drone-papers.

15. Weber, 2016.

16. Shaw and Akhter, 2014; see also Shaw, 2013; Dillon and Reid, 2001.

17. John Naughton, 2016, "Death by Drone Strike, Dished Out by Algorithm," *The Guardian,* 21 February 2016.

18. Klaidman, 2012: 41.

19. Bousquet, 2018.

20. Rose, 2001; Weber, 2016.

21. Khalili, 2012.

22. Gregory, 2017: 214; see also Wilcox, 2017.

23. David S. Could, 2011, "Anatomy of an Afghan War Tragedy," *Los Angeles Times,* 10 April 2011.

24. Jeremy Scahill and Glenn Greenwald, 2014, "The NSA's Secret Role in the U.S. Assassination Program," *The Intercept,* 10 February 2014, https://theintercept.com/2014/02/10/the-nsas-secret-role.

25. Scahill and Greenwald, 2014. See also United Nations General Assembly, 2014.

19. WOMEN AND CHILDREN

1. This accusation does not include instances of proximate shielding, where the allegation pertains to whole populations without distinctions, or even to voluntary human shields, which tend to include both male and female adults.

2. Kinsella, 2016a.

3. Seybolt, Aronson, and Fischhoff, 2013.

4. Allinson, 2015: 120.

5. Cavallaro, Sonnenberg, and Knuckey, 2012: 40.

6. Gregory, 2006b: 637.

7. Kinsella, 2016b: 175. See also Charlesworth, Chaiton, and Chinkin. 2000.

8. Kinsella, 2006; see also Carpenter, 2006; Wilke, 2018.

9. Alexandra Ma, 2019, "ISIS Fighters Reportedly Used Their Wives and Children as Human Shields before US-Backed Forces Destroyed the Last Shred of Their 'Caliphate,'" *Business Insider,* 25 March 2019.

10. Ma, 2019.

11. Ma, 2019.

12. For a critique of this position, see Scott, 2017.

13. For a similar accusation of how brown men are currently using women of color in Europe, see Farris, 2017.

14. The Tea Party's official website supported and published Jim Gilchrist's report on migrants using women and children as human shields in 2014 at https://www.teaparty.org/jim-gilchrist-illegal-alien-children-used-political-human-shields-47103/ (accessed in August 2018, now removed).

15. See Galeano, 1973; and Klein, 2007.

16. Elisabeth Malkin, 2019, "Fact Checking Trump's Claim That Mexico Sent Migrants to the Border," *New York Times,* 6 February 2019.

17. Maegan Vazquez, 2018, "Trump Admits 'There's No Proof' of His 'Unknown Middle Easterners' Caravan Claim," *CNN,* 23 October 2018.

18. RT News, 2018, "Migrant Caravan Using Women & Children as Human Shields to Break into Mexico—Pompeo," 19 October 2018; and US Department of Homeland Security, 2018, *Myth vs Fact: Caravan,* fact sheet, 1 November 2018, https://www.dhs.gov/news/2018/11/01/myth-vs-fact-caravan.

20. SPECTACLE

1. Robert Mackey and Maher Samaan, 2015, "Caged Hostages from Syrian President's Sect Paraded through Rebel-Held Suburb," *New York Times,* 1 November 2015.

2. Human Rights Watch, 2015.

3. Human Rights Watch, 2015.

4. Debord, 2012. Social media has indeed provided new possibilities for engaging mainstream media, but in an age when politics has become a frenzied contest over representation and when political actors are considered irrelevant unless they are trending, the spectacle becomes a vital tool of communication. Concurrently, it tends to illuminate social patterns and political relations between and within various communities. Aaltola, 2009.

5. Weber, 2002.

6. Tuan, 2013.

7. Cited in Mackey and Samaan, 2015.

8. Secular Syria (@syria_true), 2015, "Barbarian traitors attempt to save their lives, they use #HumanShields in #Syria #Douma!!," Twitter, 4:55a.m., 1 November 2015, https://twitter.com/syria_true/status/660802303063105536.

9. Cited in Human Rights Watch, 2015.

10. i24 News, 2015, "At Least 50 Civilians Dead in New Syria Regime Bombardment on Douma: Reports," 22 August 2015, https://www.i24news.tv/en/news/international/middle-east/82981–150822-at-least-56-civilians-dead-in-syria-regime-bombardment-in-douma-reports.

11. Hobsbawm, 1994.

12. Aaltola, 2009.

13. League of Nations, 1936c: 645.

14. Bargu, 2013; Bargu, 2014.

15. Sivakumaran, 2012.

16. Neilson, 1999.

17. Justin Rowlatt, 2017, "Why Indian Army Defended Kashmir 'Human Shield' Officer," BBC News, 31 May 2017.

18. Madhura Chakraborty, 2017, "Troubles in the Valley: A Youth Used as a Human Shield by the Army," *QRIUS,* 30 April 2017.

19. Rowlatt, 2017.

20. "BJP leader Earns on Wound of Kashmiris by Selling 'Human Shield' T-Shirts," 2018, *Kashmir Gazette,* March 31, 2018.

21. Rowlatt, 2017.

22. Rowlatt, 2017.

23. Gregory, 2004.

24. "Report of the Committee Appointed by the Government of India," 1920.

25. Cited in Khalili, 2010: 423.

26. Gordon and Perugini, 2016b.

27. Partha Chatterjee, 2017, "In Kashmir, India Is Witnessing Its General Dyer Moment," *The Wire,* 2 June 2017.

28. Ieshia Evans, 2016, "I Wasn't Afraid. I Took a Stand in Baton Rouge Because Enough Is Enough," *The Guardian,* 22 July 2016.

29. Evans, 2016.

30. The Black Lives Matter movement had been established just two years earlier by Patrisse Cullors, Alicia Garza, and Opal Tometi in the wake of the acquittal of George Zimmerman, the killer of seventeen-year-old Trayvon Martin. The three women had called on black people to protest the antiblack racism permeating the United States. See Garza, 2014: 23–28.

31. Evans, 2016.

32. Garza, 2014: 23–28.

21. COMPUTER GAMES

1. Card, 2010.

2. Moffett, Cubie, and Godden, 2017.

3. Tarja Susi, Mikael Johannesson, and Per Backlund, 2007, "Serious Games: An Overview," http://www.scangame.dk/downloads/HS-IKI-TR-07-001_PER .pdf.

4. Krulak, 1997.

5. Macedonia, 2002a.

6. Carpenter, 2013; Der Derian, 2009.

7. For an analysis of computer games for military recruitment, see Stahl, 2009.

8. Dale North, 2015, "155M Americans Play Video Games, and 80% of Households Own a Gaming Device," *Venture Beat,* 14 April 2015.

9. Wesley Yin-Poole, 2019, "The British Army Needs 'Binge Gamers,' 'Snow Flakes' and 'Me Me Me Millennials,'" *Eurogamer,* 3 January 2019.

10. Stahl, 2009: 48.

11. Stahl, 2009: 6.

12. Macedonia, 2002a: 157–67.

13. Andersen and Kurti, 2009.

14. Cited in Macedonia, 2002b.

15. One study found that the players of online first-person shooter games were almost exclusively young men (mean age about 18 years) who spend a lot of their leisure time on gaming (about 2.6 hours per day). Jansz and Tanis, 2007.

16. Philip Alston and Hina Shamsi, 2010, "A Killer above the Law," *The Guardian,* 8 February 2010.

17. Sharkey, 2011.

18. Macedonia, 2002b.

19. Colzato et al., 2010.

20. Brown, 2015.

21. Stein, 2002: 2.

22. Dead Rights Retribution, Xbox 36, https://www.amazon.com/Dead-Rights-Retribution-Xbox-360/dp/B001URRH12/ref.

23. Tom Clancy's Splinter Cell: Conviction, https://www.giantbomb.com/tom-clancys-splinter-cell-conviction/3030-20464/.

24. Turning Point: Fall of Liberty—PC, https://www.amazon.com/Turning-Point-Fall-Liberty-PC/dp/B000R2QSTI?th=1.

22. PROTEST

1. Klein, 2017: 223.

2. Sam Levin, 2016, "Dakota Access Pipeline Protests: UN Group Investigates Human Rights Abuses," *The Guardian,* 31 October 2016.

3. Adam Linehan, 2016, "'Where Evil Resides': Veterans 'Deploy' to Standing Rock to Engage the Enemy—The US Government," *Task & Purpose,* 21 November 2016.

4. Christopher Mele, 2016, "Veterans to Serve as 'Human Shields' for Dakota Pipeline Protesters," *New York Times,* 29 November 2016.

5. Balko, 2013.

6. Feigenbaum, 2017.

7. Balko, 2013.

8. Bond, 1974.

9. Hannah Strange and James Badcock, 2017, "Catalonian Referendum Violence Plunges EU into Crisis as '90pc of Voters Back Independence,'" *The Telegraph,* 2 October 2017; Mariana Zuniga and Harriet Alexander, 2017, "Venezuela Rocked by Deadly Protests during Controversial Election for 'Super Power' Assembly," *The Telegraph,* 31 July 2017.

10. Arsenault, 2007.

11. Amy Willis, 2015, "White Students Form a Human Shield around Black Protesters to Save Them," *Metro,* 21 October 2015.

12. Arendt, 2013. For a conception of state and corporate crime that is dependent not on the violation of the law but rather on conceptions of civil society, see Green and Ward, 2004.

13. For a history of the barricade and how it evolved, see Hazan, 2016.

14. Martial Law Stories, 2015, "In Photos: 1980s Strike at Globe Steel," *Martial Law Chronicles Project,* 22 September 2015.

15. Schock, 2005.

16. Sumsky, 1992.

17. Schock, 2005.

18. Caute, 1988; Brenda Stoter, 2013, "Egyptians Form Human Shields to Protect Female Protesters," *Al-Monitor,* 3 July 2013.

19. Arendt, 2013.

20. Mark Molloy, 2014, "Palestinians Tweet Tear Gas Advice to Protesters in Ferguson," *The Telegraph,* 15 August 2014.

21. @MariamBarghouti, 2014, "Always make sure to run against the wind /to keep calm when you're teargassed, the pain will pass, don't rub your eyes! #Ferguson Solidarity," Twitter, 8:07 p.m., 13 August 2014.

22. Molloy, 2014.

23. Goodale, 2006; Merry, 2006.

24. Patrick Howley, 2014, "Protest Rules: White Michael Brown Protesters Told to Serve as Human Shields for Black Protesters," *Daily Caller,* 27 November 2014.

25. Eternity Martis, 2014, "Dear Angry White People, the Ferguson Protest Was Not About You," *Huffington Post,* 27 January 2014.

26. Martis, 2014.

27. Bargu, 2013; see also Mahrouse, 2014.

28. Bargu, 2016.

29. Seventy percent of Gaza's population are refugees whose family has been dispossessed of its land as a result of the creation of the State of Israel. Gordon, 2008.

30. Israel Defense Forces (@IDF), 2018, "Do you know where your children are?" Twitter, 8:36 a.m., 14 May 2018.

31. "Israel Demands UN Condemn Hamas's Use of Children, Civilians as Human Shields," 2018, *Times of Israel,* May 14, 2018.

32. Gregory, 2006b.

33. Butler, 2015.

34. Lieblich and Shinar, 2017.

REFERENCES

Aaltola, Mika. 2009. *Western Spectacle of Governance and the Emergence of Humanitarian World Politics*. London: Palgrave Macmillan.

Aldrich, George H. 1991. "Compliance with International Humanitarian Law." *International Review of the Red Cross Archive* 31, no. 282.

Alexander, Amanda. 2007. "The Genesis of the Civilian." *Leiden Journal of International Law* 20, no. 2.

Allinson, Jamie. 2015. "The Necropolitics of Drones." *International Political Sociology* 9, no. 2 (June): 113–27.

Alter, W. 1936. "Les hôpitaux et les dangers de la guerre aérienne." *International Review of the Red Cross* 18, no. 4.

Amnesty International. 1999. "Kosovo: Amnesty International Concerns relating to NATO Bombings." London: AI, May 18.

———. 2000. "NATO/Federal Republic of Yugoslavia: 'Collateral Damage' or Unlawful Killings? Violations of the Laws of War by NATO during Operation Allied Force." London: AI.

———. 2009. *Unlock the Camps in Sri Lanka: Safety and Dignity for the Displaced Now*. London: AI.

———. 2017. *At Any Cost: The Civilian Catastrophe in West Mosul, Iraq*. London: AI.

Amoore, Louise. 2016. "Cloud Geographies Computing, Data, Sovereignty." *Progress in Human Geography* 42, no. 1.

Andersen, Robin, and Marin Kurti. 2009. "From America's Army to Call of Duty: Doing Battle with the Military Entertainment Complex." *Democratic Communiqué* 23, no. 1.

Anghie, Anthony. 2007. *Imperialism, Sovereignty and the making of International Law* Cambridge, UK: Cambridge University Press.

Arendt, Hannah. (1963) 1990. *On Revolution*. New York: Penguin Books.

———. 1973. *The Origins of Totalitarianism*. New York: Mariner Books.

———. 2013. *The Human Condition*. Chicago: University of Chicago Press.

Armstrong, Charles K. 2010. "The Destruction and Reconstruction of North Korea, 1950–1960." *Asia-Pacific Journal* 6, no. 51.

Aron, Raymond. 1965. *The Century of Total War.* New York: Beacon Press.

Arrowsmith, Pat. 1972. *To Asia in Peace: Story of a Non-Violent Action Mission to Indo-China.* London: Sidgwick & Jackson.

Arsenault, R. 2007. *Freedom Riders: 1961 and the Struggle for Racial Justice.* Oxford and New York: Oxford University Press.

Asad, Talal. 2015. "Reflections on Violence, Law, and Humanitarianism." *Critical Inquiry* 41, no. 2: 390–427.

Attewell, Wesley. 2015. "Ghosts in the Delta: USAID and the Historical Geographies of Vietnam's 'Other' War." *Environment and Planning A. Economy and Space* 47, no. 11.

Austin, John L. 1975. *How To Do Things with Words.* Cambridge, MA: Harvard University Press.

Bhabha, Homi K. 1994. *The Location of Culture.* London and New York: Routledge.

Badsey, Stephen. 2014. *The Franco-Prussian War 1870–1871.* London: Bloomsbury.

Baer, George W. 1976. *Test Case. Italy, Ethiopia, and the League of Nations.* Stanford, CA: Hoover Institution Press.

Balko, Radley. 2013. *Rise of the Warrior Cop: The Militarization of America's Police Forces.* New York: Public Affairs.

Bantekas, Ilias, and Lutz Oette. 2013. *International Human Rights Law and Practice.* Cambridge, UK: Cambridge University Press.

Bargu, Banu. 2013. "Human Shields." *Contemporary Political Theory* 12, no. 4.

———. 2014. *Starve and Immolate: The Politics of Human Weapons.* New York: Columbia University Press.

———. 2016. "Bodies against War: Voluntary Human Shielding as a Practice of Resistance." *American Journal of International Law* 110.

Bartolini, Giulio. 2012. "The Impact of Fascism in the Italian Doctrine of International Law." *Journal of the History of International Law* 14, no. 2.

Baudendistel, Rainer. 2006. *Between Bombs and Good Intentions: The Red Cross and the Italo-Ethiopian War, 1935–36.* Oxford and New York: Berghahn Books.

Baxter, Richard R. 1963. "The First Modern Codification of the Law of War: Francis Lieber and General Orders No. 100." *International Review of the Red Cross Archive* 3, no. 25.

Bedjaoui, Mohammed. 1961. *Law and the Algerian Revolution.* Brussels: Publications of the International Association of Democratic Lawyers.

Beevor, Anthony. 2009. *D-Day: The Battle for Normandy.* New York: Penguin.

———. 2011. *Crete: The Battle and the Resistance.* London, UK: Hachette.

Bell, Duncan. 2016. *Reordering the World: Essays on Liberalism and Empire.* Princeton, NJ, and Woodstock, Oxfordshire, UK: Princeton University Press.

Bellamy, Alex. J. 2012. *Massacres and Morality: Mass Atrocities in an Age of Civilian Immunity.* Oxford, UK: Oxford University Press.

Benvenisti, Eyal, and Doreen Lustig. 2017. "Taming Democracy: Codifying the Laws of War to Restore the European Order, 1856–1874." *University of Cambridge Faculty of Law Research Series,* Paper No. 28/2017.

Best, Geoffrey. 1994. *War and Law since 1945.* London: Clarendon Press.

Bigelow, Albert. 1959. *The Voyage of the Golden Rule: An Experiment with Truth.* New York: Doubleday.

Blomley, Nicholas, and Geraldine Pratt. 2001. "Canada and the Political Geographies of Rights." *The Canadian Geographer/Le Géographe Canadien* 45, no. 1.

Bodin, Jean. 1992. *On Sovereignty.* Cambridge, UK: Cambridge University Press.

Bond, James. 1974. *Rules of Riot: Internal Conflict and the Law of War.* New Jersey: Princeton University Press.

Bonfils, Henry. 1898. *Manuel de droit international public (droit des gens).* Paris: A. Rousseau.

Boot, Max. 2013. *Invisible Armies: An Epic History of Guerrilla Warfare from Ancient Times to the Present.* New York: Liveright.

Bourdieu, Pierre. 1986. "The Force of Law: Toward a Sociology of the Juridical Field." *Hastings Law Journal* 38.

Bousquet, Antoine. 2018. *The Eye of War: Military Perception from the Telescope to the Drone.* Minneapolis: University of Minnesota Press.

Braidotti, Rosi. 2013. *The Posthuman.* Cambridge, UK: Polity.

"British Relations with the Neighbouring Tribes on the North-West Frontier of India and the Military Operations Undertaken against Them during the Year 1897–1898." 1898. *Military Operation on the North-West Frontier of India,* vol. 1. *Parliamentary Papers.*

Brown, Wendy. 2015. *Undoing the Demos: Neoliberalism's Stealth Revolution.* Cambridge, MA: MIT Press.

Bugnion, François. 2003. *The International Committee of the Red Cross and the Protection of War Victims.* New York: Macmillan Education.

Burke, Roland. 2010. *Decolonization and the Evolution of International Human Rights.* Philadelphia: University of Pennsylvania Press.

Burrowes, Robert. 1991. "The Gulf War and the Gulf Peace Team." *Social Alternatives* 10, no. 2.

Butler, Judith. 2009. *Frames of War: When Is Life Grievable?* London: Verso.

———. 2015. "Human Shields." *London Review of International Law* 3, no. 2.

Bynum, Victoria E. 1998. "'White Negroes' in Segregated Mississippi: Miscegenation, Racial Identity, and the Law." *Journal of Southern History* 64, no. 2.

Callwell, Charles Edward. 1906. *Small Wars: Their Principles and Practice.* London: Harrison & Sons.

Caprari, Amanda M. 2009. "Lovable Pirates—The Legal Implications of the Battle between Environmentalists and Whalers in the Southern Ocean." *Connecticut Law Review* 42.

Card, Orson Scott. 2010. *Ender's Game.* New York: Macmillan.

Carlton, Michael. 2010. *Cruiser: The Life and Loss of HMAS Perth and Her Crew.* Sydney, Australia: Random House.

Carpenter, Charli R. 2006. *"Innocent Women and Children": Gender, Norms and the Protection of Civilians.* Aldershot, UK: Ashgate.

———. 2013. "Beware the Killer Robots: Inside the Debate over Autonomous Weapons." *Foreign Affairs,* 3.

Carter, April. 1977. "The Sahara Protest Team." In *Liberation Without Violence: A Third Party Approach,* edited by Paul Hare and Herbert Blumberg, 126–48. Totowa, NJ: Rowman & Littlefield.

Carvin, Stephanie. 2010. "The US Department of Defense Law of War Manual—an Update." In *Yearbook of International Humanitarian Law,* edited by M.N. Schmitt, L. Arimatsu, and T. McCormack, 13. The Hague, Neth.: T.M.C. Asser Press.

Catton, Philippe. 1999. "Counter-Insurgency and Nation Building: The Strategic Hamlet Programme in South Vietnam, 1961–1963." *International History Review* 21, no. 4.

Cavallaro, James, Stephan Sonnenberg, and Sarah Knuckey. 2012. *Living under Drones: Death, Injury and Trauma to Civilians from US Drone Practices in Pakistan.* Stanford, CA, and New York: International Human Rights Clinic at Stanford Law School and Global Justice Clinic at NYU School of Law. https://law .stanford.edu/publications/living-under-drones-death-injury-and-trauma-to- civilians-from-us-drone-practices-in-pakistan/.

Caute, David. 1988. *The Year of the Barricades: A Journey through 1968.* New York: Harper and Row.

Chamayou, Grégoire. 2015. *A Theory of the Drone.* New York: New Press.

Charlesworth, Hilary, Sam Chaiton, and C.M. Chinkin. 2000. *The Boundaries of International Law: A Feminist Analysis.* Manchester, UK: Manchester University Press.

Césaire, Aimé. 1972. *Discourse on Colonialism.* New York: Monthly Review Press.

Chambers, John W. 1999. *The Oxford Companion to American Military History.* New York: Oxford University Press.

Charney, Jonathan I. 1993. "Universal International Law." *American Journal of International Law* 87, no. 4.

Chickering, R., and Förster, S., eds. 2000. *Great War, Total War: Combat and Mobilization on the Western Front 1914–1918.* Cambridge, UK: Cambridge University Press.

Chimni, B.S. 1993. *International Law and World Order.* Cambridge, UK: Cambridge University Press.

———. 2006. "Third World Approaches to International Law: A Manifesto." *International Community Law Review* 8, no. 3.

Churchill, Winston. 1897. "Our Account with the Boers." *Churchill Papers* (CHAR 1/19/1–21). Cambridge, UK: Churchill Archives Centre.

———. 2013. *The Boer War: London to Ladysmith via Pretoria and Ian Hamilton's March.* New York: Bloomsbury Academic.

Clausewitz, Carl von. *On War.* 2007. Oxford: Oxford University Press.

Cohen, Stanley. 2013. *States of Denial: Knowing about Atrocities and Suffering.* London: John Wiley & Sons.

"Column 513: Boer Hostages on Trains." 1902. *Parliamentary Debates,* 4th series, vol. 102.

"Column 1025: Business of the House and Adjournment for Easter." 1902. *Parliamentary Debates,* 5th ser., vol. 105.

"Columns 509–531: South African War—Conduct of War—Terms Settlement." 1901. *Parliamentary Debates,* 4th ser., vol. 92.

"Columns 707–708: Boer Hostages on Trains." 1902. *Parliamentary Debates,* 4th ser., vol. 103.

Colzato, Lorenza S., Pieter J. A. van Leeuwen, Wery P. M. van den Wildenberg, and Bernhard Hommel. 2010. "DOOM'd to Switch: Superior Cognitive Flexibility in Players of First Person Shooter Games." *Frontiers in Psychology* 1: 8.

Concentration Camps Commission. 1902. *Report on the Concentration Camps in South Africa by the Committee of Ladies Appointed by the Secretary of State for War.* London: Eyre & Spottiswoode, printed for His Majesty's Stationery Office.

Cordesman, Anthony H. 2004. *The Ongoing Lessons of Afghanistan: Warfighting, Intelligence, Force Transformation, and Nation Building.* Working draft. Washington, DC: Center for Strategic and International Studies. https://csis-prod .s3.amazonaws.com/s3fs-public/legacy_files/files/media/csis/pubs/afghanlessons .pdf.

Correspondence and Report from His Majesty's Consul at Boma Respecting the Administration of the Independent State of the Congo. 1904. Africa, no. 1. Command Papers. London: Harrison and Sons.

Corrie Family, eds. 2009. *Let Me Stand Alone: The Journals of Rachel Corrie.* New York: W. W. Norton.

Crawford, Emily. 2015. *Identifying the Enemy Civilian Participation in Armed Conflict.* Oxford: Oxford University Press.

Crawford, Neta. 2013. *Accountability for Killing: Moral Responsibility for Collateral Damage in America's Post-9/11 Wars.* New York: Oxford University Press.

Croser, Caroline. 2007. "Networking Security in the Space of the City: Eventful Battlespaces and the Contingency of the Encounter." *Theory & Event* 10, no. 2.

Çubukçu, Ayça. 2017. "Thinking Against Humanity." *London Review of International Law* 5, no. 2.

Cushman, John H. 1966. "Pacification: Concepts Developed in the Field by the RVN 21st Infantry Division." *Army* 16.

Darcy, Shane. 2003. "The Evolution of the Law of Belligerent Reprisals." *Military Law Review* 175.

Day, David. 1987. *The Whale War.* New York: Routledge & Kegan Paul.

Debord, Guy. 2012. *Society of the Spectacle.* London: Bread and Circuses.

Del Boca, Angelo. 1996. *I gas di Mussolini.* Roma: Editori Riuniti.

Della Porta, Donatella, Mario Diani, and Lynn Mastellotto. 2003. "'No to the War with No Ifs or Buts': Protests against the War in Iraq." *Italian Politics* 19.

Der Derian, James. 2009. *Virtuous War: Mapping the Military-Industrial-Media-Entertainment-Network.* New York: Routledge.

Dewachi, Omar. 2017. *Ungovernable Life: Mandatory Medicine and Statecraft in Iraq.* Stanford, CA: Stanford University Press.

Dill, Janina. 2014. *Legitimate Targets?: Social Construction, International Law and Us Bombing*. Cambridge, UK: Cambridge University Press.

———. 2016. "The DoD Law of War Manual and the False Appeal of Differentiating Types of Civilians." *Just Security*, December 1, 2016.

Dillon, Michael, and Julian Reid. 2001. "Global Liberal Governance: Biopolitics, Security and War." *Millennium* 30, no. 1: 41–66.

Dinstein, Yoram. 2002. "Unlawful Combatancy." *Israel Yearbook on Human Rights* 32: 247–70.

———. 2004. *The Conduct of Hostilities under the Law of International Armed Conflict*. Cambridge, UK: Cambridge University Press.

Dörmann, Knut. 2003. *Elements of War Crimes under the Rome Statute of the International Criminal Court: Sources and Commentary*. Cambridge UK: Cambridge University Press.

Douglas, Valentine. 2014. *The Phoenix Program. America's Use of Terror in Vietnam*. New York: Open Road.

Douzinas, Costas. 2007. *Human Rights and Empire. The Political Philosophy of Cosmopolitanism*. London: Routledge.

Downes, Alexander B. 2008. *Targeting Civilians in War*. Ithaca: Cornell University Press.

Doyle, Arthur Conan. 1901. "The Derailing of Trains." *The Times*, 5 September 1901.

Doyle, Arthur Conan. 1902. *The War in South Africa: Its Cause and Conduct*. London: Smith, Elder.

Draper, John. 1870. *History of the American Civil War*. New York: Harper and Brothers.

Du Bois W. E. B. 1935. "Inter-Racial Implications of the Ethiopian Crisis: A Negro View." *Foreign Affairs* 19, no. 1.

Dunlap, Charles. 2001. "Law and Military Interventions: Preserving Humanitarian Values in 21st-Century Conflicts." Paper delivered at the conference Humanitarian Challenges in Military Intervention, Carr Center for Human Rights Policy, Harvard University, 29 November 2001.

———. 2008. "Lawfare Today: A Perspective." *Yale Journal of International Affairs*, 3.

———. 2015. "Human Shields and the DOD Law of War Manual: Can't We Improve the Debate?" *Just Security*. June 25, 2015.

———. 2016a. "Exclusive: Hays Parks on Human Shields and Restrictive Rules of Engagement." *Lawfire*, October 17, 2016.

———. 2016b. "No Good Options against ISIS Barbarism? Human Shields in 21st-Century Conflicts." *American Journal of International Law* 110 (unbound ed.).

Durand, André, and Pierre Boissier. 1984. *From Sarajevo to Hiroshima: History of the International Committee of the Red Cross*. Geneva: Henry Dunant Institute.

Elliott, H. W. 1995. "Hostages or Prisoners of War: War Crimes at Dinner." *Military Law Review* 149.

Enloe, Cynthia. 1990. *Bananas, Beaches and Bases: Making Feminist Sense of International Politics*. Berkeley: University of California Press.

Erakat, Noura. 2019. *Justice for Some: Law and the Question of Palestine.* Stanford, CA: Stanford University Press.

Erwood, Steve. 2011. *The Greenpeace Chronicles: 40 Years of Protecting the Planet.* Amsterdam: Greenpeace International.

Eslava, Luis, Michael Fakhri, and Vasuki Nesiah. 2017. *Bandung, Global History, and International Law. Critical Pasts and Pending Futures.* Cambridge, UK: Cambridge University Press.

Eslava, Luis, and Sundhya Pahuja. 2011. "Between Resistance and Reform: TWAIL and the Universality of International Law." *Trade, Law and Development* 3, no. 1.

Esmeir, Samera. 2012. *Juridical Humanity.* Stanford CA: Stanford University Press.

Ezzo, W. Matthew, and Amos N. Guiora. 2009. "A Critical Decision Point on the Battlefield–Friend, Foe or Innocent Bystander." In *Security: A Multidisciplinary Normative Approach,* edited by Cecilia M. Bailliet, 91–116. Leiden, Netherlands: Brill.

Falby, Allison. 2004. "Maude Royden's Guildhouse: A Nexus of Religious Change in Britain between the Wars." In *Historical Papers 2004: Canadian Society of Church History,* edited by Bruce L. Guenther. https://csch-sche.ca/historical-papers/historical-papers-canadian-society-of-church-history/2004-historical-papers/.

Fanon, Frantz. 1952. *Peau noire, masques blancs.* Paris: Éditions du Seuil.

———. 2017. *Alienation and Freedom.* Edited by Jean Khalfa and Robert J. C. Young. London: Bloomsbury.

Farris, Sara. 2017. *In the Name of Women's Rights: The Rise of Femonationalism.* Durham, NC: Duke University Press.

Fassin, Didier. 2007. "Humanitarianism as a Politics of Life." *Public Culture* 19, no. 3.

Fast, Larissa. 2014. *Aid in Danger: The Perils and Promise of Humanitarianism.* Pennsylvania: University of Pennsylvania Press.

Federal Ministry of Defense, Germany. 2013. *Law of Armed Conflict Manual.* Berlin: Federal Ministry of Defense.

Feigenbaum, Anna. 2017. *Tear Gas: From the Battlefields of WWI to the Streets of Today.* New York: Verso Books.

Feldman, Ilana, and Miriam Ticktin, eds. 2010. *In the Name of Humanity: The Government of Threat and Care.* Durham, NC: Duke University Press.

Fields, Craig I., and Pillip A. Odeen. 2004. *Defense Science Board: 2004 Summer Study on Transition to and from Hostilities.* Washington DC: Department of Defense.

Finkelstein, Norman. 2018. *Gaza: An Inquest into Its Martyrdom.* Oakland: University of California Press.

Fitzmaurice, Malgosia. 2015. *Whaling and International Law.* Cambridge, UK: Cambridge University Press, .

Fletcher, Sheila. 1989. *Maude Royden: A Life.* Oxford, UK: Blackwell.

Förster, Stig. 1987. "Facing 'People's War': Moltke the Elder and Germany's Military Options after 1871." *Journal of Strategic Studies* 10, no. 2.

Foucault, Michel. 1988. *Technologies of the Self: A Seminar with Michel Foucault.* Amherst: University of Massachusetts Press.

Foucault, Michel, and François Ewald. 2003. *"Society Must Be Defended": Lectures at the Collège de France, 1975–1976*. New York: Macmillan.

Fujitani, Takashi, Geoffrey M. White, and Lisa, Yoneyama. 2001. *Perilous Memories: The Asia-Pacific War(s)*. Durham, NC: Duke University Press.

Galeano, Eduardo. 1973. *Open Veins of Latin America. Five Centuries of the Pillage of a Continent*. New York: Monthly Review Press.

Gallay, Allan. 2002. *The Indian Slave Trade: The Rise of the English Empire in the American South, 1670–1717*. New Haven, CT: Yale University Press.

Gandhi, Mahatma. 1939. *Hind Swaraj, or, Indian Home Rule*. Ahmedabad, India: Navajivan Publishing House.

———. (1942) 1962. *Nonviolence in Peace & War*, I. Edited by Mahadev Desai. Ahmedabad: Navajivan Publishing House.

Gardam, Judith. 2004. *Necessity, Proportionality and the Use of Force by States*. Cambridge, UK: Cambridge University Press.

Garraway, Charles. 2011. "Changing Character of the Participants in War: Civilianization of Warfighting and the Concept of Direct Participation in Hostilities." *International Law Studies Series: US Naval War College* 87.

Garza, Alicia. 2014. "A Herstory of the #BlackLivesMatter Movement." In *Are All the Women Still White?: Rethinking Race, Expanding Feminisms,* edited by Janell Hobson. New York: State University of New York Press.

Gaudreau, Julien. 2003. "The Reservations to the Protocols Additional to the Geneva Conventions for the Protection of War Victims." *International Review of the Red Cross*, no. 849.

Geinitz, Christian. 2000. "The First Air War Against Noncombatants: Strategic Bombing of German Cities in World War I." In *Great War, Total War: Combat and Mobilization on the Western Front 1914–1918,* edited by Roger Chickering and Stig Förster. Cambridge, UK: Cambridge University Press.

Geneva Convention Relative to the Treatment of the Prisoners of War (Third Geneva Convention). 12 August 1949. 75 U.N.T.S. 135. https://ihl-databases.icrc.org/applic/ihl/ihl.nsf/vwTreaties1949.xsp.

Geneva Convention Relative to the Protection of Civilian Persons in Time of War, (Fourth Geneva Convention). 12 August 1949. 6 U.S.T. 3516, 75 U.N.T.S. 287. https://ihl-databases.icrc.org/applic/ihl/ihl.nsf/vwTreaties1949.xsp.

German Imperial Foreign Office. 1915. *Die völkerrechtswidrige Führung des belgischen Volkskriegs* [The Belgian peoples' war: A violation of international law]. Berlin: Auswärtiges Amt. English translation: *The German Army in Belgium: The White Book of May 1915*. 1921. New York: B. W. Huebsch.

Gilman, Nils. 2003. *Mandarins of the Future: Modernization Theory in Cold War America*. Baltimore: John Hopkins University Press.

Givoni, Michal. 2016. *The Care of the Witness: A Contemporary History of Testimony in Crises*. New York: Cambridge University Press.

Goodale, Mark. 2006. "Toward a Critical Anthropology of Human Rights." *Current Anthropology* 47, no. 3.

Gordon, Neve. 2008. *Israel's Occupation*. Berkeley: University of California Press.

———. 2012. "No Justice for Rachel Corrie." *The Nation,* August 31, 2012.

———. 2014. "Human Rights as a Security Threat: Lawfare and the Campaign against Human Rights NGOs." *Law & Society Review* 48, no. 2: 311–44.

Gordon, Neve, and Perugini, Nicola. 2016a. "Human Shields, Sovereign Power, and the Evisceration of the Civilian." *American Journal of International Law* 110 (unbound ed.).

———. 2016b. "The Politics of Human Shielding: On the Resignification of Space and the Constitution of Civilians as shields in Liberal Wars." *Environment and Planning D: Society and Space* 34, no. 1.

———. 2019. "'Hospital Shields' and the Limits of International Law." *European Journal of International Law* 30, no. 2: 439–63.

Gottlieb, Roger S. 2003. *This Sacred Earth: Religion, Nature, Environment.* New York: Routledge.

Government of Saudi Arabia. 2016. *Joint Incidents Assessment Team (JIAT) on Yemen Responds to Claims on Coalition Forces' Violations in Decisive Storm Operations.* Saudi Press Agency, May 16, 2016. https://www.spa.gov.sa/viewstory .php?lang=en&newsid=1524799.

Graham, Stephen. 2009. "Cities as Battlespace: The New Military Urbanism." *City* 13, no. 4.

———. 2011. *Cities under Siege: The New Military Urbanism.* London: Verso Books.

Grandin, Greg. 2019. *The End of the Myth: From the Frontier to the Border Wall in the Mind of America.* New York: Metropolitan Books.

Gray, Christine. 2018. *International Law and the Use of Force.* Oxford, UK: Oxford University Press.

Great Britain, Committee on Alleged German Outrages. 1915. *Report of the Committee on Alleged German Outrages Appointed by His Britannic Majesty's Government and Presided over by The Right Hon. Viscount Bryce.* New York: MacMillan.

Green, Penny, and Tony Ward. 2004. *State Crime: Governments, Violence and Corruption.* London: Pluto Press.

Gregory, Derek. 2004. *The Colonial Present: Afghanistan, Palestine, Iraq.* Oxford, UK: Blackwell.

———. 2006a. "'In Another Time-Zone, the Bombs Fall Unsafely . . .': Targets, Civilians, and Late Modern War." *Arab World Geographer* 9, no. 2.

———. 2006b. "The Death of the Civilian." *Environment and Planning D: Society and Space* 24, no. 5.

———. 2011a. "The Everywhere War." *Geographical Journal* 177, no. 3.

———. 2011b. "From a View to a Kill Drones and Late Modern War." *Theory, Culture & Society* 28, no. 7–8.

———. 2016. "The Hospital Raids," *Geographical Imaginations Blog,* September 25, 2016.

Gregory, Thomas. 2017. "Targeted Killings: Drones, Noncombatant Immunity, and the Politics of Killing," *Contemporary Security Policy,* 38, no. 2.

Gross, Michael L. 2015. *The Ethics of Insurgency.* Cambridge, UK: Cambridge University Press.

Grotius, Hugo. 2005. *The Rights of War and Peace*. Indianapolis: Liberty Fund.

Grovogui, Siba N'Zatioula. 1996. *Sovereigns, Quasi Sovereigns, and Africans: Race and Self-Determination in International Law*. Minneapolis: University of Minnesota Press.

Gusterson, Hugh. 2004. "The Seven Deadly Sins of Samuel Huntington." In *Why America's Top Pundits Are Wrong: Anthropologists Talk Back*, edited by Catherine Besteman and Hugh Gusterson. Berkeley: University of California Press.

Habibzadeh, Farrokh. 2018. "Economic Sanction: A Weapon of Mass Destruction." *Lancet*, 392 no. 10150.

Hague Convention No. 2 with Respect to the Laws and Customs of War on Land and its annex: Regulations concerning the Laws and Customs of War on Land. 29 July 1899. https://ihl-databases.icrc.org/ihl/INTRO/150.

Hague Convention No. 4 Respecting the Laws and Customs of War on Land and its annex: Regulations concerning the Laws and Customs of War on Land. 18 October 1907. https://ihl-databases.icrc.org/ihl/INTRO/195.

Hall, Stuart, Chas Critcher, Tony Jefferson, John Clarke, and Brian Roberts. 2013. *Policing the Crisis: Mugging, the State and Law and Order*. London: Palgrave Macmillan.

Hall, William E. 1890. *A Treatise on International Law*. Oxford: Clarendon Press.

Hammer, Ellen. 1944. "The Taking of Hostages in Theory and Practice." *American Journal of International Law* 38.

Halpern, Orit. 2015. *Beautiful Data: A History of Vision and Reason since 1945*. Durham, NC: Duke University Press.

Haque, Adil Ahmad. 2015. "The Defense Department's Indefensible Position on Killing Human Shields." *Just Security*, June 22, 2015.

———. 2017. *Law and Morality at War*. Oxford: Oxford University Press.

Hartman, Saidiya. 1997. *Scenes of Subjection: Terror, Slavery, and Self-Making in Nineteenth-Century America*. New York: Oxford University Press.

Hathaway, Oona, and Scott Shapiro. 2017. *The Internationalists: How a Radical Plan to Outlaw War Remade the World*. New York: Simon and Schuster.

Hazan, Eric. 2016. *A History of the Barricade*. London: Verso Books.

Henckaerts, Jean-Marie, and Louise Doswald-Beck. 2005. *Customary International Humanitarian Law*. ICRC/Cambridge, UK: Cambridge University Press.

Hendon, Bill and Stewart Elizabeth. 2008. *An Enormous Crime. The Definitive Account of American POWs Abandoned in South Asia*. New York: Thomas Dunne Books.

Himmiche, Ahmed, Nicolás D. Fernández, Virginia Hill, Lucy Mathieson, and Joel Salek. 2014. *Final Report of the Panel of Experts on Yemen Established Pursuant to Security Council Resolution 2140*. United Nations Security Council. UN Doc. S/2016/73.

Hobbes, Thomas. 1991. *Leviathan*. Cambridge, UK: Cambridge University Press.

Hobhouse, Emily. 1901. *Report of a Visit to the Camps of Women and Children in the Cape and Orange River Colonies*. London: Friars Printing Association.

Hobsbawm, Eric. 1994. "Barbarism: A User's Guide." *New Left Review* 206 (July-August).

Holmes, John. 2015. "Expert Military Report." In *Report: On the Second Mandate of the Presidential Commission of Inquiry into Complaints of Abductions and Disappearances*, edited by Maxwell P. Paranagama, Mano Ramanathan, and Suranjana Vidyaratne. Colombo: Sri Lanka Government: 210–45.

Horne, John, and Alan Krame. 2001. *German Atrocities, 1914: A History of Denial*. New Haven, CT: Yale University Press.

Howard, Michael. 2005. *The Franco-Prussian War: The German Invasion of France 1870–1871*. New York: Routledge.

Hozier, Henry, and William Adams. 1872. *The Franco-Prussian War: Its Causes, Incidents, and Consequences*. Vol. 2. London: W. Mackenzie.

Huntington, Samuel. 1968. "The Bases of Accommodation." *Foreign Affairs* 46, no. 4.

Hurd, Ian. 2017. *How to Do Things with International Law*. Princeton, NJ: Princeton University Press.

Hull, Isabel V. 2006. *Absolute Destruction: Military Culture and the Practices of War in Imperial Germany*. Ithaca, NY: Cornell University Press.

———. 2014. *A Scrap of Paper: Breaking and Making International Law during the Great War*. Ithaca: Cornell University Press.

Human Rights Watch. 2000. *Civilian Deaths in the NATO Air Campaign*. New York: HRW, February. https://www.hrw.org.

———. 2001. *Under Orders: War Crimes in Kosovo*. New York: HRW, October. https://www.hrw.org/report/2001/10/26/under-orders/war-crimes-kosovo.

———. 2009. *War on the Displaced: Sri Lankan Army and LTTE Abuses against Civilians in the Vanni*. New York: HRW. https://www.hrw.org/report/2009/02/19/war-displaced/sri-lankan-army-and-ltte-abuses-against-civilians-vanni.

———. 2010. *World Report 2010: Sri Lanka, Events of 2009*. New York: HRW. https://www.hrw.org/worldreport/2010/country-chapters/sri-lanka.

———. 2015. *Syria: Armed Groups Use Caged Hostages to Deter Attacks*. New York: HRW. https://www.hrw.org/news/2015/11/02/syria-armed-groups-usecaged-hostages-deter-attacks.

———. 2017. *Flawed Justice: Accountability for ISIS Crimes in Iraq*. New York: HRW. https://www.hrw.org/report/2017/12/05/flawed-justice/accountability-isis-crimes-iraq.

Hunter, Robert, and Kumi Naidoo. 2012. *Warriors of the Rainbow: A Chronicle of the Greenpeace Movement from 1971 to 1979*. Fremantle, Australia: Fremantle Press.

Ignatieff, Michael. 2003. *Empire Lite*. London: Vintage.

Imperial Cabinet of Russia. 1868. *Declaration Renouncing the Use, in Time of War, of Explosive Projectiles Under 400 Grammes Weight*. 29 November–11 December 1868, Saint Petersburg. https://ihl-databases.icrc.org/ihl/full/declaration1868.

Institute of International Law. 1880. The Laws of War on Land. Oxford, UK, adopted September 9, 1880.

International Committee of the Red Cross. 1934. Draft International Convention on the Condition and Protection of Civilians of Enemy Nationality Who Are on Territory belonging to or occupied by a Belligerent. Tokyo.

———. 1938. *Report on the Proposed Convention for the Establishment of Hospital Towns and Areas.* ICRC Resolution No. 11. Geneva.

———. 1946. *Preliminary Conference of National Red Cross Societies for the Study of Conventions and of Various Problems Relative to the Red Cross,* series 1, vol. 3. Geneva, 26 July–3 August 1946.

———. 1947a. *Report of the Commission of Government Experts for the Study of Conventions for the Protection of War Victims: Report of the Third Commission.* Vol. 3, "Condition and Protection of Civilians in Times of War." Geneva.

———. 1947b. *Report on the Work of the Conference of Government Experts for the Study of the Conventions for the Protection of War Victims.* Geneva, 14–26 April 1947.

———. 1949a. *Final Record of the Diplomatic Conference of Geneva of 1949,* vol. 1. Geneva.

———. 1949b. *Final Record of the Diplomatic Conference of Geneva of 1949,* vol. 2, sec. A. Geneva.

———. 1949c. *Final Record of the Diplomatic Conference of Geneva of 1949,* vol. 2, sec. B. Geneva.

———. 1949d. *Final Record of the Diplomatic Conference of Geneva of 1949,* vol. 3. Geneva.

———. 1965. "Letter on Application of Geneva Conventions in Viet-Nam, and Replies of the United States and Republic of Viet-Nam." *International Legal Materials* 4, no. 6.

International Crisis Group. 2009. "Crisis in Sri Lanka." ICG Board of Trustees statement, 20 April 2009. https://www.crisisgroup.org/asia/south-asia/sri-lanka/crisis-sri-lanka.

———. 2010. *Sri Lanka: A Bitter Peace,* Asia Briefing no. 99. New York: ICG.

International Tribunal for the Prosecution of Persons Responsible for Serious Violations of International Humanitarian Law Committed in the Territory of the Former Yugoslavia since 1991. 2000. *Final Report to the Prosecutor by the Committee Established to Review the NATO Bombing Campaign against the Federal Republic of Yugoslavia,* 13 June 2000.

Jain, Pankaj. 2016. *Dharma and Ecology of Hindu Communities: Sustenance and Sustainability.* London: Routledge.

Janin, Albert S. 2007. "Engaging Civilian-Belligerents Leads to Self-Defense: Protocol I Marriage." *Army Lawyer* 410.

Jansz, Jeroen, and Martin Tanis. 2007. "Appeal of Playing Online First Person Shooter Games." *Cyber Psychology & Behavior* 10, no. 1: 133–36.

Jochnick, Chris. 1999. "Confronting the Impunity of Non-state Actors: New Fields for the Promotion of Human Rights." *Human Rights Quarterly* 21, no. 1.

Jochnick, Chris, and Roger Normand. 1994. "The Legitimation of Violence: A Critical History of the Laws of War." *Harvard International Law Journal,* 35.

Johnson, Lyndon B. 1967. "Address on U.S. Policy in Vietnam Delivered Before a Joint Session of the Tennessee State Legislature." 15 March 1967, Nashville, TN. American Presidency Project, https://www.presidency.ucsb.edu/node/237953.

Jones, Craig. 2016. "Travelling Law: Targeted Killing, Lawfare and the Deconstruction of the Battlefield." In *American Studies Encounters the Middle East,* edited by A. Lubin and M. M. Kraidy. Chapel Hill, NC: University of North Carolina Press.

Jones, Samuel. 1911. *The Siege of Charleston.* New York: Neale.

Julliot, Charles L. 1936. "Aviation et Croix-Rouge." *International Review of the Red Cross* 18, no. 210: 433–64.

Junod, Marcel. 1951. *Warriors without Weapons.* London: Cape.

Kakel, Carroll P., III. 2013. *The Holocaust as Colonial Genocide: Hitler's Indian Wars in the 'Wild East.'"* London, UK: Palgrave Macmillan.

Kalshoven, Frits, and Leisbeth Zegveld. 2011. *Constraints on the Waging of War: An Introduction to International Humanitarian Law.* Cambridge, UK: Cambridge University Press.

Kaplan, Louis. 2015. "Photographic Patriotism: Arthur Mole's Living Photographs." In *Living Photographs—Arthur Mole.* Paris: RVB Books.

Kaplan, Louis. 2001. "A Patriotic Mole: A Living Photograph." *New Centennial Review* 1.

Kasher, Asa, and Amos Yadlin. 2005a. "Assassination and Preventive Killing." *SAIS Review* 25, no. 1: 41–57.

———. 2005b. "Military Ethics of Fighting Terror: An Israeli Perspective," *Journal of Military Ethics,* 4, no. 1.

Kennedy, David. 2009. *Of War and Law.* Princeton NJ: Princeton University Press.

Kennedy, Duncan. 2008. "A Left/Phenomenological Alternative to the Hart/Kelsen Theory of Legal Interpretation." In *Legal Reasoning: Collected Essays.* Aurora, CO: Davies Group.

Khalili, Laleh. 2010. "The Location of Palestine in Global Counterinsurgencies." *International Journal of Middle East Studies* 42, no. 3: 413–33.

———. 2012. *Time in the Shadows: Confinement in Counterinsurgencies.* Stanford, CA: Stanford University Press.

Khatchadourian, Raffi. 2007. "Neptune's Navy." *New Yorker,* October 29, 2007.

Kilcullen, David. 2010. *Counterinsurgency.* Oxford, UK: Oxford University Press.

Kinsella, Helen. 2006. "Gendering Grotius: Sex and Sex Difference in the Laws of War." *Political Theory* 34, no. 2: 161–91.

———. 2011. *The Image before the Weapon: A Critical History of the Distinction between Combatant and Civilian.* Ithaca, NY: Cornell University Press.

———. 2016a. "Gender and Human Shielding." *American Journal of International Law* 110: 305–10.

———. 2016b. "Gender and International Humanitarian Law." In *Handbook of Gender in World Politics,* edited by Jill Steans and Daniela Tepe-Belfrage, 171–77. Cheltenham, UK, and Northampton, MA: Edward Elgar Publishing.

Klaidman, Daniel. 2012. *Kill or Capture: The War on Terror and the Soul of the Obama Presidency.* New York: Houghton Mifflin Harcourt.

Klein, Naomi. 2007. *The Shock Doctrine: The Rise of Disaster Capitalism.* New York: Metropolitan Books/Henry Bolt.

———. 2017. *No is Not Enough: Resisting Trump's Shock Politics and Winning the World We Need.* Chicago: Haymarket Books.

Knights, Michael. 2003. "Air War Targetting: Sparing Civilians." *World Today* 59, no. 4.

Kolb, Robert. 1997. "Origin of the Twin Terms *Jus ad Bellum* and *Jus in Bello.*" *International Review of the Red Cross* no. 320.

Koskenniemi, Martti. 2001. *The Gentle Civilizer of Nations: The Rise and Fall of International Law 1870–1960.* Cambridge, UK: Cambridge University Press.

Koskodan, Kenneth. 2011. *No Greater Ally: The Untold Story of Poland's Forces in World War II.* London: Bloomsbury Publishing.

Kosto, Adam. 2012. *Hostages in the Middle Ages.* Oxford, UK: Oxford University Press.

Krebs, Paula. 1999. *Gender, Race, and the Writing of Empire: Public Discourse and the Boer War.* Cambridge, UK: Cambridge University Press.

Krulak, Charles. 1997. "Military Thinking and Decision Making Exercises," Marine Corps Order 1500.55. Department of the Navy Headquarters United States Marine Corps, Washington DC.

Kuntsman, Adi, and Rebecca L. Stein. 2015. *Digital Militarism: Israel's Occupation in the Social Media Age.* Stanford, CA: Stanford University Press.

L. D. 1936. "Á propos de la visibilité du signe de la Croix-Rouge." *International Review of the Red Cross* 18, no. 207.

Labanca, Nicola. 2015. *La guerra d'Etiopia 1935–1941.* Bologna: Il Mulino.

Lawrence, Mark Atwood. 2008. *The Vietnam War: A Concise International History.* New York: Oxford University Press.

Laws of War on Land (Oxford Manual, drafted by Gustave Moynier and unanimously adopted by Institute of International Law). 9 September 1880, Oxford. https://ihl-databases.icrc.org/ihl/INTRO/140.

League of Nations. 1936a. "90th Session of the Council, Annex 1587." *League of Nations Official Journal,* February 1936.

———. 1936b. "91st Session of the Council, Annex 1952." *League of Nations Official Journal,* April 1936.

———. 1936c. "Ninety-Second Session of the Council, Annex 1597." *League of Nations Official Journal,* 17, no. 6 (June).

Lee, Harper. 2010. *To Kill a Mockingbird.* New York: Random House.

Lewy, Guenter. 1978. *America in Vietnam.* New York: Oxford University Press.

Liano, Alejandro. 1929. *Ethiopie: empire des nègres blancs.* Paris: Éditions Pierre Roger.

Lieber, Francis. 1863. *General Orders No. 100: Instructions for the Government of Armies of the United States, in the Field* [Lieber Code]. New York: D. van Nostrand.

Lieblich, Eliav, and Shinar, Adam. 2017. "The Case against Police Militarization." *Michigan Journal of Race and Law* 23, no. 1.

Lindqvist, Sven. 2001. *A History of Bombing.* London: Granta Publications.

Lipkes, Jeff. 2007. *Rehearsals: The German Army in Belgium, August 1914.* Leuven, Belgium: Leuven University Press.

Little, Roger. 1995. *Nègres blancs: représentations de l'autre autre*. Paris: L'Harmattan.

"Lords Sitting of Wednesday, 15th March 1939." 1939. *House of Lords (Hansard) Sessional Papers*, 5th ser., vol. 112.

Lowe, Lisa. 2015. *The Intimacies of Four Continents*. Durham, NC: Duke University Press.

Luard, Evan. 1989. *The History of the United Nations*, vol. 2: *The Age of Decolonization 1955–1965*. London: Macmillan.

Macedonia, Michael. 2002a. "Games, Simulation, and the Military Education Dilemma." In *Internet and the University: 2001 Forum*. Louisville, CO: Educause.

———. 2002b. "Games Soldiers Play." *IEEE Spectrum* 39, no. 3.

MacKay, Don. 1995. "Nuclear Testing: New Zealand and France in the International Court of Justice." *Fordham International Law Journal* 19.

Mackenzie D. R. 1934. "Liberia and the League of Nations." *Journal of the Royal African Society* 33, no. 133.

MacQueen, Norrie. 2011. *Humanitarian Intervention and the United Nations*. Edinburgh: Edinburgh University Press.

Mahrouse, Gada. 2014. *Conflicted Commitments: Race, Privilege, and Power in Solidarity Activism*. Montreal: McGill-Queen's Press.

Mamdani, Mahmood. 2001. "A Brief History of Genocide." *Transition* 10, no. 3.

———. 2009. *Saviors and Survivors: Darfur, Politics and the War on Terror*. New York: Pantheon Books.

Mantilla, Giovanni. 2019. "Social Pressure and the Making of Wartime Civilian Protection Rules." *European Journal of International Relations*, 23 August 2019, 1–26.

Mbembe, Achille. 2003. "Necropolitics." *Public Culture* 15, no. 1.

McTaggart, David, and Robert Hunter. 1979. *Greenpeace III: Journey into the Bomb*. New York: William Morrow.

Mégret, Frédéric. 2006. "From 'Savages' to 'Unlawful Combatants': A Postcolonial Look at International Humanitarian Law's 'Other.'" In *International Law and Its "Others,"* edited by Anne Orford. Cambridge, UK: Cambridge University Press.

———. 2010. "A Cautionary Tale from the Crusades? War and Prisoners in Conditions of Normative Incommensurability." In *Prisoners in War,* edited by Sibylle Scheipers, 23–38. New York: Oxford University Press.

Melzer, Nils. 2009. *Direct Participation in Hostilities Under International Humanitarian Law*. Geneva: International Committee of the Red Cross.

Meron, Theodor. 1989. *Human Rights and Humanitarian Norms as Customary Law*. Oxford, UK: Clarendon Press.

———. 1998. "Francis Lieber's Code and Principles of Humanity." *Columbia Journal of Transnational Law* 36.

———. 2000. "The Humanization of Humanitarian Law." *American Journal of International Law* 94, no. 2.

Merry, Sally. 2006. *Human Rights and Gender Violence: Translating International Law into Local Justice*. Chicago: University of Chicago Press.

Ministère des Affaires Étrangères, Government of France. 1915. *Les violations des lois de la guerre par l'Allemagne.* Paris et Nancy: Librairie Berger-Levrault.

Ministère de la Défense, France. 2012. *Manuel du droit des conflits armés.* Paris.

Ministry of Defense, Sri Lanka. 2011. *Humanitarian Operation Factual Analysis.* Colombo: Sri Lanka Government, July 2011.

Ministry of Foreign Affairs, State of Israel. 2015. *The 2014 Gaza Conflict: Factual and Legal Aspects.* Jerusalem: Israel Ministry of Foreign Affairs.

Ministry of Justice and Ministry of Foreign Affairs, Kingdom of Belgium. 1918. *Reply to the German White Book of the 10th May 1915, "Die völkerrechtswidrige Führung des belgischen Volkskriegs."* War of 1914–1916. English translation, London: His Majesty's Stationery Office. https://archive.org/details/cu31924027863996.

Mitchell, John G., and Constance L. Stallings. 1970. *Ecotactics: The Sierra Club Handbook for Environmental Activists.* New York: Pocket Books.

Moffett, Luke, Dug Cubie, and Andrew Godden. 2017. "Bringing the Battlefield into the Classroom: Using Video Games to Teach and Assess International Humanitarian Law." *Law Teacher* 51, no. 4.

Moltke, Helmuth von, and Daniel Hughes. 1995. *Moltke on the Art of War: Selected Writings.* New York: Ballentine Books.

Moorehead, Caroline. 1999. *Dunant's Dream: War, Switzerland and History of the Red Cross.* New York: Harper Collins Publishers.

Morgan, Edmund. 2003. *American Slavery, American Freedom.* New York: W. W. Norton.

Morsink, Johannes. 1999. *The Universal Declaration of Human Rights: Origins, Drafting, and Intent.* Philadelphia: University of Pennsylvania Press.

Moses, Dirk. 2020. *The Problems of Genocide: Permanent Security and the Language of Transgression.* Cambridge: Cambridge University Press.

Moyn, Samuel. 2010. *The Last Utopia: Human Rights in History.* Cambridge, MA: Harvard University Press.

Mulhearn, Donna. 2010. *Ordinary Courage: My Journey to Baghdad as a Human Shield.* Australia: Pier 9.

Mulvaney, Kieran. 2003. *The Whaling Season: An Inside Account of the Struggle to Stop Commercial Whaling.* London: Island Press.

Murray, J. O. 1911. *The Immortal Six Hundred: A Story of Cruelty to Confederate Prisoners of War.* Roanoke, VA: Stone Printing and Manufacturing.

Mussolini, Vittorio. 1937. *Voli Sulle Ambe.* Firenze: Sansoni.

Nabulsi, Karma. 1999. *Traditions of War: Occupation, Resistance, and the Law.* Oxford, UK: Oxford University Press.

Nash, David. 1999. "The Boer War and Its Humanitarian Critics." *History Today* 49, no. 6.

National Defense Authorization Act for Fiscal Year 2018, Sec. 1057: "Annual Report on Civilian Casualties in Connection with United States Military Operations." 12 December 2017 (Public Law 115–91). https://www.congress.gov/bill/115th-congress/house-bill/2810/text.

National Security Strategy of the United States. August 1991. Preface, "A New World Order," by George H. W. Bush. Washington, DC: White House. https://www .hsdl.org/?view&did=460714.

Neilson, Brett. 1999. "Barbarism/Modernity: Notes on Barbarism." *Textual Practice* 13, no. 1.

Newton, Michael, and Larry May. 2014. *Proportionality in International Law.* Oxford, UK: Oxford University Press.

Nguyên Giáp, Võ. (1961) 2014. *People's War. People's Army.* Marxists Internet Archive, https://www.marxists.org/archive/giap/1961-pwpa.pdf. First published in English, Hanoi: Foreign Languages Publishing House.

Nordquist, Myron, and Satya N. Nandan. 2011. *United Nations Convention on the Law of the Sea 1982: A Commentary.* Vol. 7. Dordrecht: Martinus Nijhoff.

Norwegian Refugee Council/Internal Displacement Monitoring Centre. 2009. *Sri Lanka: Continuing Humanitarian Concerns and Obstacles to Durable Solutions for Recent and Longer-Term IDPs.* 10 November 2009. https://www.refworld .org/docid/4afa784b2.html.

Nybakken, Oscar E. 1939. "Humanitas Romana." *Transactions and Proceedings of the American Philological Association 70.*

Oatis, Steven J. 2004. *A Colonial Complex: South Carolina's Frontiers in the Era of the Yamasee War, 1680–1730.* Lincoln: University of Nebraska Press.

Obregón, Liliana. 2007. "Between Civilisation and Barbarism: Creole Interventions in International Law." *Third World Quarterly* 27, no. 5.

Odysseos, Louiza, and Fabio Petito. 2007. *The International Political Thought of Carl Schmitt: Terror, Liberal War, and the Crisis of Global Order.* New York: Routledge.

Official Commission of the Belgian Government. 1915. *Reports on the Violation of the Rights of Nations and the Laws and Customs of War.* London: Harrison and Sons, printed under the Authority of His Majesty's Stationery Office.

Official Records of the Diplomatic Conference on the Reaffirmation and Development of International Humanitarian Law Applicable in Armed Conflicts, vol. 5. 1978. Bern: Federal Political Department. https://www.loc.gov/rr/frd/Military_Law /pdf/RC-records_Vol-5.pdf.

Oppenheim, Lassa. 1912. *International Law: A Treatise.* New York: Longmans Green.

Orford, Anne. 2003. *Reading Humanitarian Intervention: Human Rights and the Use of Force in International Law.* Cambridge, UK: Cambridge University Press.

———, ed. 2006. *International Law and its "Others."* Cambridge, UK: Cambridge University Press.

———. 2010. "The Passions of Protection: Sovereign Authority and Humanitarian War." In *Contemporary States of Emergency,* edited by Didier Fassin and Mariella Pandolfi. Brooklyn, NY: Zone Books.

Owens, Patricia. 2015. *Economy of Force: Counterinsurgency and the Historical Rise of the Social.* Cambridge, UK: Cambridge University Press.

Özsu, Umut. 2015. "'In the Interests of Mankind as a Whole': Mohammed Bedjaoui's New International Economic Order." *Humanity: An International Journal of Human Rights, Humanitarianism, and Development* 6, no. 1.

———. 2019. "Determining New Selves: Mohammed Bedjaoui on Algeria, Western Sahara, and Post-Classical International Law." In *The Battle for International Law: North-South Perspectives in the Decolonization Era,* edited by Jochen von Bernstorff and Philipp Dann, ch. 15. Oxford, UK: Oxford University Press,

Pahuja, Sundhya. 2011. *Decolonising International Law: Development, Economic Growth, and the Politics of Universality.* Cambridge, UK: Cambridge University Press.

Pakenham, Thomas. 1979. *The Boer War.* London: Weidenfeld and Nicolson.

Pankhurst, Richard. 1997. "Il bombardamento fascista sulla Croce Rossa durante l'invasione dell'Etiopia." *Studi piacentini* 21.

———. 1999. "Italian Fascist War Crimes in Ethiopia: A History of Their Discussion, from the League of Nations to the United Nations (1936–1949)." *Northeast African Studies.* 6, no. 1–2.

Paranagama, Maxwell P., Mano Ramanathan, and Suranjana Vidyaratne, eds. 2015. *Report: On the Second Mandate of the Presidential Commission of Inquiry into Complaints of Abductions and Disappearances.* Colombo: Sri Lanka Government.

Parfitt, Rose. 2011. "Empire des Nègres Blancs: The Hybridity of International Personality and the Abyssinia Crisis of 1935–36." *Leiden Journal of International Law* 24, no. 4.

———. 2019. *The Process of International Legal Reproduction: Inequality, Historiography, Resistance.* Cambridge, UK: Cambridge University Press.

Parks, W. Hays. 1983. "Linebacker and the Law of War." *Air University Review* 34, no. 12.

———. 2010. "National Security Law in Practice: The Department of Defense Law of War Manual." Address to the American Bar Association Standing Committee on Law and Security. jnslp.com/wp-content/uploads/2010/11/aba-speech-11082010-final-as-given.pdf.

Pavolini, Alessandro. 1936. "Nuova e schiacciante prova dell'abuso dell'emblema della Croce Rossa in Etiopia." *Il Corriere della Sera,* January 5, 1936.

Perugini, Nicola, and Neve Gordon. 2015. *The Human Right to Dominate.* New York: Oxford University Press.

———. 2017. "Distinction and the Ethics of Violence: On the Legal Construction of Liminal Subjects and Spaces." *Antipode* 49 no. 5.

———. 2019. "Between Sovereignty and Race: The Bombardment of Hospitals in the Italo-Ethiopian War and the Colonial Imprint of International Law." *State Crime* 8, no. 1: 104–25.

Perret, Françoise, and François Bugnion. 2009. *Histoire du Comité international de la Croix-Rouge.* Vol. 4, *De Budapest à Saigon, 1956–1965.* Geneva: Georg Editeur/CICR.

Phillipson, Coleman. 1911. *The International Law and Custom of Ancient Greece and Rome.* London: Macmillan.

Pictet, Jean, Hans-Peter Gasser, Sylvie-So Junod, Claude Pilloud, Jean De Preux, Yves Sandoz, Christophe Swinarski, Claude F. Wenger, and Bruno Zimmermann. 1987. *Commentary on the Additional Protocols: Of 8 June 1977 to the Geneva Conventions of 12 August 1949*. Dordrecht: Martinus Nijhoff.

Pillet, Antoine. 1901. *Les lois actuelles de la guerre*. Paris: A. Rousseau.

Pillet, Antoine. 1916. *La guerre actuelle et les droits des gens*. Paris: Pedone.

Pitts, Jennifer. 2018. *Boundaries of the International: Law and Empire*. Cambridge, MA: Harvard University Press.

Phuong-Lan, Bui Thi. 2003. "When the Forest Became the Enemy and the Legacy of American Herbicidal Warfare in Vietnam." PhD Thesis in History of American Civilization, Harvard University, Graduate School or Arts and Sciences.

Plant, Glen. 1983. "Civilian Protest Vessels and the Law of the Sea." *Netherlands Yearbook of International Law* 14.

———. 2002. "International Law and Direct Action Protests at Sea: Twenty Years On." *Netherlands Yearbook of International Law* 33.

Pratt, Edwin A. 1915. *Rise of Rail Power: In War and Conquest 1833–1914*. London: P. S. King.

Project of an International Declaration concerning the Laws and Customs of War (Brussels Declaration). 27 August 1874, Brussels. https://ihl-databases.icrc.org /ihl/INTRO/135.

Prosecutor v. Radovan Karadžić. 2016. International Criminal Tribunal for the Former Yugoslavia, 26 March 2016.

Prosecutor v. Ramush Haradinaj, Idriz Balaj, Lahi Brahimaj, rev. 4th amended indictment. 2011. International Criminal Tribunal for the Former Yugoslavia, 21 January 2011.

Prosecutor v. Ratko Mladić. 2017. International Criminal Tribunal for the Former Yugoslavia, 27 November 2017.

Protocol I Additional to the Geneva Conventions of 12 August 1949, and relating to the Protection of Victims of International Armed Conflicts. 8 June 1977. 1125 U.N.T.S. 3. https://ihl-databases.icrc.org/ihl/INTRO/470.

Ramet, Sabrina P. 2011. *Serbia and the Serbs in World War Two*. Berlin: Springer.

Read, Simon. 2015. *Winston Churchill Reporting: Adventures of a Young War Correspondent*. Boston: Da Capo Press.

Reagan, Ronald. 1987. "Message to the Senate Transmitting a Protocol to the 1949 Geneva Conventions." Reagan Library, January 29, 1987. https://www .reaganlibrary.gov/research/speeches/012987b.

Reisman, W. Michael, and William K. Leitzau. 1991. "Moving International Law from Theory to Practice: The Role of Military Manuals in Effectuating the Law of Armed Conflict." *International Law Studies* 64.

"Report of the Committee Appointed by the Government of India to Investigate the Disturbances in the Punjab, etc." 1920. *House of Commons Parliamentary Papers*, 1–191.

Reynolds, John. 2017. *Empire, Emergency, and International Law*. Cambridge UK: Cambridge University Press.

Rey-Schyrr, Catherine. 2007. *Histoire du Comité international de la Croix-Rouge.* Vol. 3, *De Yalta à Dien Bien Phu, 1945–1955.* Geneva: Georg Editeur/CICR.

Risse, Thomas, Stephen C. Ropp, and Kathryn Sikkink. 1999. *The Power of Human Rights: International Norms and Domestic Change.* Cambridge, UK: Cambridge University Press.

Rochat, Giorgio. 1971. *Militari e politici nella preparazione della campagna d'Etiopia.* Milano: Franco Angeli.

———. 1988. "L'impiego dei gas nella guerra d'Etiopia, 1935–36." *Rivista di Storia Contemporanea* 17, no. 1.

Rogers, A. P. V. 2010. "The United Kingdom Manual of the Law of Armed Conflict." In *National Military Manuals on the Law of Armed Conflict,* edited by Nobuo Hayashi. Oslo: Torkel Opsahl Academic EPublisher.

Rogers, A. P. V., and P. Malherbe. 1999. *Fight It Right: Model Manual on the Law of Armed Conflict for Armed Forces.* Geneva: ICRC.

Roman, Alfred. 1884. *The Military Operations of General Beauregard.* New York: Harper & Bros.

Rose, Nikolas. 2001. "The Politics of Life Itself." *Theory, Culture & Society.* 18, no. 6: 1–30.

Rosén, Frederik. 2016. *Collateral Damage: A Candid History of a Peculiar Form of Death.* New York: Hurst.

Rosen, Richard D. 2009. "Targeting Enemy Forces in the War on Terror: Preserving Civilian Immunity." *Vanderbilt Journal of Transnational Law* 42, no. 3.

Royden, A. Maude. Files. Women's Library Archive. London School of Economics.

———. 1915. *The Great Adventure: The Way to Peace.* London: Headly, Fellowship of Reconciliation.

———. 1932. "The Peace Army." In *Sermon,* 1–8. London: Guildhouse.

———. 1933. "The Peace Army." *Friendship: Journal of the Friends' Hall and Walthamstow Educational Settlement,* May-June 1933.

———. 1941. "The Failure of the Pacifists." *Survey Graphic,* December 1941.

———. 1949. "Master Christian?" In *Gandhi Memorial, Peace Number,* edited by Kshitis Roy. Santinketan, India: Santinketan Press.

Royden, A. Maude, Herbert Gray, and Richard Sheppard. 1932. "Unarmed Peace Army." *Daily Express,* 26 February 1932.

Rubinstein. Amnon, and Yaniv Roznai. 2011. "Human Shields in Modern Armed Conflicts: The Need for a Proportionate Proportionality." *Stanford Law and Policy Review* 22, no. 1.

Said, Edward. 1980. *The Question of Palestine.* New York: Vintage Books.

Safeguarding Health in Conflict. 2017. *Impunity Must End: Attacks on Health in 23 Countries in Conflict in 2016.* Boston: Physicians for Human Rights.

Sassòli, Marco. 2003. "Legitimate Targets of Attacks under International Humanitarian Law." *HPCR Policy Brief.*

———. 2010. "Taking Armed Groups Seriously: Ways to Improve their Compliance with International Humanitarian Law." *Journal of International Humanitarian Legal Studies* 1, no. 1.

Sassòli, Marco, Antoine Bouvier, and Anne Quintin. 2011. *How Does Law Protect in War?* Geneva: ICRC.

Sayer, Ian, and Dronfield, Jeremy. 2019. *Hitler's Last Plot: The 139 VIP Hostages Selected for Death in the Final Days of World War II.* New York: Da Capo Press.

Schabas, William A. 2019. *The Trial of the Kaiser.* Oxford, UK: Oxford University Press.

Scheffer, David. 2012. *All the Missing Souls: A Personal History of the War Crime Tribunals.* Princeton, NJ: Princeton University Press.

Scheipers, Sibylle. 2015. *Unlawful Combatants: A Genealogy of the Irregular Fighter.* New York: Oxford University Press.

———. 2018. *On Small War: Carl von Clausewitz and People's War.* Oxford, UK: Oxford University Press.

Schmitt, Carl. 2004. *Theory of the Partisan: A Commentary/Remark on the Concept of the Political.* New York: Telos Press .

———. 2006. *The Nomos of the Earth in the International Law of the Jus Publicum Europaeum.* East Lansing: Michigan State University Press.

Schmitt, Michael. 2005. "Humanitarian Law and Direct Participation in Hostilities by Private Contractors or Civilian Employees." *Chicago Journal of International Law* 5.

———. 2008. "Human Shields in International Humanitarian Law." *Columbia Journal of Transnational Law* 47, no. 2.

———. 2009. "Targeting and International Humanitarian Law in Afghanistan." *International Law Studies* 85: 307–39.

———. 2010. "Deconstructing Direct Participation in Hostilities: The Constitutive Elements." *New York University Journal of International Law and Politics* 42.

———. 2012. "Human Shields in International Humanitarian Law." In *Essays on Law and War at the Fault Lines.* The Hague: T.M.C. Asser Press.

Schock, Kurt. 2005. *Unarmed Insurrections: People Power Movements in Nondemocracies.* Minneapolis: University of Minnesota Press.

Schoenekase, Daniel P. 2004. "Targeting Decisions Regarding Human Shields." *Military Review* 84, no. 5.

Scott, Joan Wallach. 2017. *Sex and Secularism.* Princeton, NJ: Princeton University Press.

Scott, Robert. 1891. *The War of the Rebellion: A Compilation of the Official Records of the Union and Confederate Armies.* Series 1, vol. 35, part 2. Washington, DC: Government Printing Office.

Scudi umani a Baghdad: Un diario a molte voci. 2005. Rome: Manifesto Libri.

Seybolt, Taylor B., Jay D. Aronson, and Baruch Fischhoff. 2013. *Counting Civilian Casualties: An Introduction to Recording and Estimating Non-Military Deaths in Conflict.* Oxford, UK: Oxford University Press.

Sharkey, Noel. 2011. "Automating Warfare: Lessons Learned from the Drones." *Journal of Law, Information and Science* 21: 140–54.

Shaw, Ian. 2013. "Predator Empire: The Geopolitics of US Drone Warfare." *Geopolitics* 18, no. 3: 536–59.

Shaw, Ian, and Majed Akhter. 2014. "The Dronification of State Violence." *Critical Asian Studies* 46, no. 2.

Shaw, Martin. 2005. *The New Western Way of War: Risk-Transfer War and Its Crisis in Iraq.* Cambridge, UK: Polity.

Sheehan-Dean, Aron. 2019. *The Calculus of Violence.* Cambridge, MA: Harvard University Press.

Sherman, William. 1875. *Memoirs of General William T. Sherman,* vol. 2. New York: D. Appleton.

Shiva, Vandana. 2016. *Staying Alive: Women, Ecology, and Development.* New York: North Atlantic Books.

Shue, Henry, and David Wippman. 2001. "Limiting Attacks on Dual-Use Facilities Performing Indispensable Civilian Functions." *Cornell International Law Journal* 35.

Skaff, Jonathan K. 2012. *Sui-Tang China and Its Turko-Mongol Neighbors.* Oxford, UK: Oxford University Press.

Skerker, Michael. 2004. "Just War Criteria and the New Face of War: Human Shields, Manufactured Martyrs, and Little Boys with Stones." *Journal of Military Ethics* 3, no. 1.

Sivakumaran, Sandesh. 2012. *The Law of Non-International Armed Conflict.* Oxford, UK: Oxford University Press.

Slim, Hugo. 2007. *Killing Civilians: Method, Madness, and Morality in War.* New York: Oxford University Press.

———. 2015. *Humanitarian Ethics.* New York: Oxford University Press.

Smith, Rupert. 2006. *The Utility of Force: The Art of War in the Modern World.* London: Penguin Books.

Spaight, James. 1911. *War Rights on Land.* New York: Macmillan.

Spies, S.B. 1977. *Methods of Barbarism? Roberts and Kitchener and Civilians in the Boer Republics, January 1900-May 1902.* Cape Town: Human & Rousseau.

Stahl, Roger. 2009. *Militainment, Inc.: War, Media, and Popular Culture.* New York: Routledge.

Starobin, Paul. 2017. *Madness Rules the Hour: Charleston, 1860 and the Mania for War.* New York: Public Affairs.

Stead, William Thomas. 1901. *Methods of Barbarism: The Case for Intervention.* London: Mobray House.

Stein, Yael. 2002. *Human Shield: Use of Palestinian Civilians as Human Shields in Violation of High Court of Justice Order.* Jerusalem: B'Tselem.

Sumsky, Victor V. 1992. "The City as Political Actor: Manila, February 1986." *Alternatives* 17, no. 4: 479–92.

Swiss Federal Council. 1978a. *Official Records of the Diplomatic Conference on the Reaffirmation and Development of International Humanitarian Law Applicable in Armed Conflicts (1974–1977),* vol. 3. Bern: Federal Political Department.

———. 1978b. *Official Records of the Diplomatic Conference on the Reaffirmation and Development of International Humanitarian Law Applicable in Armed Conflicts. Geneva (1974–1977),* vol. 14. Bern: Federal Political Department.

Temuge, Tolga. 2005. "Scudo: Protezione; persona che difende o protegge." In *Scudi umani a Baghdad: Un diario a molte voci*. Rome: Manifesto Libri.

Teshale, Tibebu. 1996. "The 'Anomaly' and 'Paradox' of Africa." *Journal of Black Studies* 26, no. 4.

Thaler, Mathias. 2018. *Naming Violence: A Critical Theory of Genocide, Torture and Terrorism*. New York: Columbia University Press.

Townsend, John Ferrars. 1860. *The South Alone Should Govern the South, and African Slavery Should Be Controlled By Those Only Who Are Friendly To It*. Charleston, SC: Steam Power Presses of Evans and Cogswell.

Tracy, James. 1996. *Direct Action: Radical Pacifism from the Union Eight to the Chicago Seven*. Chicago: University of Chicago Press.

Treaty Banning Nuclear Weapon Tests in the Atmosphere, in Outer Space and Under Water. 5 August 1963. U.S.T. 1313, T.I.A.S. No. 5433, 480 U.N.T.S. 43. http://disarmament.un.org/treaties/t/test_ban.

Truninger, Florianne, and François Bugnion. 1994. "The International Committee of the Red Cross and the Indochina War—From the Japanese Defeat to the Geneva Agreements (1945–1954)." *International Review of the Red Cross Archive* 34, no. 303.

Tse-tung, Mao. 1917. "A Study of Physical Education." *New Youth*, April 1917.

———. (1961) 1989. *Mao Tse-tung on Guerrilla Warfare*. Translated by Samuel B. Griffith. FMFRP 12–18. Washington, DC: US Marine Corps, Department of the Navy.

Tuan, Yi-Fu. 2013. *Landscapes of Fear*. New York: Pantheon.

Turner, Victor. 1969. *The Ritual Process: Structure and Anti-Structure*. New York: Transaction Publishers.

Turse, Nick. 2013. *Kill Anything That Moves: The Real American War in Vietnam*. New York: Metropolitan Books.

Tyner, James A. *War, Violence, and Population: Making the Body Count*. New York: Guilford Press.

UK War Office. 1914. *Manual of Military Law*. London: Her Majesty's Stationery Office.

———. 1958. *The Law of War on Land, being Part III of the Manual of Military Law*. London: Her Majesty's Stationery Office.

United Nations Commission on Human Rights. 1999. *Report of the Working Group on Enforced or Involuntary Disappearances*. E/CN.4/2000/64. 21 December 1999.

———. 2006. *Report of the Special Rapporteur on Extrajudicial, Summary or Arbitrary Executions*. E/CN.4/2006/53. 8 March 2006.

United Nations Convention on the Law of the Sea. 1982. UN Doc. A/CONF.62/. Done at Montego Bay, 10 December 1982.

United Nations General Assembly. 2014. *Report of the Special Rapporteur on the Promotion and Protection of Human Rights and Fundamental Freedoms while Countering Terrorism*. UN Doc. A/69/397.

United Nations Human Rights Council. 2014. *Resolution Ensuring Respect for International Law in the Occupied Palestinian Territory, including East Jerusalem*. UN Doc. A/HRC/RES/S-21/1. 24 July 2014.

———. 2015a. *Report of the Independent Commission of Inquiry Established Pursuant to Human Rights Council Resolution S-21/1.* UN Doc. A/HRC/29/CRP.4. 24 June 2015.

———. 2015b. *Report of the OHCHR Investigation on Sri Lanka (OISL).* UN Doc. A/HRC/30/CRP.2. 16 September 2015.

United Nations Security Council. 1990. *Security Council Resolution 678* (Iraq-Kuwait). UN Doc. S/RES/678. 29 November 1990.

———. 1992. *Security Council Resolution 770* (Bosnia and Herzegovina). UN Doc. S/RES/770. 13 August 1992.

———. 1993a. *Security Council Resolution 819* (Bosnia and Herzegovina). UN Doc. S/RES/819. 16 April 1993.

———. 1993b. *Security Council Resolution 827* (International Criminal Tribunal for the former Yugoslavia [ICTY]). UN Doc. S/RES/827. 25 May 1993.

———. 2016. *Security Council Resolution 2286 on Protection of the Wounded and Sick, Medical Personnel and Humanitarian Personnel in Armed Conflict.* UN Doc. S/RES/2286. 3 May 2016.

United Nations Secretary-General. 2011. *Report of the Secretary-General's Panel of Experts on Accountability in Sri Lanka.* 31 March 2011.

United Nations War Crimes Commission. 1948a. *Law Reports of Trials of War Criminals,* vol. 4. London: published for the UN War Crimes Commission by H.M.S.O.

———. 1948b. *Law Reports of Trials of War Criminals,* vol. 11. London: published for the UN War Crimes Commission by H.M.S.O.

———. 1949. *Law Reports of Trials of War Criminals,* vol. 24. London: published for the UN War Crimes Commission by H.M.S.O.

US Central Intelligence Agency. 2003. *Putting Noncombatants at Risk: Saddam's Use of "Human Shields."* CIA Library General Reports, January 2003.

US Department of the Army. 1956. *The Law of Land Warfare.* Washington, DC: US Government Printing Office.

US Department of Defense, Office of General Counsel. 2015. *Law of War Manual.* Washington, DC: DoD.

———. 2016. *Law of War Manual,* rev. Washington, DC: DoD.

US Department of State. 1999. *The Ethnic Cleansing of Kosovo: Fact Sheet Based on Information from U.S. Government Sources,* June 4, 1999.

US Marine Corps. 1940. *Small Wars Manual.* Washington, DC: US Government Printing Office.

US War Department, Office of the Chief of Staff. 1914. *Rules of Land Warfare.* Washington, DC: US Government Printing Office.

Van Dijk, Boyd. 2018. "Human Rights in War: On the Entangled Foundations of the 1949 Geneva Conventions." *American Journal of International Law* 112, no. 4: 553–82.

Van Schaack, Beth. 2016. "Human Shields: Complementary Duties under IHL." *American Journal of International Law* 110 (unbound ed.).

———. 2019. "The Law and Policy of Human Shielding." In *Complex Battlespaces: The Law of Armed Conflict and the Dynamics of Modern Warfare,* edited by

Winston S. Williams and Christopher M. Ford. New York: Oxford University Press.

Vattel, Emer de. 2008. *The Law of Nations: Or Principles of the Law of Nature Applied to the Conduct of Nations and Sovereigns*. Indianapolis: Liberty Fund.

Veuthey, Michel. 1983. *Guerilla et droit humanitaire*. Geneva: Comité international de la Croix Rouge.

Vietnam Task Force, Office of the Secretary of Defense. 2011. *Evolution of the War— Counterinsurgency: The Kennedy Commitments (1961–1963)*. Part IV, B. 1. National Archives, declassified 2011 per Executive Order 13526, Section 3.3. (Pentagon Papers) https://catalog.archives.gov/id/5890493.

Virilio, Paul. 1989. *War and Cinema: The Logistics of Perception*. London: Verso.

Vourkoutiotis, Vasilis. 2003. *Prisoners of War and the German High Command*. Palgrave Macmillan.

Walzer, Michael. 2016. "The Risk Dilemma." *Philosophia* 44, no. 2: 289–93.

Wawro, Geoffrey. 2005. *The Franco-Prussian War: The German Conquest of France in 1870–1871*. Cambridge, UK: Cambridge University Press.

Wynne, Graeme C., Wilfrid Miles, and Cyril Falls. 1927. *History of the Great War Based on Official Documents: Military Operations, France and Belgium, 1914 May July; The German Diversion Offensive and the First Allied Counter Offensive*. London: Macmillan.

Weber, Jutta. 2016. "Keep Adding: On Kill Lists, Drone Warfare and the Politics of Databases." *Environment and Planning D: Society and Space* 34, no. 1: 107–25.

Weber, Samuel. 2002. "War, Terrorism, and Spectacle: On Towers and Caves." *South Atlantic Quarterly* 101, no. 3.

Weber, Thomas. 1996. *Gandhi's Peace Army. The Shanti Sena and Unarmed Peacekeeping*. New York: Syracuse University Press.

Weheliye, Alexander. 2014. *Habeas Viscus: Racializing Assemblages, Biopolitics, and Black Feminist Theories of the Human*. Durham, NC: Duke University Press.

Weiss, Gordon. 2011. *The Cage: The Fight for Sri Lanka and the Last Days of the Tamil Tigers*. New York: Random House.

Weizman, Eyal. 2012. *The Least of All Possible Evils: Humanitarian Violence from Arendt to Gaza*. London, UK: Verso Books.

———. 2017. *Forensic Architecture: Violence at the Threshold of Detectability*. Cambridge, MA: MIT Press.

Wenger, Andreas, and Simon J. Mason. 2008. "The Civilianization of Armed Conflict: Trends and Implications." *International Review of the Red Cross* 90, no. 872: 835–52.

Weyler, Rex. 2004. *Greenpeace: How a Group of Ecologists, Journalists, and Visionaries Changed the World*. Vancouver: Raincoast Books.

Wheeler, Nicholas J. 2002. *Saving Strangers: Humanitarian Intervention in International Society*. Oxford, UK: Oxford University Press.

White House. 2006. "Barack Obama: Press Conference by the President after Meeting with National Security Officials." 4 August 2006. https://obamawhitehouse

.archives.gov/the-press-office/2016/08/04/press-conference-president-after-meeting-national-security-officials.

Whiteman, Marjorie M. 1968. *Digest of International Law Vol. 10.* Washington: Department of Defense.

Wieviorka, Annette. 2006. *The Era of the Witness.* Ithaca, NY: Cornell University Press.

Wilcox, Lauren. 2017. "Embodying Algorithmic War: Gender, Race, and the Post-human in Drone Warfare." *Security Dialogue* 48, no. 1.

Wilke, Christiane. 2018. "How International Law Learned to Love the Bomb: Civilians and the Regulation of Aerial Warfare in the 1920s." *Australian Feminist Law Journal* 44, no. 1.

Williams, Michael. 1996. "Hobbes and International Relations: A Reconsideration." *International Organization* 50, no. 2.

Wilson, Thomas. 2016. *The Ashley Cooper Plan: The Founding of Carolina and the Origins of Southern Political Culture.* Chapel Hill: University of North Carolina Press.

Wilson, Trevor. 1979. "Lord Bryce's Investigation into Alleged German Atrocities in Belgium, 1914–15." *Journal of Contemporary History* 14, no. 3.

Winthrop, William. 1920. *Military Law and Precedents.* Washington, DC: US Government Printing Office.

Witt, John. 2012. *Lincoln's Code: The Laws of War in American History.* New York: Simon & Schuster.

Wittner, Lawrence. 1970. *Rebels against War: The American Peace Movement, 1941–1960.* New York: Columbia University Press.

Whyte, Jessica. 2018. "The Dangerous Concept of the Just War: Decolonization, Wars of National Liberation, and the Additional Protocols to the Geneva Conventions." *Humanity: An International Journal of Human Rights, Humanitarianism, and Development* 9, no. 3.

Wolfe, Patrick. 2016. *Traces of History: Elementary Structures of Race.* London: Verso Books.

Young, Alvin Lee. 2009. *The History, Use, Disposition and Environmental Fate of Agent Orange.* New York: Springer.

Zander, Patrick G. 2017. *Hidden Armies of the Second World War: World War II Resistance Movements.* California: ABC-CLIO.

Zedong, Mao. 1968. *Military Writings.* Peking: Foreign Languages Press.

Zelko, Frank. 2013. *Make It a Green Peace: The Rise of a Countercultural Environmentalism.* New York: Oxford University Press.

Zolo, Danilo. 2009. *Victors' Justice: From Nuremberg to Baghdad.* London: Verso.

INDEX

activists: antinuclear activists, 97; international solidarity activists, 109–11, 110 fig.16; nuclear activism, 96, 108; in Palestine, 5, 13, 108–16. *See also* antimilitary activism; Corrie, Rachel; Greenpeace; Hurndall, Tom; International Solidarity Movement (ISM)

Additional Protocols, 132–35, 146. *See also* Protocol II of 1977; Protocol I of 1977

aerial bombardments: in armed conflicts, 151; black letter law, 152, 154–56; culpability determination for, 152–54, 153 fig.20; during Italo-Ethiopian War, 229nn4–5; war on terror and, 156–58. *See also* hospitals

Afghanistan, 38, 135, 156, 168, 181, 242n21

African Americans: Black Lives Matter movement, 11, 199–200, 200 fig.31, 211, 213–14, 217, 249n30; Black Panther militants, 96; Civil War human shielding and, 22; Zimmerman acquittal, 249n30

agency, proximity and, 163–64, 244n21

Agroville Program, 89, 90

Albright, Madeleine, 121

Alexander II, Czar of Russian Empire, 224n21

Algerian National Liberation Front, 133

allocating blame for violence: during Franco-German War, 30, 44; in Gaza, 165, 171, 215; during Italo-Ethiopian War, 68; in Kosovo, 123–24; mobilizing human shields as weapon of, 10; naturalization of gender and, 187; in Sri

Lanka, 205–6; during Vietnamese resistance, 92; during war on ISIS, 160, 162, 165, 205–6; during war on terror, 135–36; during WWII, 85

ambiguity in shielding situations (term), 8, 62, 150

Amelioration of the Condition of the Wounded and Sick in Armies in the Field, 79

American Revolution, 86, 93

America's Army (computer game), 202

Amnesty International, 46, 52, 126, 160

anticolonialism: Additional Protocols and, 132; Bandung Conference, 132–33; liberation struggles, 81, 134, 140; transnational black anticolonial consciousness, 60

antimilitary activism: overview, 108–9; active civilians, 112–13; humanitarian shielding action, 110 fig.16, 111–12; Human Shield Action group, 110, 112–13, 114; as resistance in Iraq and Palestine, 13, 108–16; Royden on, 53–54; suicide, 114–16, 115 fig.17

antinuclear movement, 97, 103

antiwar movement, 57, 103

Aquino, Corazon, 212

Arbour, Louise, 125

Army Battlezone (computer game), 201

Army of Two (computer game), 11, 204, 205 fig.33

Arrowsmith, Pat, 108–9

al-Assad, Bashar, 156, 191, 193, 194

Austin, John, 245n28
Awlaki family, 246n7

Bandung Conference, 132–33, 239n24
barbarism: overview, 14; accusations of
against children, 187–88; in computer
games, 206–7; during Franco-German
War, 30, 41, 49; German WWI violations as, 13, 44–45, 49, 51; images and,
193–95; international law and, 193–95;
Italo-Ethiopian War depictions of, 13,
62; Mexican-American War, 18; during
Second Boer War, 41, 42
Barghouti, Mariam, 213
Bargu, Banu, 195, 214
battlespace, 162–63, 182
Bedjaoui, Mohammed, 133
Belgian Congo, 46
The Belgian's People War (German White
Book), 48–49, 50–51
Belgium: Brussels Declaration of 1874, 41,
224n21; chronicling the use of human
screens by, 49–51; documenting Ger-
man atrocities, 45–48, 227n9; German
response to allegations from, 48–49;
occupation of, 13, 42, 43; reports on
Belgian Congo, 46
Berger, Gottlob, 230n9
Bigelow, Albert, 97
Bishnoi sect, 98, 99
black letter law, 152, 154–56
Black Lives Matter movement, 11, 199–200,
200 fig.31, 211, 213–14, 217, 249n30
Black Panthers, 96
Black Shawl, Loreal, 208–9
Blériot, Louis, 151
Boer War, Second: overview, 13, 35–37, 42;
Churchill and, 36 fig.5; counterinsurgency dilemmas during, 37–39; debates
over human shields during, 51; first-class
human shields during, 41–42, 50;
selective humanitarianism during,
39–41; treatment of noncombatants
during, 226n29
Bosnia: Kosovo war comparisons, 121–23;
Mladic, Ratko, 124, 126; NATO warfare strategy in, 118; UN shields in,
119–21

Bosnia-Herzegovina, 117, 119
Bousquet, Antoine, 180
Braidotti, Rosi, 100
Brodrick, John, 41, 42
Brown, Michael, 213
Brussels Declaration of 1874, 41, 224n21
Bryce, James, 42, 50
Bui Thi Phuong-Lan, 233n34
Bush, George W., 111–12, 135, 136
Butler, Judith, 137

Call of Duty (computer game), 202
Callwell, Charles Edward, 37, 226n10
Card, Orson Scott, 201, 202
Casement, Roger, 45–46
Central Intelligence Agency (CIA), 90, 111
Cereti, Carlo, 62
Chaco War, 231n21
Charleston, siege of: overview, 16–18;
bombing of, 17 fig.3, 20, 21; civilians
during, 144–45; Foster on, 19, 21; Jones
on, 17–18, 21
chemical warfare, 93–95, 94 fig.12
children and human shielding: overview,
14, 185; accusations of barbarism
toward, 187–88; during Civil War, 22;
drone warfare deaths, 179, 184; effects
of military-aged males (MAM) classifi-
cation on, 186; in Gaza, 215–17, 216
fig.36; gender and passivity of, 186–87;
in images during Italo-Ethiopian War,
65, 66 fig.11, 67; ISIS and, 187–88;
migrants and, 247n14; by Viet Cong,
91; during World War I, 47–48; xenophobia and, 189 fig.26, 189–90
China: Mao Tse-Tung, 27, 86–87, 89, 90,
91, 93, 94, 236n3; peace army and, 55–56,
58 fig.7, 58–59; Shanghai occupation, 13.
See also Sino-Japanese War
Chipko movement, 98, 99 fig.13
Chirac, Jacques, 120
Christians, 31, 54, 56, 80, 110
Churchill, Winston, 35–36, 36 fig.5, 37, 38
CIA (Central Intelligence Agency), 90, 111
civil disobedience: overview, 208–9, 209
fig.35; as act of war, 14–15, 208–18;
framing of civilians as human shields,
215–17; human barricades, 211–13;

militarized police, 209–11; paradox of shielding, 213–15

Civilian Convention, 81–83, 131–32, 232n20. *See also* Convention Relative to the Protection of Civilian Persons in Time of War

civilian protections, lack of: overview, 71–72, 77; laws of war expansion, 76–77; lethal weapons and, 230n15; Nazi human shielding as, 13, 71–77; no crime without law (*nullum crimen sine lege*) principle, 72–74, 124; precarious balance, 74–75

civilians: overview, 8, 14; agency and, 163–64; changing status of, 8; civilian brutalizations during conflicts, 231n21; civilianhood extension, 80–81; civilian immunity, 225n41; civilian protection codification efforts, 76–77; civilian shields, 83–84; civilian status erosion, 140; civilian value increase, 79–80; colonial imprint, 168–69; deaths during Vietnam War, 91, 92; definitions of, 81; drone warfare deaths, 179, 183–84; enemy civilians defined, 232n11; extending civilianhood, 80–81; guilt, assignment of, 166–67; humanitarian shielding action, 235n14; Hurdnall, Tom, 236n25; inadequate protections for, 76–77; increasing value of, 79–80; irregular specter, 165–66; legitimate reprisals and, 32; passive civilians, 81–83; percentages of proximate shields, 161–63; as resistance fighters, 225n41; targeting of civilian sites, 60–61; trapped in midst of war on ISIS, 14, 159–69; use of, 224n21; weaponization of, 3–5, 76, 78, 175–76, 176 fig.25; WWII use of, 73–74, 76. *See also* peace army; proximity

Civil War: overview, 13, 16–18, 25; codification and, 7; disavowing the human, 24–25; gradations of humanity, 22–24; hostage use during, 223nn30,32; Jones, Samuel, 222–23n22; Lee, Robert E., 223n32; Lieber Code, 19–21; shared values assumption, 18–19; Sherman, William T., 222n5, 223n22; Union

forces use of prisoners of war as human shields, 222n5, 223n22; use of civilian shields, 222–23n22, 223n32; weapon of the strong, 21. *See also* Charleston, siege of

Clark, Wes, Jr., 208

The Clash of Civilizations (Huntington), 90

Clausewitz, Carl von, 179

codification: overview, 13, 78, 85; civilianhood extension, 80–81; civilian value increase, 79–80; Geneva Conventions, 13, 78–85; lethal protection, 84–85; Lieber Code, 7; passive civilians, 81–83; from prisoner shields to civilian shields, 83–84; proportionality principle, 146

Cold War, 88, 96, 118, 123, 123n3, 140, 244n15

collateral damage, 9, 135, 137, 138, 147, 184, 186, 207

colonialism: anticolonialism, 60; colonial present, 14; colonial process of formation, 239n24; colonial spaces, 245n29

colonial wars: aerial bombardments, 45; international law and, 81; Second Boer War as, 35, 37, 42

combatant/noncombatant distinction: during Civil War, 20–21; during Franco-German War, 29–30, 31; *Law of War Manual* (2015) and, 137–38; laws of armed conflict and, 72; laws of war and, 8; of Mao Tse-tung, 86

Committee of Ladies, 40

Committee on Alleged German Outrages in Belgium, 50

computer games: overview, 11, 14, 201–2; *America's Army,* 202; *Army Battlezone,* 201; *Army of Two,* 11, 204, 205 fig.33; *Call of Duty,* 202; *Dead to Right: Retribution,* 206–7; gamer statistics, 250n15; in-home gaming, 202–4, 203 fig.32; human shield function in, 11, 204–6, 205 fig.33–34; human shields in virtual wars, 14, 201–7; involuntary shielding in, 14, 185, 206; *The Last of Us,* 11, 204, 205 fig.34; recruitment and, 202–4; *Splinter Cells,* 207; *Turning Point: Fall of Liberty,* 207; virtual barbarity in, 206–7

emblems: overview, 13, 60–61, 70; League of Nations, 67–68; media images of, 64 fig.8, 65 fig.9, 66 fig.10–11; misuse of Red Cross emblem, 63, 68–69, 154–55; perfidy accusations, 62–67; racialized law, 69–70; Red Crescent flags in Libya, 151; Red Cross Medical Facilities during Italo-Ethiopian War, 13, 60–70; white negro designation, 61–62, 229n12

Emmich, Otto von, 43–44

Empire Club, 240n32

Ender's Game (Card), 201

Enloe, Cynthia, 47

environmental shielding: overview, 10, 13, 96–98; by Bishnoi sect, 98, 99; Chipko movement, 98–99, 99 fig.13; debates over herbicidal warfare, 95; environment life matters, 98–100, 99 fig.13; gender and, 234n21; herbicidal warfare, 93–95, 94 fig.12; human sacrifice in war and, 101; human shielding on the high seas, 106–7, 235n36; Mururoa, 100–103, 101 fig.14, 106; save the whales campaign, 103–5, 105 fig.15

Erakat, Noura, 37

Eslava, Luis, 239n24

ethics: Civil War and, 7; in computer games, 204; debates over, 8, 45; ethical calculations, 6; ethical framing, 176–78; of humanitarian shielding action, 235n14; IDF's info-war framing and, 176–78; international conventions and, 30; *Law of War Manual* (2015) and, 137–38; military virtue, 31; moral cartography, 174–75; nonhuman and, 13; nonviolent ethics, 57–59, 109; proportionality principle and, 145; resistance strategies and, 15; responsibility to protect (R2P), 118; of violence, 6, 9–10. *See also* humane violence; humanitarian wars; laws of war

Ethiopia: overview, 60–61; images during Italo-Ethiopian War, 63–67, 64 fig.8, 65 fig.9, 66 fig.10–11; League of Nations and, 60, 61–62, 67–68, 229n12; perfidy accusations, 62–67; white negro designation, 61–62, 229n12. *See also* Italo-Ethiopian War

ethnic cleansing, 51, 118, 119

Evans, Ieshia, 11, 199–200, 200 fig.31

evidence gathering: reports and, 51; war crime accusations and, 227n9; during WWI, 49–51

eyewitness testimonies: war crime accusations and, 227n9; during WWI, 50

Fakhri, Michael, 239n24

Fanon, Frantz, 229n12

Fawcett, Millicent, 40, 45, 53

Feigenbaum, Anna, 210

Flights over the Amba Mountains (Mussolini), 60

fog of war (term), 179, 183

Foster, John G., 17, 19, 20, 21, 22, 24–25, 144–45

Frames of War (Butler), 245n8

framing: of civilians as human shields, 140, 165–66, 215–17, 239n19, 245n28; ethical framing, 176–78; functioning as speech acts, 245n28; of ISIS as barbarians, 187–88; rationalizing violence during WWI and, 51–52

France: chronicling the use of human screens by, 49–51; First Indochina War, 88; nuclear testing, 100–103, 101 fig.14, 104, 106; Paris Peace Conference of 1919, 51; Rapid Reaction Force, 120. *See also* Franco-German War

Francis, Pope, 160

Franco-German War: overview, 13, 26–28, 34; civilians as resistance fighters in, 225n41; counterinsurgency during, 28; debates after, 8; *francs-tireurs,* 27 fig.4; international law and, 29–30, 165; irregular shielding and, 33–34; legal use of human shields, 13, 26–34; medical immunity breaches during, 67; noble human shields during, 5, 29–30, 32; paradigm shift after, 31–33; in shadow of the law during, 30–31

francs-tireurs (free shooters), 27 fig.4, 27–28, 29, 30, 72

Gambetta, Léon, 26

Gandhi, Mahatma, 4, 54–55, 98, 228n11

Garza, Alicia, 249n30

human rights law, 145
human rights violations: commissions to
    investigate, 40, 45–46; NGOs and,
    46, 52
Human Rights Watch, 46, 52, 126, 144
human screens (term), 3, 49–51
Human Shield Action group, 109, 112–13,
    114
human vulnerability, 5–6, 6 fig.2
Hunter, Robert, 96, 104–5
Huntington, Samuel, 90
Hurdnall, Tom, 114, 236n25
Hussein, Saddam, 108, 109, 111, 113

ideology operations, 8
Ignatieff, Michael, 236n3
illegal shielding, 61
images: barbarism and, 193–95; cinemato-
    graphic techniques, 245n8; during
    Italo-Ethiopian War, 63–67, 64 fig.8, 65
    fig.9, 66 fig.10–11, 193, 194–95; mind
    bomb images, 100–101, 103; of Red
    Cross Medical Facilities, 64 fig.8, 65
    fig.9, 66 fig.10–11; of Syrian warfare,
    194. See also spectacle
imperialism: anti-imperialism of Mao
    Tse-tung, 236n3; benign imperialism,
    236n3; voluntary shielding challenges
    to, 2. See also colonialism
India: Bishnoi sect, 98, 99; Chipko move-
    ment, 98–99, 99 fig.13; human shielding
    in Kashmir, 195–98, 197 fig.29, 199, 200,
    217; Shanti Sena (Indian peace army),
    228n11
indigenous populations: anticolonial
    liberation struggles and, 81; crimes
    against, 13; extermination of, 78
Indochina War, First, 88
info-war: overview, 14, 170–72, 171 fig.22,
    178; ethical frame, 176–78; Operation
    Cast Lead, 245n1; Operation Pillar of
    Cloud, 245n1; social media and Gaza
    Wars, 14, 170–78; weaponizing civil-
    ians, 175–76, 176 fig.25; "What Would
    You Do? campaign, 172–75, 173 fig.23,
    174 fig.24
inhumane strategy adoption: Belgium
    occupation and, 45; chronicling the use

of human screens, 49–51; civilian
    immunity and, 33–34, 225n41; during
    Italo-Ethiopian War, 61, 62–63; nonvio-
    lent ethics and, 57; by Viet Cong, 91
insurgents: Additional Protocols and, 135;
    during Franco-German War, 27–28; as
    irregulars, 33; Law of War Manual
    (2015) on, 137, 138; Mao's influence on,
    87; in Vietnam, 91. See also Vietnamese
    resistance
International Committee of the Red Cross,
    68–69, 76, 77, 79, 124, 151, 154,
    231nn20,24, 232n13; accusations of
    targeting of, 67; article 24, 232n23; cities
    of refuge/hospital towns proposal,
    231n24; civilian protection codification
    and, 76–77, 79; on ecological warfare,
    95; founding of, 20; on human shielding
    debates, 68–69; League of Nations and,
    76; principle of proportionality and,
    75–76; reports by, 46; on upholding
    Geneva Conventions in Vietnam, 92
International Criminal Court, 124, 241n16
International Criminal Tribunal for
    Rwanda, 124
International Criminal Tribunal for the
    Former Yugoslavia, 117–28; overview,
    14, 117–18, 127–28; establishment of,
    123; humanitarian lawfare, 123–24; as
    humanitarian lawfare, 123–24; immu-
    nity, 124–27, 128 fig.19; investigations of
    human shielding in Bosnia, 119–20;
    Kosovo and, 237n27; politics of, 125, 128
    fig.19; refugee shields, 121–23; UN
    shields in Bosnia, 119–21, 120 fig.18
International Crisis Group, 144
international law: of armed conflict,
    241n16; Belgian occupation and, 42,
    44; colonial wars and, 81; decolonial
    process of transformation of, 239n24;
    effects of Franco-German War on,
    31–33; expected protection by, 5; found-
    ers of, 31; Franco-German War and,
    29–30, 165; involuntary shielding and,
    83–84, 93, 239n19; Law of Armed Con-
    flict and, 239n19; Lieber code and, 20;
    national liberation struggles and,
    239n29; new interpretations of, 145;

paradigm shift over basis of, 31–32; perfidy, 62–63, 175; racialization of, 69–70; rights on high seas, 106–7; *Rules of Land Warfare* and, 238n9; Treaty of London of 1839, 44; Vietnamese resistance and, 92; voluntary shielding and, 84, 239n19

International Solidarity Movement (ISM), 1–2, 114–16, 115 fig.17, 163, 236n25

involuntary shielding: overview, 14; agency and, 163–64; during Belgian invasion of 1915, 53; in computer games, 14, 185; gender and, 185; history of, 2; human vulnerability and, 6; international law and, 83–84, 93, 239n19; in Iraq, 111; *Law of War Manual* (2015) and, 137; noble human shields, 5, 29–30, 32; percentages of, 161–63; practicing of, 205–6; proportionality analysis of, 147–50; proximate shielding and, 160–61, 163–64, 167; refugee shields, 121–23; shielding zones, 142–45; UN shields in Bosnia, 120–21; Vietnamese resistance and, 93; during war on terror, 137; weaponization and, 3–4

Iraq: overview, 14, 108–9; active civilians, 8–9, 112–13; antimilitary activism in, 13, 108–16; civilian proximity, 85; economic sanctions against, 109; glue uniting activists, 110 fig.16; humanitarian shielding action, 111–12, 235n14; Human Shield Action group in, 109–11; Hurdnall, Tom, 236n25; Hussein, Saddam, 108, 109, 111, 113; international volunteers in, 4, 5; involuntary shielding in, 111; media references to human shields in, 245n29; Mosel campaign, 9, 14, 159–61, 161 fig.21, 164–67, 169, 170, 205; suicide, 114–16, 115 fig.17

irregulars: overview, 13, 26–28, 34; counterinsurgency and, 28, 29–30; definitions of, 34; *francs-tireurs*, 27 fig.4; ISIS and specter of, 165–66; as legal use of human shields in Franco-German War, 13, 26–34; legitimacy of, 33–34, 224n21; as noble human shields, 5, 29–30, 32; paradigm shift and, 31–33; in shadow of the law, 30–31; shielding of, 33–34. *See*

also insurgents; partisans; resistance fighters; terrorists

ISIS (Islamic State in Iraq and Syria): overview, 159–61, 161 fig.21; agency and, 163–64; civilians trapped in midst of war on, 14, 159–69; colonial imprint, 168–69; framing as barbarians, 187–88; guilt, assigning, 166–67; humanitarian shielding action, 235n14; human vulnerability and, 5, 6 fig.2; Mosul campaign, 9, 14, 159–61, 161 fig.21, 164–67, 169, 170, 205; percentages of proximate shields, 161–63; Raqqa campaign, 4, 9, 10, 162; use of human shields, 5, 6 fig.2, 9

ISM (International Solidarity Movement), 1–2, 114–16, 115 fig.17, 163, 236n25

Israel: overview, 14; arguments against war crimes accusations, 170; bombing of medical facilities in, 156–57; Corrie civil lawsuit, 115–16; denial of protections to Gaza civilians, 217; dual-use accusations, 173–74, 174 fig.24; framing of civilians as human shields in, 165, 215–17; infographics, 171–76, 173 fig.23, 176 fig.25; Israel Defense Forces (IDF), 165, 171–72, 173 fig.23, 174 fig.24, 175–76, 176 fig.25, 215–16, 216 fig.36; medical facility bombings by, 156, 157; Operation Protective Edge, 170, 172–73; Palestinian uprising, second, 114; perfidy accusations by, 175; proximate human shields and, 160; refugees from creation of State of, 251n29; Reisner, Daniel, 129–30; shielding practices, 206; social media use, 171–72, 174 fig.24, 175–76, 176 fig.25; UN Human Rights Council resolution, 170–71, 171 fig.22. *See also* Corrie, Rachel; Gaza Wars; Israel Defense Forces (IDF)

Israel Defense Forces (IDF), 165, 171–72, 173 fig.23, 174 fig.24, 175–76, 176 fig.25, 215–16, 216 fig.36

Italo-Ethiopian War, 60–70; overview, 13, 60–61, 70; aerial bombardments, 151, 229nn4–5; civilian brutalizations, 231n21; images during, 63–67, 64 fig.8, 65 fig.9, 66 fig.10–11; Italian

Italo-Ethiopian War *(continued)*
colonialism, 229n4; League of Nations, 67–68; Mao Tse-Tung and, 86; media images of, 64 fig.8, 65 fig.9, 66 fig.10–11; misuse of Red Cross emblem during, 68–69; perfidy accusations during, 62–67; racialized law, 69–70; white negro designation, 61–62

Italy: aerial bombardments in Libya, 151; League of Nations and, 67–68; liberation struggles and, 93. *See also* Italo-Ethiopian War

Jackson, Andrew, 18
Jambheshwar (guru), 98
Japan: Sino-Japanese War, Second, 86; Tokyo war crimes trials, 74; whaling industry, 104; WWII use of civilians, 74. *See also* Sino-Japanese War
Jefferson, Thomas, 18
Johnson, Lyndon B., 90, 91, 92, 93
Jones, Samuel, 16–18, 19, 20, 21, 22, 24–25, 144, 222–23n22
Junod, Marcel, 68–69
jus ad bellum criteria, 44, 58
jus in bello regulations, 44, 58, 145

Karadzic, Radovan, 126
Kashmir, 14, 195–99, 196 fig.28, 197 fig.29, 200, 217
Kennedy, David, 238n4
Kennedy, Duncan, 130
Kennedy, John F., 89, 90
Kinsella, Helen, 185, 187
Kitchener, Herbert, 41
Korean War, 155
Koriša incident, 122, 127
Kosovo: International Criminal Tribunal for the Former Yugoslavia and, 237n27; Kosovar refugee shields, 121; Kosovo Liberation Army, 121, 127; war in, 118
Kurdish forces, 159

The Last of Us (computer game), 11, 204, 205 fig.34
lawfare: defined, 123; war on terror and, 135; as weapon in Bosnia/Kosovo, 124

lawmaking tools: overview, 129–31, 139; additional protocols, 132–35; lawfare at work, 135; military handbooks as, 14, 129–39; US manuals and human shielding, 131–32; weapon of the strong, 136–39; weapon of the weak, 136–39

The Law of Land Warfare (1956), 130
Law of War Manual (2015), 8, 130–31, 135, 136–37

laws of armed conflict: active civilians and, 113; civilians and, 13, 17, 73–74; civilians of occupied lands, 80–81; in colonial wars, 35; human shields and, 7–8, 10, 12; as international humanitarian law, 78; limits of, 72; perfidy and, 62–63; principle of distinction and, 30–31; racism application of, 69–70; reprisals and, 32; violations by Viet Cong, 92. *See also* laws of war

laws of war: overview, 7–9; combatant/noncombatant distinction, 8, 34; ethics and, 6, 8; expansion of, 76–77; as international humanitarian law, 78; investigation of WWI violations of, 45, 46, 50; Italo-Ethiopian War violations of, 60–61; Laws of War on Land (Oxford Manual of 1880), 225n21; nonviolent ethics and, 57–58; principle of distinction, 7; principle of proportionality, 145–46. *See also* combatant/noncombatant distinction; laws of armed conflict; Lieber Code; manuals; principle of distinction

League of Nations: Ethiopia and, 60, 61–62, 67–68, 229n12; International Committee of the Red Cross and, 76; Italy and, 62, 67–68, 195; Liberia and, 229n9; Royden and, 56, 58–59

Lee, Robert E., 223n32
legal figure of human shield: after WWII, 81; Civil War and, 18; colonial imprint of, 168; cover ups and, 184; humane violence and, 11–12; irregulars as, 33–34; laws of war and, 7, 8; legitimizing violence and, 9–10; passive civilians as, 81; shielding zones and, 144, 150; social media and, 171–72, 176; tapping and, 177; Vietnamese resistance and, 93

legal frameworks: effects of Franco-German War on, 31–33; laws of war, 7–9; legitimizing violence, 9–10; racialized law, 69–70; Vietnamese resistance and, 91

legal use of human shields: overview, 26–28, 34; counterinsurgency as, 28; in Franco-German War, 13, 26–34; *francs-tireurs*, 27 fig.4; irregular shielding as, 33–34; noble human shields, 5, 29–30, 32; paradigm shift and, 31–33; in shadow of the law, 30–31

Leopold, King of Belgium, 46

Leviathan (Hobbes), 33–34

Liano, Alejandro, 229n12

liberal humanitarianism: overview, 35–37, 42; Churchill and, 36 fig.5; counterinsurgency dilemmas, 37–39; first-class human shields and, 41–42; limits of, 13, 35–42; selective humanitarianism, 39–41

Liberation Tigers of Tamil Eelam. *See* Tamil Tigers (Liberation Tigers of Tamil Eelam)

Liberia, League of Nation membership, 229n9

Libya, 151

Lieber, Francis, 7, 8, 20, 223n30

Lieber Code, 7–8, 169; Article 17, 131; balanced use of, 74–75; Civil War and, 19–21; Franco-German War and, 28, 30; gradations of humanity and, 22–24; hostage protection, 83, 223n30; human shielding and, 25; international law impacts of, 130, 238n10; on pace of war, 122; shielding acts in, 131

liminality, 175–76

Mackarness, Frederic, 40–41

Majuba, Battle of, 35

manuals: overview, 14, 129–31, 139; additional protocols, 132–35; Chinese reactionary manuals, 86; colonial process of formation, 239n24; decolonial process of transformation of, 239n24; French manual of 2012, 239n19; German manual of 1902, 224n21; German manual of 2013, 239n19; human shields, 239n19;

international law and, 239n24, 239n29; *Kriegs-Etappen Ordnung,* 46; lawfare at work, 135; *Law of Armed Conflict,* 239n19; *The Law of Land Warfare* (1956), 130; *Law of War Manual* (2015), 8, 130–31, 135, 136–37; military handbooks as lawmaking tools, 14, 129–39; national liberation struggles and, 239n29; norms and, 238n4; Oxford Manual of 1880, 225n21; *People's War, People's Army* (Giap), 88; *Rules of Land Warfare,* 238n9; *Small Wars* (Callwell), 37; *Small Wars Manual* (USMC), 226n10; US manuals and human shielding, 131–32, 238n2, 239n19; War Office Manual during Second Boer War, 226n29; war on terror and, 239n19; weapon of the strong, 136–39; weapon of the weak, 136–39. *See also* Lieber Code

Mao Tse-Tung, 27, 86–87, 89, 90, 91, 93, 94, 236n3

Marcos, Ferdinand, 212

Martin, Trayvon, 249n30

Martis, Eternity, 214

May, Larry, 147

McTaggart, David, 101–3, 104, 106

Médecins Sans Frontières (Doctors Without Borders), 157–58

medical facilities: overview, 151–52; attacks on, 242n21; attacks on as recurrent strategy of war, 242n21; black letters, 154–56; bombing of, 156; bombings as counterterrorism, 156–58; culpability determination, 152–53, 153 fig.20; humanizing war crimes, 158; medical immunity breaches, 67; use of as shields, 14, 151–58; violations of laws on bombing of, 73. *See also* hospitals

Metz, Siege of, 26

Mexican-American War, 18

Meyer, Richard B., 111

militainment, 203, 204

militants: Black Panther militants, 96; Hamas militants, 157, 165–66, 170–71, 175; ISIS militants, 160, 165; al-Qaeda militants, 179; surveillance technologies and, 9–10

military handbooks. *See* manuals
military intervention: definitions of military necessity, 20; reports on German WWI violations and, 44–45, 51; UN responsibility to protect and, 119
Milosevic, Slobodan, 122, 143
mind bomb images, 100–101, 103
mirroring, 88–90
Mladic, Ratko, 124, 126
Moltke, Helmuth von, 26, 28, 30, 38
moral cartography, 174–75
Mosul campaign, 9, 14, 159–61, 161 fig.21, 164–67, 169, 170, 205
Motta, Giuseppe, 77
Mulhearn, Donna, 111
Mururoa, 100–103, 101 fig.14, 104, 106
Mussolini, Benito, 60, 62, 195
Mussolini, Vittorio, 60, 62–63, 67, 68
mustard gas, 60

Nabulsi, Karma, 82
Napoleon III, Emperor of France, 26
National Committee for a Sane Nuclear Policy (SANE), 97, 99
National Liberation Front of South Vietnam, 88
National Security Agency (NSA), 182
Native Americans. *See* Standing Rock Sioux Reservation protest
NATO (North Atlantic Treaty Organization): overview, 14; in Bosnia, 119–21; humanitarian lawfare use by, 123–24; humanitarian wars and, 117–18; immunity at trial, 124–28; in Kosovo, 121–23
natural law, 31–32
Nazi human shielding, 71–77; overview, 13, 71–72, 77; Hitler and, 230n9; laws of war expansion, 76–77; mistreatment of Polish nationals under, 80; no crime without law (*nullum crimen sine lege*) principle, 72–74, 124; pacifism and, 228n1; precarious balance, 74–75
Nesiah, Vasuki, 239n24
Netanyahu, Benjamin, 170, 171 fig.22
neutrality, violations of, 44, 50
Newton, Michael, 143–44, 147
Ngo Dinh Nhu, 89
Nice, Geoffrey, 146–47, 148

9/11 terrorist attacks, 109, 135
Nixon, Richard, 210
noble human shields, during Franco-German War, 5, 29–30, 32
no crime without law (*nullum crimen sine lege*) principle, 72–74, 124
no-fire zones, 140–42, 143, 152, 205
noncombatant/combatant distinction. *See* combatant/noncombatant distinction
noncombatants: during Civil War, 16–17, 20–21; Grotius on, 230n13; noncombatant immunity, 31; during Second Boer War, 38; Vattel on, 230n13; during Vietnam War, 91
nonwhites, human shielding and, 8, 22
NSA (National Security Agency), 182
nuclear activism, 96, 108
nuclear testing: Aleutian Islands, 97, 100; Greenpeace and, 163; Marshall Islands, 97; Mururoa, 100–103, 101 fig.14, 104, 106
nullum crimen sine lege (no crime without law) principle, 72–74, 124
Nuremberg trials: overview, 13, 71–72, 77; Eichmann trial, 227n9; laws of war expansion, 76–77; mentions of human shields, 230n9; no crime without law (*nullum crimen sine lege*) principle, 72–74, 124; precarious balance, 74–75

Obama, Barack, 136, 180
O'Keefe, Kenneth, 110
Operation Desert Storm, 109
Operation Pillar of Cloud, 177
Operation Protective Edge, 170
Operation Ranch Hand, 94
Operation Rolling Thunder, 90–91
Oppenheim, Lassa, 32–33, 49, 138, 139
Our Account with the Boers (unpublished pamphlet) (Churchill), 35–36

pacifism, international: overview, 53–54, 58–59; Agroville Program, 89, 90; denunciation of, 228n1; nonviolent ethics, 57–59; passive resistance (*satyagraha*), 54–55; peace army and, 13, 56–59, 58 fig.7; Quaker pacifist sects, 228n7; Royden on, 228n1; shielding army as,

reprisals: during Belgian occupation, 44, 49; during Crete occupation, 71–72; Franco-German War and, 32, 138, 139; during Italo-Ethiopian War, 61; *Law of War Manual* (2015) and, 138; legitimate use of, 32, 41; logic of, 138, 139; purpose of, 32

resistance: overview, 108–9; active civilians, 112–13; antimilitary activism in Iraq and Palestine, 13, 108–16; during Belgian occupation, 44; Bishnoi sect, 98, 99; development of strategy of, 4; ethics and, 15; Ethiopian resistance, 62–63; Gandhi and, 4; glue uniting activists, 110 fig.16; Greek resistance on Crete, 71–72; humanitarian shielding action, 111–12; humanitarian shielding action in Iraq, 235n14; Human Shield Action group in Iraq, 109–11; Hurndall, Tom, 236n25; Iraq, 236n25; by irregulars, 28, 29–30; legality on high seas, 107; resistance fighters, 33, 225n41; *satyagraha* (passive resistance), 54–55; during Second Boer War, 36, 38; suicide, 114–16, 115 fig.17; use in environmental struggles, 96. *See also* environmental shielding; irregulars; Vietnamese resistance

responsibility to protect (R2P), 118

Roberts, Frederick Sleigh, 37–38, 41

Rochat, Giorgio, 229n4

Rome Statute, 124

Royden, A. Maude, 13, 53–59, 98, 104, 108–9, 228n1

Rugova, Ibrahim, 121

Ruhr occupation, 231n21

Rules of Land Warfare, 130

Rusk, Dean, 92

Russia, 104–5, 118

safe zones, 140–42, 143, 152, 205

Said, Edward, 246n9

SANE (National Committee for a Sane Nuclear Policy), 97, 99

Sassòli, Marco, 174

satyagraha (passive resistance), 54–55

Saudi Arabia, 108, 109, 156, 157

scale of human shielding: overview, 14, 140, 150; definitions of, 145; definitions of human shielding, 241n16; *Elements of Crimes,* 241n16; Empire Club, 240n32; International Criminal Court, 241n16; international law and, 241n16; no-fire zones, 140–42; principle of proportionality, 14, 140–50, 240n32, 241n17; proportionality algorithms, 145–47; proportionality analysis, 147–50; shielding zones, 142–45; war crimes and, 241n17. *See also* principle of proportionality

Schmitt, Carl, 91, 225n41

Schmitt, Michael, 181

Second Boer War. *See* Boer War, Second

Sedan, Battle of, 26

selective humanitarianism, 39–41

semiotic warfare, defined, 246n9

Serbs: ethnic cleansing by, 119; Kosovar refugee shields and, 121–23; lawfare as weapon, 123–24; Milosevic, 143; Milosevic, Slobodan, 122; paramilitary forces, 117, 119; tribunal investigations for human shielding, 124–28; UN shields in Bosnia, 120 fig.18, 120–21; war in Kosovo and, 118

settlers: overview, 35–37, 42; Churchill and, 36 fig.5; counterinsurgency dilemmas, 37–39; as first-class human shields, 41–42; liberal humanitarianism during Second Boer War, 13, 35–42; selective humanitarianism, 39–41

Shaw, Thomas, 41

Shea, Jamie, 125

Sheppard, Richard (Dick), 55, 56

Sherman, William T., 222n5, 223n22

shielding army, 55–57

shielding zones, 119, 142–45

Shock, Kurt, 212

Sierra Club, 97

Sino-Japanese War: overview, 13, 53–54, 58 fig.7, 58–59; civilian brutalizations, 231n21; nonviolent ethics, 57–59; passive resistance (*satyagraha*), 54–55; shielding army during, 55–57; voluntary shielding during, 13, 53–59; voluntary shielding proposal during, 55–59, 58 fig.7

Sino-Japanese War, Second, 86

Slovenia, 117

Small Wars Manual (USMC), 226n10

Smith, Rupert, 121
Snowden, Edward, 182
social contracts, 106; Hobbes and, 33–34
social media: overview, 170–72, 171 fig.22,
    178; ethical frame, 176–78; Gaza Wars
    and, 14, 170–78; Israel Defense Forces
    (IDF) on, 171–72, 174 fig.24, 175–76,
    176 fig.25, 215–16, 216 fig.36; mainstream
    media possibilities and, 248n4; weap-
    onizing civilians, 175–76, 176 fig.25;
    "What Would You Do? campaign,
    172–75, 173 fig.23, 174 fig.24
South Africa: overview, 13; colonial wars in,
    37. See also Boer War, Second
South Vietnam, 88–90, 92
South Vietnamese Army, 88–89
sovereign authority, 32, 69–70, 106–7
Spaight, James, 32–33
Spanish Civil War, 231n21
Special Committee on Decolonization, 133
spectacle, 191–200; overview, 191–92, 192
    fig.27, 200; colonial present, 14, 195–99,
    196 fig.28, 197 fig.29, 198 fig.30; dehu-
    manizing/humanizing shields, 14;
    environmental shielding as, 98; global
    spectatorship, 192–95; resistance specta-
    cle, 199–200, 200 fig.31; social media,
    248n4. See also images
Splinter Cells (computer game), 207
Sri Lankan civil war, 119; overview, 14, 140,
    150; American Civil War comparison,
    144–45; civilian deaths, 146; civilian
    proximity, 85; human shielding in, 14,
    140–50; no-fire zones, 140–42; propor-
    tionality algorithms, 145–47; propor-
    tionality analysis, 147–50; shielding
    zones, 142–45
Stahl, Roger, 203
Standing Rock Sioux Reservation protest,
    11, 208–10, 209 fig.35, 211, 215, 217
state-centric jurisprudence, 32, 33
Stead, William Thomas, 40
St. Petersburg Declaration of 1868, 30,
    230n15
Strategic Hamlet Program, 89–90
Student, Kurt, 71–73, 76
surveillance technologies: overview, 14,
    179–80, 184; cover-up, 183–84; functions

of, 183; new surveillance technologies, 9,
    180–81; post–human shielding and, 14,
    179–84; posthuman turn, 181–83
Syria: bombing of medical facilities in, 156;
    global spectatorship and, 192–93; hospi-
    tal attacks in, 242n21; images of specta-
    cle from, 195, 200; ISIS using civilians
    as human shields in, 5, 163, 187–88;
    media references to human shields in,
    245n29; media spectacle in, 191–92;
    Raqqa campaign, 4, 9, 10, 162

Tamil Tigers (Liberation Tigers of Tamil
    Eelam): overview, 14; defeat of, 140–42,
    146; proportionality algorithms, 147;
    proportionality analysis, 148–49; state
    violence against, 141; war crime accusa-
    tions and, 142–45, 146–47; warfare
    techniques of, 141
tapping, 177
Tea Party organization, 189, 247n14
terrorists, 33, 135
Third Republic of France, 26
Thompson, Robert, 89
To Kill a Mockingbird (Lee), 2, 3, 3 fig.1, 10
Tokyo war crimes trials, 74
Tometi, Opal, 249n30
trains, destruction of, 224n21; during
    Second Boer War, 36, 36 fig.5, 39, 41–42
Treaty of London of 1839, 44
Trenchard, Hugh, 153–54
Trump, Donald, 160, 190
Tuan, Yi-Fu, 193
Turner, Victor, 175–76
Turning Point: Fall of Liberty (computer
    game), 207

UN Convention on the Law of the Sea of
    1982, 235n36
United Nations: bombing of Korean medi-
    cal facilities, 155; Civilian Convention
    debates, 81–82; on drone warfare, 184;
    Human Rights Council resolution,
    170–71, 171 fig.22; on ISIS militants,
    160, 165; Israel's war crimes accusations
    by, 170; responsibility to protect (R2P),
    119; Rome Statute, 124; safe area crea-
    tion by, 119, 142; Security Council, 108,

109, 117, 119, 123; UNPROFOR, 117,
119–21, 120 fig.18, 123; UN shields in
Bosnia, 119–21
United Nations Charter, 78, 146
United Nations Protection Force
(UNPROFOR), 117
Universal Declaration of Human Rights, 78
UNPROFOR (United Nations Protection
Force), 117, 119–21, 120 fig.18, 123
UN Universal Declaration of Human
Rights, 232n13
urban spaces, 20, 162
US Planning Mission for the Sierra Leone
Special Criminal Court, 143
The Utility of Force (Smith), 121

Vattel, Emer de, 230n13
Venezuela, 211
Viet Cong, 27, 88–89, 90, 91–92, 93, 94
Viet Minh coalition, 88, 155
Vietnamese resistance: overview, 13, 86–87,
95; Arrowsmith and, 108; bombing of
medical units during, 155; chemical
warfare and, 93–95, 94 fig.12; farmers as
eco-refugees, 233n34; First Indochina
War, 87–88; herbicidal warfare, 93–95,
94 fig.12; Ho Chi Minh, 87–88; as
human shielding, 13, 86–95; leaflets
against, 91–92; mirroring strategies
during, 88–90; outlawing of, 90–93
Vinoba, Bhave, 228n11
violence: assessment of deployment of, 13;
debates over use of, 45; ethics of, 13, 37,
42, 57; giving meaning to use of, 246n9;
humane violence, 11–12; laws of war and,
7; legitimizing violence, 9–10; militarization of policing, 11; rationalizing
violence during WWI, 51–52; spatial
logic of, 244n15; state-centric jurisprudence and, 33. *See also* humane violence
viral images, 191–200; overview, 191–92, 192
fig.27, 200; colonial present, 195–99, 196
fig.28, 197 fig.29, 198 fig.30; dehuman-
izing/humanizing shields, 14; global
spectatorship, 192–95; resistance spectacle, 199–200, 200 fig.31
virtual wars. *See* computer games
Vitoria, Francisco de, 31

voluntary shielding: overview, 1–2, 53–54,
58 fig.7, 58–59; agency and, 163–64;
gender and, 185; Gulf Peace Team,
108–9; humanitarian shielding action,
111–13; Human Shield Action, 110,
112–13, 114; human vulnerability and, 6;
Hurdnall, Tom, 114, 236n25; international law and, 84, 239n19; in Iraq, 110
fig.16, 111–13; *Law of War Manual* (2015)
and, 137; laws of war and, 8; nonviolent
ethics, 57–59; passive resistance (*satyagraha*), 54–55; percentages of, 161–63;
proximate shielding and, 160–61, 163–
64, 167; as resistance, 4, 14, 15; rights on
high seas and, 106–7; role in history of
warfare, 3; shielding army, 55–57; during
Sino-Japanese War, 13, 53–59, 58 fig.7;
women and, 247n1. *See also* Corrie,
Rachel; environmental shielding
Vo Nguyen Giap, 88
vulnerability, human: environmental
shielding and, 99–100; as strategic
antiwar tool, 57; as weapon of deterrence, 5–7, 6 fig.2, 24

Wadi Hajjar, 159
War and Cinema (Virilio), 245n8
war crimes: overview, 14; Belgian investigation of, 45, 46–48, 47 fig.6; evidence
gathering, 227n9; eyewitness testimonies, 227n9; framing of civilians as
human shields and, 140; hospitals as
shields as, 158; humanizing, 158; humanizing war crimes, 158; legitimizing
warfare methods and, 67; mandate of
international courts, 124; principle of
proportionality and, 75, 145–47; proportionality principle and, 241n17; Sri
Lankan civil war, 146–47; Tokyo war
crimes trials, 74; UN responsibility to
protect from, 119. *See also* International
Criminal Tribunal for the Former
Yugoslavia; Nuremberg; Nuremberg
trials; Sri Lankan civil war
warfare, customs of: civilized/uncivilized
distinction, 51, 67; Civil War, 18–19;
Italo-Ethiopian War, 67; Mexican-
American War, 18; World War I, 45

warfare strategies, insurgents and, 135
war on terror: Additional Protocols and,
    135; aerial bombardments of medical
    facilities during, 156–58; civilian status
    erosion and, 140; as global and per-
    petual, 9; as justified, 109; nonwhites
    and, 14; war manuals and, 239n19
Warriors without Weapons (Junod), 68–69
Watson, Paul, 104–5
weaponization of civilians, 3–5, 175–76, 176
    fig.25; Bargu on, 195; codification and,
    76, 78; in computer games, 202; Israeli
    accusation of, 175–76, 176 fig.25; Netan-
    yahu on, 170; in Sri Lanka, 141; suicide
    bombers and, 141
weapon of the strong: during Civil War, 21;
    during war on terror, 136–39
weapon of the weak: during Civil War, 18,
    21; during war on terror, 136–39
weapons of mass destruction, 109
Weheliye, Alexander, 22
whale shielding, 103–5, 105 fig.15, 163
White Book (*The Belgian's People War*),
    48–49, 50–51
white negro designation: black albinos
    (term), 229n12; Italo-Ethiopian War,
    61–62; Liano on, 229n12
whiteness, activists' use of, 5, 115
Wieviorka, Annette, 227n9
Wilhelm II, emperor of German Empire,
    51
women and environmental shielding,
    Chipko movement, 98–99, 99 fig.13
women and human shielding, 185–90;
    overview, 14, 185; during Civil War, 22;
    drone warfare deaths, 179, 184; Evans,
    Ieshia, 199–200, 200 fig.31; gender and
    passivity, 186–87; Greenpeace's gender
    politics, 234n21; ISIS and, 187–88;
    migrants and, 247n14; military-aged
    males (MAM) and, 186; proximate
    shielding, 247n1; return of the barbar-
    ians, 187–88; by Viet Cong, 91; volun-
    tary shielding, 247n1; during World
    War I, 47–48; xenophobia, 189 fig.26,
    189–90; xenophobia and, 189–90

Women's International League for Peace
    and Freedom, 55
World Health Organization, 156
World War I: overview, 43–45, 52; Belgian
    occupation during, 13; chronicling the
    use of human shields during, 49–51;
    documenting German atrocities, 45–48,
    47 fig.6, 51; German bombing of hospi-
    tals during, 152–53, 153 fig.20; German
    response to human shields, 48–49;
    medical immunity breaches during, 67;
    rationalizing violence during, 51–52;
    reports during, 13, 43–52, 227n9; use of
    human shields by Germany during, 13,
    43–52; witness reports during, 227n9;
    women/children and human shielding,
    22
World War II: overview, 13, 71–72; aerial
    bombardments during, 154; codifica-
    tion following, 78; Eichmann Trial,
    227n9; involuntary shielding in, 206;
    laws of war expansion, 76–77; mentions
    of human shields, 230n9; mistreatment
    of civilians during, 80; no crime with-
    out law (*nullum crimen sine lege*) princi-
    ple, 72–74, 124; precarious balance,
    74–75; women/children and human
    shielding, 22. *See also* Nuremberg;
    Nuremberg trials

xenophobia: passivity and human shield-
    ing, 189–90; women and human shield-
    ing, 189 fig.26

Yemen: bombing of medical facilities in,
    156–57; drone warfare in, 179, 184; hospi-
    tal attacks in, 157–58, 242n21; media
    references to human shields in, 245n29
Yugoslavia, former: overview, 14, 117–18,
    127–28; humanitarian lawfare, 123–24;
    immunity, 124–27, 128 fig.19; Interna-
    tional Criminal Tribunal for the
    Former Yugoslavia, 14, 117–28; involun-
    tary shielding in, 206; refugee shields,
    121–23; UN shields in Bosnia, 119–21,
    120 fig.18

Founded in 1893,
UNIVERSITY OF CALIFORNIA PRESS
publishes bold, progressive books and journals
on topics in the arts, humanities, social sciences,
and natural sciences—with a focus on social
justice issues—that inspire thought and action
among readers worldwide.

The UC PRESS FOUNDATION
raises funds to uphold the press's vital role
as an independent, nonprofit publisher, and
receives philanthropic support from a wide
range of individuals and institutions—and from
committed readers like you. To learn more, visit
ucpress.edu/supportus.